HELENE AH

The Scientific Reproduction of Gender Inequality

A Discourse Analysis of Research Texts on Women's Entrepreneurship

Liber • Copenhagen Business School Press • Abstrakt

The Scientific Reproduction of Gender Inequality
ISBN 91-47-07424-8   (Sweden)
© 2004 Liber AB

ISBN 87-630-0123-3   (Rest of the world)

Publishers editor: Ola Håkansson
Language editor: Elisabeth Mueller Nylander
Design: Fredrik Elvander
Typeset: LundaText AB

1:1

Printed in Sweden by
Wallin och Dalholm Boktryckeri AB 2004

Distribution:
Sweden
Liber AB, Baltzarsgatan 4,
205 10 Malmö, Sweden
tel +46 40-25 86 00, fax +46 40-97 05 50
http://www.liber.se
Kundtjänst tel +46 8-690 93 30, fax +46 8-690 93 01

Denmark
DBK Logistics, Mimersvej 4
DK-4600 Koege, Denmark
phone: +45 3269 7788, fax: +45 3269 7789
www.cbspress.dk

North America
Copenhagen Business School Press
Books International Inc.
P.O. Box 605
Herndon, VA 20172-0605, USA
phone: +1 703 661 1500, toll-free: +1 800 758 3756
fax: +1 703 661 1501

Rest of the World
Marston Book Services, P.O. Box 269
Abingdon, Oxfordshire, OX14 4YN, UK
phone: +44 (0) 1235 465500, fax: +44 (0) 1235 465555
E-mail Direct Customers: direct.order@marston.co.uk
E-mail Booksellers: trade.order@marston.co.uk

The Scientific Reproduction
of Gender Inequality

Contents

Tables and Figures

Introduction

You are not born a woman, wrote Simone deBeauvoir, you become one. It is the process of becoming a woman that is of interest in this work. Feminist scholarship has since long documented the different constructions of masculinity and femininity and the resulting subordination of the feminine. But how does this happen? What are the practices involved in the ubiquitous reproduction of the current gender regime? Why does this continue in spite of so many years of feminist activism, and in spite of such widely held and confessed beliefs about the equal rights of every human being?

This work is about the processes whereby gender inequality is reproduced. I write about an area, where this would, I think, be least expected. Because of this, the analysis may be able to shed some light on how it still takes place. I have chosen to investigate constructions of gender and gender/power relations in research articles about women's entrepreneurship, published in scientific journals.

An often-held view of science is that it is supposed to accurately describe and explain reality, not create or recreate it. Researchers enjoy a status of experts in society, and knowledge produced in science is supposedly more reliable than other sorts of knowledge. This is exactly why a critical look at science is so important. Because research articles are not just innocent, objective reflections of social reality. According to the social constructionist view taken in this work, they are co-producers of social reality. Assumptions about social reality go into the research process, they are re-packaged in the research process, and they are sent out again in the form of authoritative scientific articles.

The assumptions underlying the research articles reviewed here, the methods chosen, the questions asked, and the conclusions drawn all produce a certain picture of women and their role and place in society. This picture may or may not be to women's advantage. From a feminist perspective, it seemed important to analyze this picture and lay bare the assumptions and choices underlying it, and also question them. Consequently, this work analyzes the discursive construction of the female entrepreneur, or female entrepreneurship, in research texts, from a feminist theory perspective.

The book is divided into three parts. The first part lays the necessary theoretical foundation. Chapter one, *Gender as Socially Constructed*, presents a brief overview of feminist theory. I begin by discussing feminist ideologies and feminist research from two different perspectives. The perspectives, put simply, are either that men and women are essentially similar or that they are essentially different. By introducing social constructionism I discuss a third perspective, which says that talking about essential similarities or differences between men and women does not make much sense. It is more fruitful to look at gender as something socially constructed which varies in time and place and is only loosely coupled to male and female bodies. This perspective, which is also mine, says that one should look at how gender is produced rather than at what it is. The chapter finishes with a discussion about the merits of knowledge claims from a feminist position in a scientific discourse.

In chapter two, *Entrepreneurship as Gendered*, I review how the concepts entrepreneur and entrepreneurship are discussed in economics, and in management-based research on entrepreneurship. The review leads me to think that entrepreneurship and entrepreneur are not gender-neutral concepts. To investigate this more in detail, I put the conclusion of chapter one to work, i.e. the theory of gender as something which is produced. The literature review is therefore followed by a short deconstruction, where I compare the conceptions of entrepreneur with a femininity/masculinity index that is widely used in psychological research.

In chapter three, *Defining and Applying the Concept Discourse*, I discuss the term discourse. I rely on Foucault who said that discourses are practices, which systematically form the object of which they speak. This definition indicates that it is not only what is said that counts as discourse, but also the practices by which statements are made possible. The chapter discusses what is meant by such practices, labeled here as discursive practices. The result is a list of ten points covering what to look for in the ensuing discourse analysis.

The second part presents the analysis. Chapter four, *Writing and Publishing Practices*, introduces the texts and discusses practices that control the production of such texts. I am here referring to writing and publishing practices, disciplinary regulations, and institutional support for entrepreneurship research.

In chapter five, *Research Articles on Women Entrepreneurs: Methods and Findings*, I provide an overview of methods, samples, and theory bases of the reviewed articles. The overview comprises the basis for a methodological discussion and critique. The chapter also contains a summary of the article findings.

Chapter six, *How Articles Construct the Female Entrepreneur*, looks at the arguments put forward for researching women's entrepreneurship in the first place, and it analyzes how the research constructs and positions the woman entrepreneur.

Chapter seven, *How Articles Construct Work and Family*, builds on the observation that family, which is hardly an issue in the entrepreneurship research literature, becomes a research topic when women entrepreneurs are investigated. The chapter looks at how work and family are constructed and what consequences this has.

I finish the book by tying together the theory from the first part with the results from the discourse analysis in the second part. Chapter eight, *The Scientific Reproduction of Gender Inequality*, presents the conclusions of the work. I discuss the discourse on women's entrepreneurship in research articles, the practices that produce this discourse, and suggest how one could produce this discourse differently. All the chapters have short summaries to facilitate a quick overview. I have also included three appendices with detailed information on text selection procedures and analysis techniques.

I would gratefully like to acknowledge a number of people who made this book possible. First, my gratitude goes to Leif Melin, Barbara Czarniawska, Per Davidsson, and Elisabeth Sundin who read and commented the manuscript in its entirety. I count myself fortunate for their excellent advice. I also received very helpful comments at different stages in the writing process from Howard Aldrich, Candida Brush, Erica Burman, Marta Calás, Nancy Carter, Mohamed Chaib, Silvia Gherardi, Benson Honig, Ulla Johansson, Anders W. Johansson, Deirdre McCloskey and Pernilla Nilsson. My colleagues Ethel Brundin, Jonas Dahlqvist, Annika Hall, Susanne Hansson, Emilia Florin Samuelsson, Tomas Müllern and Caroline Wigren gave me feedback along the way. Elisabeth Mueller Nylander provided excellent language checking, and the Swedish Research Council financed this project. A heartfelt thanks to all of you! With so much good advice from so many people, it is unlikely that they all agree on everything. The final responsibility is, of course, my own.

1
Gender as Socially Constructed

The field of gender theory, or feminist theory began as the study of women. There are several different ways of reasoning around the nature and place of women, but it cannot be done without an accompanying way of reasoning around men, since men and women are defined in relation to each other. The theorizing of men and masculinity was, however, until very recently only implicit. One of the main points of feminist theory is that the man is made the unspoken norm, and the woman the exception, which calls for an explanation (Hearn & Parkin, 1983; Mills, 1988; Wahl, 1996a). This chapter touches upon some of the historical developments in feminist theory in order to position this work in the current feminist theoretical landscape, and to enable a discussion of the use of a feminist perspective in science[1]. I see three main lines in feminist theory – the idea that men and women are essentially similar, the idea that they are essentially different, and the idea that talking about essences does not make any sense at all. The third position, which I take, sees gender as socially constructed and finds the distinction between the words sex and gender problematic, which is why I use them as synonyms throughout the text.

Same or Different? Feminist Ideologies

Early feminist thinking did not concern itself much with theoretical conceptualizations of gender. Fighting for the right to vote, to work, to an education, to control one's own body, and to own property were

---

1 Giving a complete overview of feminist theory or gender theory is beyond the ambition of this chapter. For useful overviews and critical discussions of feminist theories, see for example Calás & Smircich (1996), Alvesson & Due Billing (1999) or Beasley (1999).

burning issues that needed other kinds of arguments. The suffrage movement in the nineteenth century in both Britain and the United States had strong roots in liberal feminist thinking. Liberal feminism suggests that due to overt discrimination and/or systemic factors women are, compared to men, deprived of resources like education and work experience. Liberal feminism has its roots in liberal political philosophy: All human beings are seen as equal and they are essentially rational, self-interest seeking agents. Rationality is a mental capacity of which men and women have the same potential. Rationality is what makes us human, and since women and men have the same capacity for rational thinking, they are equally human. Women have achieved less than men because they were deprived of opportunities such as education, work experience, etc. (Fischer et al. 1993). If there was no discrimination, men and women could actualize their potential to the same degree. Implicit in this theory is that if discrimination disappeared, women and men would have similar behavior, preferences and accomplishments. Since the basis for the differences is thought to be discrimination against women, this means that women will become more like men. Being like a man is the standard, and rational, self-interest seeking is the norm. Liberal feminism has been criticized for ignoring other sorts of injustices, for example class discrimination, and thus not really arguing for the improvement of conditions for all women (Alvesson & Due Billing, 1999).

Socialist feminism takes class into account. Socialist feminism is influenced by Marxist theory, and there are both socialist versions and Marxist versions. The system of patriarchy (men's control of women's work and reproduction) is seen by the Marxist feminists as part of the system of capitalism. In their early versions, patriarchy was thought of as something that would vanish with the disappearance of capitalism. Feminist struggle would thus equate with class struggle. In Sweden, for example, socialist men argued that women should not fight for their issues separately, but rather they should stand united with the men in the class struggle. Solidarity was the key word.

Socialist feminists grew suspicious of this, however, observing that men of the working class in many instances formed unholy alliances with the capitalists to the detriment of women. It had been assumed that women must not compete with men for jobs, and most Swedish working class men in the 1930s valued a housewife highly and wanted to keep the female labor force out of the job market (Hirdman, 1992). Socialist feminists see patriarchy and capitalism as independent of one another. Patriarchy precedes capitalism and will most likely succeed it as well, if nothing is done to change the gender roles. The *public-private divide*, the partition of men's productive, salaried work and women's unpaid re-productive work, which made women dependant on their husbands, was seen as the base of patriarchy in the capitalistic system (Hartmann, 1986).

The private is public theme has influenced many of the social welfare reforms for which Sweden is so famous, for example the building of day care centers, individual taxation, paid parental leave, and the right to stay home with sick children for either parent. It has not been enough, however, to change the pattern of the father as the primary breadwinner and the mother as the caretaker. Instead, women work double shifts, one at work and one at home, and they still receive lower salaries and lower pensions as shown by Ahrne & Roman (1997) and Nyberg (1997).

Radical feminism grew out of the women's movement in the 1960's. Radical feminists see sexuality, or reproduction, as the basis for patriarchy. The expressions of this include rape, incest, abuse, prostitution, and pornography. Some even see the institution of marriage as the organized oppression of women. Radical feminists think that what they hold to be feminine traits, such as caring, empathy, emotional expressiveness, endurance, and common sense, are found to be lacking in men, and that these traits have been constantly devalued in patriarchal society to the detriment of all human beings. A separatist strategy is typical – female "consciousness-raising" groups and alternative political organizations meant exclusively for women and based on female values as opposed to male. The aim is to change the basic structure of society. Radical feminism envisions a new social order where women are not subordinated to men. A related belief is that of eco-feminism, i.e., the idea that women will take better care of the environment than men since "women are born environmentalists" (Anderson 1990:143).

What unites different political feminist schools is the thought that men and women are two distinct categories. Another uniting factor is the existence of two prerequisites that are usually identified as the basis for feminism, namely the recognition of women's secondary position in society and the desire to change this order. Ideas of why this is so, what actions to take, and the nature of the desired end result, distinguish the various schools.

How feminist ideologies conceive of gender is relevant to this work. To simplify, there are two main lines: The first is that women and men are essentially the same, and the second is that women and men are different from each other (and women's qualities need to be valued higher than they are). The first line of thought, most poignant in liberal feminism, is criticized for applying a male standard to women as well, with discriminatory results. The second line of thought, typical of radical feminism, is criticized for treating women and women's qualities uniformly (and indirectly men and men's qualities), as well as for privileging some women's experiences at the expense of others. Neither ideology questions the categories "woman" and "man". These are taken for granted.

Same or Different? Different Grounds for Feminist Research

Introducing feminist ideologies and feminist research under two different headlines requires some words of explanation. Few words cause as much confusion and misunderstanding as the word "feminism", writes Wahl (1996b). Feminism is broadly defined as the recognition of men's and women's unequal conditions and the desire to change this. There is a difference, though, between feminist politics, feminist ideology, and feminist research. Wahl defines feminist politics as working to create equal conditions for men and women, feminist ideology as ideas of how "things are" (and why, my remark), as well as ideas of how things ought to be. The different political views discussed in the previous section are examples of feminist ideologies. Wahl defines feminist research as the scientific production of descriptions, explanations and interpretations, based on a feminist theoretical perspective. Central ingredients to this perspective include the concept of the gender system (more on that below) and the insight that most mainstream research has been gender blind and has implicitly used the man as the standard for the individual.

There are, of course, no clear boundaries between research, ideology, and politics, just as there is no research that is totally deprived of ideology, and especially no politics without an ideology. Many feminist researchers work from an explicit ideological standpoint. Many overviews of feminist theory do not separate ideologies and research, but talk of feminist Marxist research, liberal feminist research, and so on. The 1990s have, however, produced feminist research that is somewhat less engaged and more academic/theoretical in nature, and I therefore find Wahl's separation useful, if for no other reason than to give increased clarity.

The field of gender research exploded during the 1980s and 1990s. With scientific research came discussions of epistemologies, and a useful way to categorize the field of gender research is to do it according to which epistemological position is favored. Following Harding (1987), Alvesson & Due Billing (1999) distinguish between three perspectives. The first sees sex as an unproblematic variable and could be referred to as feminist empiricism. The second differentiates women from men as knowing subjects. It includes the feminist standpoint perspective, but also psychoanalytically informed theories. The third is the post-structural perspective. I will discuss the first two in this section. The post-structural perspective is addressed later in this chapter, after an introduction of the concept of socially constructed sex.

Feminist Empiricism

Feminist empiricism sees sex as a relevant as well as unproblematic category. Sex is added to the research agenda as a category such as age or education would be. Theories and methods often remain the same as before this addition, and there is seldom any gender-specific theory development. The focus is on explaining discrimination against women by differences between the sexes, either innate, psychological differences or structural differences. This is the dominant approach in management studies, and it is well justified when it comes to research on inequalities between men and women – wage differentials, vertical and horizontal segregation, working hours, etc.

Sweden, a country that is world famous for equality, is a good example of how simply counting men and women effectively shows that more is to be done. Sweden has a very gender-segregated job market. Women dominate in the public sector and in the service industry, and they are mostly found in low-level positions. Men are usually found in the private sector and in the manufacturing industry. Top-level positions are heavily male-dominated. In 1998, 89% of all university professors were men and in 1999, 95% of all board members of listed companies were men (Statistics Sweden, 2000). Even for the same job, and with the same qualifications, Swedish women still averaged less in pay than their male counterparts in 1997 (Nyberg, 1997; Persson & Wadensjö, 1997). Similar circumstances are found in many other countries. Why this is so, and how to amend it, have been questions driving a substantial amount of research in management and organization.

The so-called "women in management" research tries to explain women's lesser achievements by differences in, for example, leadership styles. Women are likely to be described as less assertive, less competitive, less achievement oriented, and so on. However, few significant differences have been found. Results are, at best, inconclusive (Doyle & Paludi, 1998; Shackleton, 1995). The within-sex variation is much larger than the between-sex variation. This agrees with findings from psychological research. A review[2] of the psychological literature on gender differences performed by Hyde (reported in Doyle & Paludi, 1998) concludes that sex differences, in this case in verbal ability, quantitative ability, visual-spatial ability and field articulation, account for no more than 1%–5% of the population variance. The other side of this coin (i.e., when no significant differences are found) is to show that women are just as good as men. As Calás & Smircich (1996:223) put it: "Women in management" research has spent "thirty years ... researching that women are people too".

If explanations do not rest in the sex of individuals, perhaps they rest in structures? The segregated job market, with men's jobs and women's jobs, is characterized by horizontal gender segregation. Vertical gender segregation refers to the phenomenon that men usually have management positions whereas women have lower positions. There seems to be a glass ceiling, which women are not allowed to go beyond. Horizontal and vertical segregation can be found within a single organization. Jobs are gendered, with regard to content as well as position and influence. Being a secretary is for example typically associated with femininity, and being a president with masculinity. This gendered structure has consequences for those individuals who try to break the pattern, as shown by Kanter (1977) in her classic "Men and women of the corporation". The minority – for example a single woman in an otherwise male management group – becomes a highly visible token, and is seen by the majority not as an individual but as a representative of her sex. He or she therefore often becomes a victim for sex role stereotyping. The presence of a token makes the majority more acutely aware of their own sex, and they may overstate the differences and try to keep the token out. When thinking of a candidate for a management position, managers tend to choose those who are similar to themselves in background and outlook. A male manager will

---

2   The authors performed a so called meta-analysis, which is "a statistical procedure that permits psychologists to synthesize results from several studies and yield a measure of the magnitude of the gender difference. It is a statistical method for conducting a literature review" (Doyle & Paludi, 1998:13).

therefore think of a man, and when choosing among several, one that is like himself.[3] Men are said to act homosocially (Lindgren, 1996). Women also tend to stay in low-level positions not because they have no desire or ability to advance, but because they are put in a structurally dead-end position from the beginning and adapt accordingly. Numbers, power structures, and opportunity structures are thus the main explanations in Kanter's theory, not gender. A male minority in a female management group, however, would perhaps not receive an exact mirror treatment.

Statistics from "sex as a variable research" is an important and indispensable part of feminist research. It forms the basis for research based on other perspectives. When it comes to assigning traits, motives, attitudes, and so on to male and female bodies the approach is questionable. It tends to reify and recreate gender differences, and it seldom captures how the differences are produced in the first place. Calás & Smircich (1996) also criticize the research for its individualistic approach. It takes bureaucracy and hierarchical division of labor for granted and aims at improving women's chances to succeed in a system that is already given.

Women as Different from Men as Knowing Subjects

The feminist standpoint perspective sees gender as a basic organizing principle in society. It holds that women have experiences and interests that are different from men's, based on their socializing and their subordinated position. It is inspired by Marxist analysis, which says that the oppressed (the working class) has a privileged position in making any knowledge claims about oppression. Likewise, women have a privileged position in making any knowledge claims about patriarchal oppression. Women's standpoints are neglected in a patriarchal societal discourse, and this perspective wants to privilege women's interest for the purpose of social change. Standpoint theory assumes a unique woman's point of view. For standpoint feminists, this comes from the experience of subjugation. Other theories offer psychological explanations. For example, women are thought of as possessing a different rationality from men, since they stress care and wholeness more than narrow means-end rationality, as well as a different moral reasoning. Organization research from this perspective maintains that women do indeed manage and relate differently at work. This is not necessarily

---

3   Holgersson & Höök (1997) illustrates this very clearly in a report on how Swedish CEOs are recruited.

based on inherent differences, but on women being socialized differently and on the different sorts of life experiences they have as compared to men. Psycho-analytical feminism stresses early socialization. Social feminism[4], a term sometimes used in Anglo-Saxon writing, includes early socialization, but also counts later experiences in life, such as the experience of mothering, or the experience of subordination to men in school, work or marriage. The female way of doing things – being relationship-oriented, caring and democratic (Chodorow, 1988), applying a contextual instead of a means-ends rationality (Sörensen, 1982) and a different moral reasoning, applying an ethics of care instead of an ethics of justice (Gilligan, 1982) – has been marginalized and suppressed along with women themselves in traditional bureaucracies.

These ways and values are often regarded as very positive, and women's ways of doing things are seen as complementary to men's and used as an argument for more women managers. Female traits are said to be a competitive advantage for companies. Relationship orientation makes for good customer relations. More radical voices maintain that women will build better organizations, or that organizations will become more democratic and flat if more women begin to enter (Iannello, 1992). Ferguson (1984) challenges bureaucracy as based on a male rationality valuing individualism and competition and holds that organizations will have to change fundamentally in order to accommodate women. Although not unchallenged, the results and the theories from this perspective are frequently heard and discussed in the daily press and the popular press and debates. A major shortcoming is that all women risk being stuck with pre-assigned female traits, having no chance to use the "male" ones when needed, thus re-affirming the existing social order instead of changing it.

Research based on this perspective has been very productive in uncovering an unstated male bias in research and in opening up the debate for critical reformulation. Assigning all the good traits to women is, however, dubious. This perspective, along with some of the feminist empiricist research, has been criticized for essentialism, that is assuming that certain traits go naturally with male and female bodies and

---

4 North American feminist literature sometimes categorizes the field in liberal feminism (men and women are not different, really) and social feminism, (men and women are different, for good reasons, and we should use it), omitting many of the feminist ideologies and taking an objectivistic standpoint for granted. From my point of view, this is too much of a simplification, but it is understandable given the different political experience of the USA and Sweden, as well as the "liberal, positivist, behaviorist and instrumental orientations" of American mainstream organizational literature (Calás & Smircich, 1996:244).

then reifying these traits as masculine and feminine, taking little account of within-sex variation as well as historical and cultural circumstances. The perspective is also criticized for using white middle-class women as the mold, while ignoring women from other social groups. This perspective is found in the North American literature, but is largely absent in the Scandinavian research literature.

Both perspectives above are preoccupied with the sameness or difference between men and women. Both perspectives may be questioned for essentializing sex, and treating sex as an unproblematic category. The next section introduces another way of viewing sex, which questions the assumed status of these categories.

Socially Constructed Men and Women

A basic tenet of this text is that knowledge is socially constructed, as outlined by Berger & Luckmann (1966)[5], i.e., that it is impossible to develop knowledge based on any "pure" sense-data observation. "Were we to describe our experience in terms of sensory description … we would be confronted with not only uninterpreted, but an uninterpretable world", writes Czarniawska, (1997:12). It is only possible to understand the world if one has access to a language, to a pre-understanding of some sort that orders categories in a comprehensible way, as well as an understanding of the particular context where action takes place. All of these will mold one's understanding in certain directions. This understanding is created in a social context, it is socially constructed, and this goes, of course, for gender as well as for anything else.

Social constructionism does not, however, say anything about the existence of an objective reality. Social constructionism, as I interpret it, is an epistemology, not an ontology. It says that there is no way to get objective knowledge about the world, which is independent from the observer. It does not claim that a world independent from our observation is non-existent. As such, constructionism is thus often compatible with either empiricism or realism. "We need to make a distinction between the claim that the world is out there and the claim that truth is out there" (Rorty, cited in Czarniawska, 2002). The world is out there, but a user's manual does not come with it.

---

5   Some of Berger & Luckmann's main sources of inspiration were Alfred Schütz's phenomenology and George Herbert Mead's symbolic interactionism (Czarniawska, 2002).

Here is my short version of Berger & Luckmann's (1966) view on how reality becomes socially constructed. Imagine that a space ship filled with small boys lands on a deserted island on the planet Earth. The boys find the island agreeable and decide to stay. They build a society together. A few years pass and then one day a small boat runs ashore with only one survivor. The young men look at "it", amazed, since it looks almost like one of them, but not quite, so they decide that it cannot be a man. What is it then? Is it a god? Is it a slave? Is it an animal? No, not likely, they decide, since it can speak, even if they do not understand the language it uses. What is it then? A heated discussion ensues, but after weighing the arguments for and against the different alternatives, they proclaim that it is a slave. It seems a practical and agreeable choice. Berger and Luckmann call this externalizing reality. The young men decide what the slave may be used for and not, and they issue rules and regulations pertaining to the use and trade of slaves. They write a small pamphlet describing the typical characteristics and essential qualities of slaves, so that no one shall have any doubts about what a slave is like. This is called objectification of social reality.

The young men discover that they can mate with the slave and children and grandchildren are born, both boys and slaves. The little slaves, called "girls", learn that they are "beautiful" and they receive the necessary training for the performance of typical slaves' chores, such as cooking and cleaning. The little boys learn that they will grow up to become fine young men and they are trained in all the things that fine young men do, including learning the rules pertaining to the use and trade of slaves. In this way they internalize social reality and as they act according to this understanding and in turn teach it to their children, reality is continuously being re-created. No one remembers that there was a discussion about the status of that first woman ages ago. Her status as slave is by now taken for granted. It has become institutionalized, i.e., people habitually do certain things and they have a normative explanation for it.

Were the people on my island to continue living in isolation, their stories might never be challenged. There are, however, other islands in this saga, and people meet and exchange realities. New versions may come from this. There may be happily co-existing versions, or totally irreconcilable versions leading to endless fights.

With a social constructionist perspective as outlined above follows a questioning of the assumed categories of man and woman. The "essential qualities" ascribed to the slave in the example above were exactly that, ascribed qualities. A non-essentialist view of gender rejects the idea that a male or female body entails some innate, stable qualities, which determine both the body's actions and reactions to them. These are more likely to be a result of socializing and social context. Tall people might be ashamed or proud of their size, they may stoop or walk straight and they might be admired or stigmatized. From the very first moment, however, a newborn baby is duly categorized as a boy or a girl. Their bodies are filled with descriptive adjectives, with attributes, with hopes, aspirations and expectations.

A baby is called pretty, cute, strong, muscular, sweet-hearted, good-natured, brave, etc., but the words are not used haphazardly. One set of adjectives is reserved for girls, the other for boys. There is no visible difference between a baby boy and a baby girl with their diapers on, still they are treated differently, talked to differently and even held differently. The exact same baby gets different treatment depending if test subjects are told that it is a boy or that it is a girl (Jalmert, 1999). The little boys and girls are receptive and to a large extent fulfill their significant others' expectations in terms of proper gender behavior. As they grow up, they encounter endless objectifications of gender and gender differences in schools and through media. They cannot help but internalize the message. They teach their own children a similar story and thus recreate the gender difference.

The actual content of what is regarded male and female varies over time, place and social context. A very fine man in Britain in the seventeenth century was of a slender build and had a knack for the arts and for reciting poetry (the movie Orlando based on the novel by Virginia Woolf is a beautiful illustration). My grandmother did not have to worry about looking beautiful beyond her teens. Other traits were more highly valued. Today women spend money on face lifts, tummy tucks and breast surgery in their forties and fifties. A bank teller is not a high status job today. Mostly women do it. At the turn of the century it was one of the finest jobs a man could have (Reskin and Padavic as quoted in Alvesson & Due Billing, 1999). The dairy profession has undergone a similar change. It was a mystical thing, reserved for women, until milking cows was done by machines and it became a man's job (Sommestad, 1992). The point to be made is not that the true nature of men and women has not yet been revealed, but that assumptions about what is male and female are socially constructed and therefore change in time. You are not born a woman, wrote Simone deBeauvoir, you become one (1949/1986).

Social arrangements are often referred to nature, however, which confers legitimacy upon them (Mary Douglas, 1987). Nature bestows legitimacy in the most terrific ways, and is infinitely flexible and amenable to arguments. Anthropologist Douglas (ibid) writes that it is common in Africa that women do all the hard and tedious work in the fields, usually justified by the fact that men are needed for some other, superior activity. Not so among the Bamenda people in Cameron where women did all the hard and tedious work in the fields because only women and God could make things grow. Today biological arguments are back in vogue, claiming that women, because of their hormones, are by nature particularly well suited for caring and nurturing activities. They are also said to be able to bear routine jobs better than men (Robert & Uvnäs Moberg, 1994). Most grade school teachers in Sweden today are women, which nicely fits this argument. In the 1930s, interestingly, most teachers were men. A woman's natural place was at home, a hard job like a teacher's was seen as unnatural for women. If women did teach, they did not have the same pay. In a somewhat acrobatic move, Swedish member of parliament Mr. Bergquist argued in 1938 that women teachers, even if they seemed to do the same job, could not be entitled to the same pay, because due to their weaker nerves and lesser strength they could not possibly perform the same job as well as a man (Hirdman, 1992)[6]. Today, when teaching in Sweden has become a woman's job, and where the argument of 1938 is no longer possible, the salary level has decreased for the entire profession. (Voices are raised to attract more men to teaching, to "elevate the status" of the job again. However, raising the salary level might perform this trick more easily.)

Throughout these examples, men and women are seen as different. The nature of the difference has varied, but in the contemporary debate there is a tendency to think of the difference in vogue as eternal, and as grounded in nature. Even if the two debating factions have different versions of the nature of men and women, it is still the nature of men and women that is referred to. Moreover, there are seldom more than two categories allowed. Phenomena not fitting these two categories, such as homosexuality, are easily seen as "unnatural". Dichotomous thinking seems pervasive, but along with it comes hierarchical

---

6   In September 2001, there was a court settlement in Sweden determining that a hospital nurse and a hospital technician's jobs were comparable in terms of job content and requirements, but that the employer still did not break the wage discrimination law by paying the male technician more, because the market rate for technicians was higher. There *is* a private market for technicians in Sweden, but hardly for hospital nurses. The "market" was in this case used as "nature" would be in other instances.

thinking. Not only is the world divided in pairs, the elements in the pairs are ordered hierarchically. One is held as better than the other. Light is better than dark, tall is better than short, thin is better than fat, outspoken is better than introvert (Needham, 1973)[7]. The same goes for male and female, which McCloskey (1998) calls "the mother of all dichotomies". Anything "female" is almost consistently valued less than the "male", and the female is defined as something else than the male, which is the standard to be measured against. This led historian Yvonne Hirdman (1992) to formulate the concept which she calls the gender system. The gender system rests on two kinds of logic. The first is the logic of separation. It keeps men and women separate, and more importantly, it keeps anything considered "female" separate from anything considered "male". The second logic is the one of superiority. The two genders are ordered hierarchically, with the male placed above the female.

Men and women alike recreate the gender system. It is pervasive. It is perhaps easiest to see it in other places, like Afghanistan, or in other times, say Europe in the 19th century, but it would be wrong to assume that contemporary Westerners have done away with it. Some of the most flagrant cases of discrimination have disappeared, nota bene, but the hierarchy is as solid as ever, it is just expressed differently. In an experiment, I asked a group of 26 engineering students in Sweden, about half women, half men, to write down the first word that came to their mind when thinking about how "women are" and how "men are". The setting was a lecture with no explicit talk about gender. The students were about 20–25 years old. It turned out that the male students held themselves in very high regard, and the women appreciated the men as well. Men were said to be easy-going, stable, not run by emotions, adventurous, good collaborators, visionary, straight-forward, competitive, and open. Both sexes agreed, the lists of words were quite similar. Men thought that women were emotional, gossipy, had to be friends to work together, took things personally, were long-winded, in need of acknowledgment, and thrifty. Women thought that women were resentful, sneaky, insinuating, emotional, competitive in a "different way", resentful of women bosses, relationship centered, and afraid to stick out. When I asked the students to tell me what lists were positive and what lists were negative they unanimously agreed that the list of male attributes was the good one, while the list of female attributes were things better avoided.

---

7   The actual order varies in time and cultural context – when I grew up, being silent was better than outspoken. But the *ordering* seems to be pervasive.

This exercise demonstrates clearly how both men and women recreate the gender system. Hirdman (1992, p. 230) asks herself why the gender system is so stable. Why do not only men, "good ones" as well as "bad ones", but also women support the system so consistently? Why does a young, bright engineering student think of women as resentful, insidious and sneaky while she holds her male colleagues to be easy-going, straightforward and stable?

Hirdman gives two explanations. One is the individual explanation, on the level of sexuality. Men and women are dependent on each other if the species is to survive. Because of this dependence, people follow the rules, people do and think the things that are considered "male" and "female", or they risk being without a partner. Holmberg (1993) did a symbolic interactionist study on how gender is constructed in young, egalitarian couples without children, and found that they were not very egalitarian after all, and the woman was the driving force in upholding the male norm. The other explanation is on the level of society, writes Hirdman. She holds that the gender system is the base for other orders, social, economical as well as political. A change in the power relationship between the sexes would change other power centers as well, and the other power centers would quite naturally resist this.

> A change of relationships between men and women is therefore always a revolutionary change. And as we know, societies do not tolerate revolutions. This tells us why so many techniques have been developed in order to prevent the basic gender system from exposure. Oppression of women is a societal neurosis that cannot be acknowledged. That would make the societal superego crumble and fall. So facts are denied, by women as well as by men. They use the technique of repression, that is, denying oppression, or the techniques of diminishing or ridiculing, or by pseudo-problematizing, that is, arguing that other circumstances are the important ones, or, by the most audacious technique of all, the technique of reversed analysis, saying that it is in fact the women who decide (Hirdman, 1992, p. 230 f, my translation).

Regarding gender as socially constructed implies thus not only a rejection of the idea that men and women can be described by their essential qualities, it also implies that a power perspective – gender relations, rather than gender *per se* is of interest. Gender becomes a fleeting and malleable concept, which is far from the fixed and stable idea envisioned by the "same or different" theories described previously.

The Post-structural Perspective

The post-structural perspective builds on an understanding of gender as socially constructed. It does not take the categories men and women for granted. Gender is not considered property but "a relationship which brings about redefinitions of subjectivities and subject positions over time, both as products and as producers of social context" (Calás & Smircich, 1996:241). "Subjectivity" is a sense of who you are. A "subject position" is a sense of how you are positioned in relation to others. Both are affected by or constructed through gender, which is not something residing inside the human, but a relational concept, just like 'big' cannot be 'big' unless there is something other than 'big' that makes it so (Gherardi, 1995). And it is not stable. Sitting by my computer I am mainly a writer, but as I go to get my coffee and chat with colleagues I am a female colleague, positioning myself differently. Gender creeps into my relationships with my supervisors who I relate to differently depending on, among other things, their sex. At home I can be a loving wife, perhaps, or a tyrannical mother, or at other times a loving mother and an indifferent wife. I do most of the gardening at home, but only those neighbors who easily accept a woman gardener discuss pruning and fertilizing with me. The other ones talk to my husband on his occasional visits to the vegetable garden, or wait until winter when the men in the neighborhood meet around the snow shovels. I experience myself differently in all of these situations, and I position myself differently, but I can never steer clear of gender.

Gender thus becomes something that permeates all these instances, but it is unstable and ambiguous. Concepts like man, woman, male and female are falsely unitary concepts. The meaning of these concepts is socially constructed at each and every turn. The meaning of gender varies between different contexts, even for the same individual. Bronwyn Davies explains this as follows:

> Individuals, through learning the discursive practices of society, are able to position themselves within those practices in multiple ways, and to develop subjectivities both in concert with and in opposition to the ways in which others choose to position them. By focusing on the multiple subject positions that a person takes up and the often contradictory nature of those positionings, and by focusing on the fact that the social world is constantly being constituted through the discursive practices in which individuals engage, we are able so see individuals not as the unitary beings that humanist theory would have them be, but as the complex, changing, contradictory creatures that we each experience ourselves to be, despite

our best efforts at producing a unified, coherent and relatively static self (Davies, 1989:xi).

Looking for a unitary "me" or "woman" behind the mother, gardener, student, colleague, subordinate, etc., would thus be an impossible feat according to the post-structural perspective, which advocates the idea of multiple selves, or a "fragmented" identity. Instead of "uncovering" how reality is, poststructuralist research looks for how reality is constructed in different contexts. Calás & Smircich (1996:219) write that feminist, post-structural research sees discourses about men and women – expressed and constituted by language – and their accompanying power relationships as the central research topic.

Post-structural organization research would, for example, criticize the variable-research for simplifying things far too much. A major fault is that sex is seen as an explanation rather than as a starting point for research. It polarizes men and women, ignores their similarities and common interests, neglects cultural and historical differences, ignores local, contextual circumstances and does not consider age, class, race and ethnicity. It would also criticize the feminist standpoint perspective for privileging some women at the expense of others, and for making the values and experiences of upper/middle class white women the standard for all women.

Instead of looking at physical men and women, such research has studied the construction of concepts such as leadership, organization and business administration using gender as an analytical tool (Martin 1990; Acker, 1992; Calás & Smircich, 1992,). These concepts have been found to be far from the neutral, straight-forward things that they are usually treated as in our daily discourse and management literature. Leadership, for example, was found to be constructed around a male norm, and a "woman leader" would almost by definition be a deviation from how a leader typically is envisioned. Post-structural organizational analysis reveals the involvement of organization theory in reproducing gendered arrangements. The task for a post-structural feminist organizational scientist is to "challenge and change the dominant and colonizing organizational discourse, over and over again" (Calás & Smircich, 1996:245).

So what is gender, then?

It should be clear by now that this work, in tune with the post-structural perspective, conceives of gender as socially constructed. Not enough is said on this topic, however. Let me start with the semantics. The term gender was introduced as a useful tool to differentiate between biological sex (bodies with male or female reproductive organs) and socially constructed sex, which was a result of upbringing and social interaction (Acker, 1992; Lindén & Milles, 1995). Gender and its components (roles, norms, identity) were seen as varying along a continuum of femininity and masculinity and should be thought of as independent of a person's biological sex. The word gender can also be used to refer to things other than people. Jobs can be gendered, for example (Doyle & Paludi, 1998). Gender may be envisioned as a social arrangement, based on differences that are determined by sex, specific to each social context (Danius, 1995).

The concept gender is a very useful tool for demonstrating how sex is socially constructed, but its use runs into several problems. The first problem is that it has been co-opted by normal science as well as daily conversation and is today used in the same sense as sex. Whereas surveys used to ask you to fill out your sex, in English-speaking countries today they now ask for your gender. The original distinction has been lost.

A more complicated problem is the question of what comes first – sex or gender? Danius (1995) writes that the Greek physiologist Galenos only acknowledged one physiological sex. Man and woman were thought to be physiologically the same, they were just equipped with inverted versions of their sexual organs. Attention was put on similarities, not differences. The idea of the male/female physiology was a social creation. This idea lived up until the renaissance when the idea of two, physiologically different bodies became prominent and attention was put on differences. These differences were indeed found, and a long array of psychological and moral differences were constructed and explained by the physiological ones.

The seemingly unproblematic physical definition of a man or a woman gets more complicated, however, as science develops more sophisticated measuring devices. Using biological definitions, there are at least seventeen different sexes based on anatomy, genes, hormones, fertility and so on (Davies, 1989 Kaplan & Rogers, 1990). Transsexuals who are "women born in male bodies" (or the reverse) are unsettling reminders of the ambiguity of sex. Therefore, acknowledging only two genders seems like a social and pragmatic construct with a questionable base in physiology.

The distinction between sex and gender may have been a useful pedagogical device, but it reifies the heterosexual male and female body as something essential, solid and natural, and as the constant reference point for socially constructed sex. It says that there is a divide between that which is constant (nature, the body) and that which is variable (culture) which indicates a false clarity (Eduards, 1995). The body should more properly be regarded as discursively constructed, just as much as all the things we attach to it. The conclusion to this is that sex – or gender (same thing) – should be regarded as a socially and discursively constructed phenomenon that is culturally, historically and locally specific.

Doing away with the body as a solid concept does present problems, though. There are practical problems. How do you name a man or a woman with such a fluid view of the body? Even if the body is seen as a constructed phenomenon, the idea of the body is still the basis for the construction of gender.

There are communication problems as well. How do you design a study and communicate your results with a definition of sex/gender that is so counter to common sense? "Have you ever seen a gender", asked Mary Daly, a prominent figure in the American women's movement, (quoted in Eduards, 1995:64) pointing to the distance between actual men and women and their scientific representations.

Moreover, there are political problems. How can you produce research with a liberating aim if you cannot picture women or men as a group? What policy can you possibly recommend based on research with no positive ground for knowledge and a knowing subject? How can local and fragmented policies ever be strong enough to change a system that oppresses women? Is not a deconstruction always subject to another deconstruction? "Feminists beware!" say the critics, who think that such a fragmented and heterogeneous perspective undermines the feminist project. There are difficulties and dangers in talking about women as a single group but there are also dangers in not being able to talk of women as a single group. Young (1995:188) writes, "Clearly, these two positions pose a dilemma for feminist theory. On the one hand, without some sense in which 'woman' is the name of a social collective, there is nothing specific to feminist politics. On the other hand, any effort to identify the attributes of that collective appears to undermine feminist politics by leaving out some women whom feminists ought to include."

To address the problem, Young introduces the concept of gender as seriality, from Sartre. It offers a way of thinking of women or men as a social collective without requiring that all of them have common attributes or a common situation. A series is "a social collective whose members are unified passively by the object around which their actions are oriented or by the objectified results of the material effects of the actions of others" (Young 1995:199). Sartre calls this "practico-inert realities". Young exemplifies with Sartre's description of people waiting for a bus as such a series. They relate to one another minimally, and they follow the rules of bus waiting. They relate to the material object, the bus and to the social practices of public transportation. In that sense they are a series. They are not a group, in Young's sense, since they have no common experiences, identities, actions or goals. If the bus does not show up, though, they might become a group. They might start to talk to each other, share experiences of public transportation and perhaps decide to share a taxi. In a series, a person experiences others, but also his or herself as an Other, as an anonymous someone. In the line, I would see myself as a person waiting for the bus. With this comes constraints, that I experience as given or natural.

Sartre developed the concept to explain social class, but it is just as useful for gender. As a woman I may not always identify with other women, but I have to relate to the "practico-inert realities" of, for example, menstruation. Not only the biological phenomenon but also the social rules of it, along with the associated material objects. I must relate to gendered language, to clothing, to gendered divisions of space, to a sexual division of labor, and so on. I must relate to the fact that those in my surroundings label me as a woman. Women relate in infinite ways, but relate they must. And so must men. Thinking of gender as seriality avoids essentializing sex while still allowing for the conceptualization of women or men as categories.

I find the idea of seriality very useful. In this work, I will treat men and women as categories. An individual will be assigned to a category based on which sort of body (of two possible, admittedly simplified) he or she was born, for the simple reason that everyone else does so. However, if I can avoid it, no assumptions about items such as qualities, traits, natural predispositions, purposes, common experiences, and identities will be made. Instead, I will study how these are constructed.

Knowledge Claims from a Feminist Position

As noted above, feminist theory can mean different things. Uniting the different feminist perspectives, however, is the recognition of women's subordination to men, and the desire to do something about this. Women's subordination is thus a starting point. Enough research exists to support this claim; it does not have to be shown again and again by feminist studies. What is more interesting to show is *how* this is accomplished. A feminist theory perspective would entail the challenging of knowledge produced in a field from a feminist perspective, to reappraise the methods used, and to provide alternative ways of theorizing, that may have social and political consequences (Calás & Smircich, 1996).

Is there a place for such a position in a scientific discourse? Yes, says Donna Haraway (1991), who claims that a partial position is all that is available. She notes that the idea of an objectivist epistemology, with its accompanying terms "validity" and "reliability", is an idea, or ideal, which can never be attained. Holding on to it would be pretense. For something to be valid in objectivist science, there should ideally be something *outside* of science legitimating it – the belief in an outer, objective world mirrored in science through objective, neutral methods. This idea is a myth, as sociologists of science have long since argued (Kuhn, 1970; Latour & Woolgar, 1979; McCloskey, 1985). What you look for and how you look affects what you see and there is no way to get around this. Science is, like everything else, socially constructed. It operates through persuasion and argumentation. Arguments that seem to be grounded in something beyond the scope of argumentation will of course give the arguer the upper hand, which is why the idea of science as neutral has staying power. It is a useful rhetorical tool.

Does this mean that anything goes? No. Haraway notes that objectivism is, at its extreme, the "god-trick of seeing everything from nowhere ... the false vision promising transcendence of all limits and responsibility", but she is equally wary of what she holds to be the "other side" of this dimension: post-modern, relativist knowledge "where every claim to truth is the subject of further deconstruction" (Haraway, 1991:189–190). She says "relativism is a way of being nowhere while claiming to be everywhere equally" (ibid: 191). Relativism is the twin of objectivism. Both deny a partial perspective. Both are unrealistic ideas. Objectivism is impossible to attain, and no one can be guilty of relativism, since it is only possible to see from *somewhere*, from a position. Haraway calls this *situated knowledge*[8].

Situated knowledge is knowledge that speaks from a position in time and space. It is "embodied" knowledge as opposed to free-float-

---

8   See also Berger & Luckmann (1966:59) who write about knowledge as *local,* and Lyotard (1979/1991) who replaces the idea of grand narratives as explanations for social reality with "local, time-bound and space-bound determinisms".

ing knowledge that speaks from nowhere. Haraway says to develop knowledge from the standpoint of the subjugated, not because they are "innocent" positions, but because "they are least likely to allow denial of the critical and interpretative core of all knowledge" (ibid:191).

"The woman's point of view" is, of course, too much a simplification since there is no *singular* such position. As Haraway (1991:192) says, "one cannot 'be' either a cell or molecule – or a woman, colonized person, laborer, and so on – if one intends to see and see from these positions critically". As pointed out before, however, I do not claim any essential meaning of "woman", but look for what different texts have to say about woman as a category. I also write from the position of a Scandinavian woman, with experience of a welfare state that differs from most of the countries represented in the analyzed texts. This perspective sensitizes me to certain things in the texts that I might not have noticed if I was a US citizen, for example. My position is marginal in a third sense as well, namely in regard to the research community I study. US scholars and journals and certain kinds of research practices dominate the texts I have chosen. These practices might have escaped my notice if I were a US scholar myself. I thus make use of my marginal position, but of course this position also shapes the results.

Situated knowledge is articulately based on politics and ethics, and "partiality and not universality is the condition of being heard to make rational knowledge claims," says Haraway (1991:191). She does not mean that feminist research provides truer versions of the area of study. Using a feminist perspective is ultimately a political choice. Using *any* perspective is a political, or value based choice, I would add, since all science reproduces or challenges a particular social construction of reality, whether admitting it or not. However, to challenge gender arrangements is the explicit aim here.

A partial perspective is antithetical to relativism in Haraway's sense, since it means that you can choose between theories based on values. It is not about true or false, but about judging politically and morally good or bad theories and testing them within the network that science constitutes. "Science is judged, possible explanations compete. Proposed theories are tested for their ability to 'fit' with other theories, with intuitive feelings about reality – and also for their ability to fit with any kind of data that can be generated by observation and measurement" writes Anderson (1990:77). So, not everything goes.

Are there any guidelines for a discourse analysis, then? Winther Jörgensen & Phillips (1999) write that a discourse analysis should try to adhere to three rules. I have used these as guidelines for my work. The first such rule is *coherence*. The claims made must be consistent throughout the work. A related concept is the demand for *transparency*. The reader should be able to follow how the work was conducted and the material should be presented in enough detail for the reader to be able to make his or her own judgments about the conclusions. The third rule is *fruitfulness*. Does the analysis contribute to new ways of understanding a phenomenon? Does it enable new ways of thinking about women's entrepreneurship? Does it contribute to raising the awareness of discourse as a form of social praxis that maintains power relationships?

A feminist perspective also entails an interest in change. Using a social constructionist approach opens up the possibility for change by looking at things differently. Social arrangements are amazingly stable and difficult to change, but they are in principle contingent. This premise is used to question that which is taken for granted so that new questions may be asked to what is already known. It acts as an alienating lens (Söndergaard, 1999). It is this Verfremdung from everyday knowledge that opens possibilities for change. You "move something from the field of the objective to the field of the political, from the silent and obvious to something you can be for or against, opening up for discussion, critique and therefore change" (Winther Jörgensen & Phillips, 1999:165, my translation). I would like the results of this work to enable new sorts of thoughts on the topic of women's entrepreneurship.

The book may also give a new, interesting slant to entrepreneurship research in general, and to research on female entrepreneurs in particular. The field of entrepreneurship research is so far rather a-theoretical. Most studies have aimed at cataloguing the properties of successful businesses or the traits of successful (and unsuccessful) entrepreneurs. Women's entrepreneurship has mostly been studied from the very limited perspective of the differences between men and women. Discourse analysis offers analytical tools that are not commonly used in entrepreneurship research, and social constructionism introduces an expanded research area compared to most entrepreneurship research I have come across so far. Tales about entrepreneurship, as constitutive of social reality, become important.

Summary

The aim of this chapter was to introduce how this work envisions gender, or sex. Most of feminist ideology and feminist research do not question "woman" and "man" as natural categories. Attention is put on differences – in traits, in experiences, in structures, and in conditions – to explain the lesser position of women in society. Problems with these views are that they either use a male norm as the standard, or create a female norm which privileges white, middle-class heterosexual women in the West and excludes others. Poststructuralist feminist research avoids essentializing and polarizing men and women, and sees gender, including the body, as a socially and discursively constructed phenomenon that is culturally, historically, and locally specific.

Omitting the body as the fixed point for assigning gender, presents practical as well as political problems, however. To avoid this, I use the concept of gender as seriality. "Woman" and "man" are still treated as categories, but I do not assume any specific qualities, traits, purposes, common experiences, etc., for any category. Instead, I study how these are constructed.

Revisiting the purpose, *to analyze the discursive construction of the female entrepreneur/female entrepreneurship in research texts from a feminist theory perspective*, this chapter has dealt with how to conceive of "construction", "female", and "feminist perspective". I will study how "femaleness" is conceived of or constructed in the texts from a feminist theory perspective, which entails the recognition of women's secondary position in society and the desire to challenge this order. From this perspective, it becomes important to study in what ways research texts about female entrepreneurs position women. I discussed the concept "situated knowledge" and concluded that this is a feminist and critical study that aims at adhering to the criteria of consistency, transparency, and, above all, for its ability to open up for new ways of thinking about the object of study. The following chapter is devoted to a discussion of yet two more terms in the purpose formulation, namely "entrepreneur" and "entrepreneurship".

2

Entrepreneurship as Gendered

Defining the essence of entrepreneurship has occupied, and continues to occupy scholars from the 16th century and onward. I shall not try to define it, for two reasons. First, the epistemological position in this study does not acknowledge essences. If there is no essence as to what constitutes a man or a woman, it would be highly inconsistent to discuss the essence of what is an entrepreneur. Secondly, I do not study entrepreneurship as such, but how others, using the concept, perceive it. I believe, however, that many of the thoughts in the various definitions of entrepreneurship and of the entrepreneur as a person will be present in, and important for, the discourse about women's entrepreneurship. For this reason, I will take the reader through a brief tour of the definitions in economics and in management research on entrepreneurship[1]. The literature review points to a certain gendering of the entrepreneurship concept. For this reason, I proceed to look at the definitions through feminist eyes and attempt a deconstruction of the concept.

Entrepreneurship in Economics

The Physiocrats, Classical and Neo-classical Thinkers

In the context of economic theory, according to Hébert & Link's (1988) comprehensive review, on which I base this section of the chap-

---

1   Entrepreneurship is also discussed in, for example, education, where it is seen more as "creativity" than something pursued for economic gains. Theories on entrepreneurship in sociology, where present, also take a different angle. Likewise entrepreneurship in everyday discourse may have connotations beyond the ones discussed here. This review is restricted to the literature in economics and entrepreneurship research journals (with a base in economics and management) that the studied entrepreneurship researchers primarily rely on.

ter, the word entrepreneur first appeared in France. They trace the beginning to Cantillon (1680s?–1734; birth date unknown) who was a banker and financier in France. He wrote a famous essay, *Essai sur la nature du commerce en general*, which circulated privately among a small group of French economists but was not published until 1755. Cantillon defined the entrepreneur as someone who engages in exchanges for profit and exercises business judgment in the face of uncertainty. The uncertainty refers to the future sales price for goods on their way to final consumption. Entrepreneurs conducted all the production, circulation and exchange in a market economy and could thus be producers, merchants, arbitrageurs, or even robbers. (Cantillon made his own fortune by pulling out of an inflationary scheme in due time.) Cantillon saw entrepreneurship as a function, situated at the heart of the market economy.

Cantillon had a group of followers called The Physiocrats among whom Quesnay (1694–1774), who formulated the first mathematical general equilibrium system, added the role of capital, which Turgot (1727–1781) in turn defined as a special function, but still tied to the entrepreneur. One could be a capitalist without being an entrepreneur, but not vice versa. Baudeau (1730–1792) made the entrepreneur an innovator as well – someone who invents new techniques or ideas to reduce costs and increase profits. He also went beyond his predecessors in stressing the importance of the ability, intelligence and organizational skills of the person carrying out the entrepreneurial function.

Say (1767–1832), who belonged to the same tradition of thinkers, divided human industry into three steps – knowledge of how to do something, the application of this knowledge to a useful purpose (the entrepreneurial step), and the actual production that requires manual labor. The entrepreneurial step required sound judgment, one of the key features of Say's entrepreneur, making entrepreneurship synonymous with management.

Destutt de Tracy (1754–1836) envisioned the whole of society as nothing but a continual succession of exchange. Commerce and society was the same thing, wherefore entrepreneurship became a very wide function. He also theorized how entrepreneurs did what they could to influence legislation and institutional arrangement to their advantage, thus making them "political entrepreneurs". Saint-Simon (1760–1825), finally saw the entrepreneur as the astute business leader who piloted society into the era of industrialism. He was both the skilled manager and the visionary of society.

Whereas the French chiefly saw the entrepreneur as a risk bearer or a production coordinator, the English stressed the role of the capitalist. Adam Smith did not separate the function of the capitalist from that of the entrepreneurs, which set the standard for thoughts to come. The consequence was confusion between the concepts interest (the capitalist's reward) and profit (the entrepreneur's reward).

Through Ricardo and Marx, capitalists were seen as extorting labor for illegitimate purposes. A consequence was that entrepreneurial profit was also regarded as something illegitimate. Adam Smith recognized the role of technical innovation, but assigned this to a separate group of people, the "philosophers or men of speculation, whose trade it is not to do anything, but to observe everything; and who, upon that account, are often capable of combining together the powers of the most distant and dissimilar objects" (Smith cited in Hébert & Link, 1988:48).

John Stuart Mill (1876–1873) also equated the entrepreneur with the capitalist, although he noted the need for superior business talents. "If pressed, individual writers of the period would probably have denied it", write Hébert & Link, (1988:55) "but the impression left by British classical economics is that each business practically runs itself."

German thinkers were more astute in theorizing the entrepreneurial function. Von Thünen, for example, writing in 1850 conceptualized "entrepreneurial gain" as profit minus interest on invested capital, insurance against business losses and the wages of management. There is thus something, which is neither return on capital nor foreseeable risk, nor management compensation, but the reward for taking an entrepreneurial, uninsurable risk.

So there is a theoretical difference between entrepreneurship and management. A manager could sleep well having done his day of work, maintained von Thünen, but the entrepreneur had sleepless nights during which he, through much anxiety, came up with new and better solutions for the enterprise. So his entrepreneur was both an innovator and a risk bearer. An able person as well, according to Mangoldt, who maintained that the entrepreneurial profit was the rent of ability, wherefore the entrepreneur should be counted as a separate factor of production.

The thinkers discussed so far belong to classical economics. Neoclassical economists were concerned with the fundamental laws of price formation. Austrian thinkers from this era conceptualized the entrepreneur as the one who transformed goods from one stage to another in the production chain, involving time, risk and uncertainty

(Menger); a capitalist (Böhm-Bawerk); or a jack-of-all-trades (Wieser). The latter saw him as director, leader, employer, owner, capitalist, and innovator with perception, foresight, and courage.

Walras, a French economist who lived between 1834 and 1910, developed the theory of general, static equilibrium. He saw the entrepreneur neither as the capitalist, nor as the firm manager but rather as an intermediary between production and consumption, drawn to situations of disequilibrium where opportunities for profits reside. An economy in a state of equilibrium would, however, make him superfluous. Marshall's (1842–1924, British) entrepreneur was essentially a manager, but not just anyone could be a manager. Marshall was inspired by Darwin and had almost an evolutionary view on the development of entrepreneurs. His entrepreneur was a man of exceptional virtue who led the economic and moral progress of society, but this went mostly unrecognized.

> This imagination gains little credit with the people, because it is not allowed to run riot; its strength is disciplined by a stronger will; and its highest glory is to have attained great ends by means so simple that no one will know, and non but experts will even guess, how a dozen other expedients, each suggesting as much brilliancy to the hasty observer, were set aside in favour of it (Marshall, in Hébert & Link, 1988:76).

US theorist Amasa Walker (1700–1875) and his son Francis A. Walker (1840–1897) were more interested in separating the function of the entrepreneur from the capitalist but less keen on separating it from management. This made them emphasize the extraordinary abilities of the entrepreneurs. A successful entrepreneur had "the power of foresight, a facility for organization and administration, unusual energy, and other leadership qualities – traits that are generally in short supply" (ibid:85). This differential ability earned him his profit. The younger Walker even differentiated between four levels of entrepreneurs with different degrees of qualifications:

> "First we have those rarely-gifted persons ... whose commercial dealings have the air of magic; who have such power of foresight; who are so resolute and firm in temper that apprehensions and alarms and repeated shocks of disaster never cause them to relax their hold or change their coarse; who have such command over men that all with whom they have to do acquire vigor from the contact." Next, in descending order, is a class of high-ordered talent, persons of "natural mastery, sagacious, prompt and resolute in their avocation"; followed by those who do reasonably

well in business, although more by diligence then by genius; and finally ... those "of checkered fortunes, sometimes doing well, but more often ill ..." (Hébert & Link, 1988:86 citing Walker).

Knight (1885–1972) was, according to Hébert & Link, the US economist who most carefully examined entrepreneurship. First, he differed between insurable risk, of which you may calculate the probabilities, and uninsurable uncertainty, the most important of which being future demand. The presence of the latter transforms society into an "enterprise organization", where the function of the entrepreneurs becomes pivotal. He distinguished between management and entrepreneurship, but the manager became an entrepreneur if he "exercised judgment involving liability to error", without which profits could not exist.

Thus the economists have debated the dividing line between the entrepreneur, the innovator, the capitalist, and the manager; debated the role of risk and uncertainty and on who bears it; and tried to theorize the essence and role of profits. They all seemed to envision the entrepreneur as a man, and one of exceptional character, whether hero or maverick, and they all saw entrepreneurial activity as the response to some exogenous force exerted on the market system. Schumpeter, borrowing from Marx, Sombart, Weber, Walras, Menger, Wieser, and Böhm-Bawerk was to change this, and place the entrepreneur center stage as the driver of economic development. Since his thinking is paramount to modern theories of entrepreneurship, I will devote some more space to his ideas.

Schumpeter

Schumpeter's classic "The theory of economic development" was first published in German in 1911. An English edition was published in 1934. Schumpeter's main contribution to economics was to introduce the theory of "economic development", which is conceptualized differently than general equilibrium theory. Economic development comes from within the capitalist system, and it comes in bursts rather than gradually. Economic development is accompanied by economic growth, but it is more than that. It brings qualitative changes or "revolutions" which radically transform old equilibriums. "Add successively as many mail coaches as you please, you will never get a railroad thereby", said Schumpeter, to explain the difference (Schumpeter, 1934/1983:64). Adding a railroad, however, would displace other means of traffic, which made him label this process "creative destruction" as well.

Schumpeter suggested that innovation and economic development can be achieved in five different ways: (a) the introduction of new goods, (b) the introduction of new methods of production, (c) the opening up of a new market, (d) the conquest of a new source of supply of raw materials or half-manufactured goods, or (e) the carrying out of a new organization of any industry, such as the creation of a monopoly or the breaking up of one.

Schumpeter called the carrying out of any one of these "enterprise" and the person who does this is the "entrepreneur". His gain is the profit that can be reaped until a new equilibrium has emerged. He does not necessarily bear the economic risk, however, the banker who furnishes the necessary credit does that. Schumpeter's entrepreneur is not the same as a business owner/manager either since the latter does not necessarily carry out new combinations but may merely operate an established business.

Schumpeter was reluctant to assign entrepreneurs to a special social class or to a special vocation, since he conceptualized the entrepreneurial function rather than the person, but still, someone has to carry the function. Who is this person and what motivates him? It was always a "he" – perhaps superfluous to note since Schumpeter was an Austrian aristocrat writing at the beginning of the last century[2]. More than his gender distinguished the entrepreneur, however.

> While in the accustomed circular flow every individual can act promptly and rationally because he is sure of his ground and is supported by the conduct ... of all other individuals, who in turn expect the accustomed activity from him, he cannot simply do this when he is confronted by a new task. While in the accustomed channels his own ability and experience suffice for the normal individual, when confronted with innovations he needs guidance ... Where the boundaries of routine stop, many people can go no further (Schumpeter, 1934/1983:78–80).

Entrepreneurs are a special type, and unusual. Many men can sing, he says, but the Carusos are rare. First, his intuition and daring makes an entrepreneur take the right decision even though he does not have complete information. Secondly, he has the ability to go beyond fixed habits of thinking. "This mental freedom presupposes a great surplus force over the everyday demand and is something peculiar and rare in

---

2   Until the early 1980's scientific texts customarily referred to the individual as "he", irrespective of if the texts talked about men or women. Since then, it has become politically incorrect, but it is still very common.

nature" writes Schumpeter (1934/1983:86). Thirdly, he is able to withstand the opposition coming from the social environment against one who wishes to do something new.

> Surmounting this opposition is always a special kind of task which does not exist in the customary course of life, a task which also requires a special kind of conduct. In matters economic this resistance manifests itself first of all in the groups threatened by the innovation, then in the difficulty in finding the necessary cooperation, finally in the difficulty in winning over consumers (ibid:87).

The entrepreneurs carry out economic leadership, but, as Schumpeter writes, "the personality of the capitalistic entrepreneur need not, and generally does not, answer to the idea most of us have of what a 'leader' looks like, so much so that there is some difficulty in realizing that he comes from within the social category of leader at all" (ibid:89). He leads the means of production into new channels, and he leads (unwillingly) imitators into the field, undercutting his own profits, but the only person he needs to convince is the banker and the service he renders takes a specialist to appreciate.

> Add to this the precariousness of the economic position both of the individual entrepreneurs and of entrepreneurs as a group, and the fact that when his economic success raises him socially he has no cultural tradition or attitude to fall back upon, but moves about in society as an upstart, whose ways are readily laughed at, and we shall understand why this type has never been popular, and why even scientific critique often makes short work of it (ibid:90).

What motivates this unusual, and by others seen as odd, figure? He is more self-centered than other types, writes Schumpeter, but is in no sense a hedonist.

> Experience teaches ... that typical entrepreneurs retire from the arena only when and because their strength is spent and they feel no longer equal to their task. This does not seem to verify the picture of the economic man, balancing probable results against disutility of effort and reaching in due coarse a point of equilibrium beyond which he is not willing to go ... And activity of the entrepreneurial type is obviously an obstacle to hedonist enjoyment of those kinds of commodity which are usually acquired by incomes beyond a certain size, because their 'consumption' presupposes leisure (ibid:92).

So, if not hedonist consumption, what is it that motivates him? Schumpeter sees three things. The first is "the dream and the will to found a private kingdom, usually, but not necessarily, also a dynasty" (ibid:93). He says that this is the nearest approach to medieval lordship possible to modern man, and that it offers a sense of power and independence, particularly for those who have no other means of achieving social distinction. The second motive is the will to conquer: "the impulse to fight, to prove oneself superior to others, to succeed for the sake, not of the fruits of success, but of success itself. From this aspect, economic action becomes akin to sport – there are financial races, or rather boxing-matches." (ibid:93). "Finally", writes Schumpeter, "there is the joy of creating, of getting things done, or simply of exercising one's energy and ingenuity. This is akin to a ubiquitous motive, but nowhere else does it stand out as an independent factor of behavior with anything like the clearness with which it obtrudes itself in our case. Our type seeks out difficulties, changes in order to change, delights in ventures." (ibid:93–94) .

Schumpeter's entrepreneur is associated with economic change, growth, and development, and the entrepreneurial function is thus positioned as a necessity and a good thing for society. The entrepreneur becomes the heroic figure who carries this function, which is so vital to society. In his introduction to the 1983 edition of "The theory of economic development", John E. Elliott writes:

> ... the entrepreneur must be a man of 'vision', of daring, willing to take chances, to strike out, largely on the basis of intuition, on courses of action in direct opposition to the established, settled patterns of the circular flow. The entrepreneur is more of a 'heroic' than an 'economic' figure: he must have 'the drive and the will to found a private kingdom' as a 'captain of industry'; the 'will to conquer', to fight for the sake of the fight rather than simply the financial gains of the combat: the desire to create new things – even at the expense of destroying old patterns of thought and action (xxi).

Economists after Schumpeter have continued the debates on the view of the entrepreneurs along the lines outlined above, departing either from a neo-classical equilibrium theory position, or from Schumpeter's position, recognized as the Austrian school (even if Schumpeter himself was not a "pure Austrian"). The study of entrepreneurship in economics spans the whole spectrum from very abstract studies of the market and pricing mechanism, to very concrete phenomena such as the firm and the individual entrepreneur. According to Hébert & Link, (1988:8) "the concept of entrepreneurship bids fair to the claim of being the most elusive concept within the purview of economics" perhaps, claim the authors, because the entrepreneur as a change agent did not fit well within equilibrium theory which had come to dominate economics. Most of the reviewed economists regard entrepreneurship in functional terms (innovation, financing, managing, risk-bearing, etc.) but Hébert & Link hold that the entrepreneur must be theorized as well and that his/her most basic features are perception, courage and action. They ask:

> What gifts of intellect, imagination, critical judgment, capacity for res-
> olute action and sustained effort, courage and detachment are required if
> a person is to bring novelty into the business scene and to shape in some
> degree its ongoing historical evolution? Is the continual and sometimes
> dramatic transformation of the means, ends and methods of business the
> work of a type of moving spirit, a class of exceptional people? If so, what
> are they like, what precisely is exceptional in their psyches, their situa-
> tions in life, their sources of inspiration? Finally, what sets their thought
> on fire and spurs them to action? (Hébert & Link 1988:7–8).

This fascination with the person carries through to entrepreneurship research, which is the topic of the next section.

The Entrepreneur in Management Research on Entrepreneurship

Entrepreneurship research has been a separate research field in management research, with its own publications, research centers, and endowed chairs since the 1970s or the early 1980s, and it is rapidly growing (Cooper et.al 2000). The field inherited the definitions of entrepreneurship from economics, with Schumpeter as the most important source of inspiration. With an understanding of entrepreneurship as "creative destruction" (Schumpeter, 1934/1983); "pure alertness to as yet unexploited – because unnoticed – opportunities" (Kirzner 1983:286); or "… the pursuit of opportunity without regard to resources currently controlled" (Stevenson (1984:5), many envisioned entrepreneurship as an act of creativity, innovation, and ingenuity. Entrepreneurs were seen as risk takers and perhaps a little bit as daredevils. The concept of growth and success and earning a good personal profit are implicit as is the contribution to economic growth in society. These definitions clearly center on process: "creative destruction, pursuit of opportunities, alertness to opportunities, breaking an equilibrium", but the person who accomplishes this is also seen as unique and important for society.

Consequently, most of the early research on entrepreneurs focused on who this person was, rather than on what this person did. The idea was that the entrepreneurial personality differed from the ordinary, and by identifying such a person it would be possible to select would-be entrepreneurs and thus stimulate entrepreneurship for the benefit of the economy. This is commonly referred to as the trait approach. It has been very productive in outlining the characteristics of entrepreneurs, but disappointingly unproductive in finding out how they differ from others. Gartner (1988:22), reviewing the psychological research, found that "when certain psychological traits are carefully evaluated, it is not possible to differentiate entrepreneurs from managers or from the general population based on the entrepreneur's supposed possession of such traits".

The entrepreneurs that one might suspect to be the true equilibrium breakers are also difficult to locate for research purposes. They are best identified after the fact, and there are not that many of them. Bill Gates and Steven Jobs do not constitute a big enough sample to be statistically significant. What researchers ended up using instead were samples of small business owners. The great majority of small business owners, both men and women, do not want their businesses to grow, however. They are content with a business of a manageable size in which they can retain control and earn enough money to support their family (Wiklund et al., 1997; Aldrich, 1999). Very few of the "entrepreneurs" in the samples of small business owners typically used in entrepreneurship research carry out any of the five different sorts of innovation leading to economic development as described by Schumpeter. Most small business owners would therefore not qualify as entrepreneurs according to Schumpeter.

The great paradox of entrepreneurship research is thus that researchers have been looking for the characteristics leading to entrepreneurship in the Schumpeterian sense among entrepreneurs of the small business owner type. This was of course not left without criticism within the field. The late 1980s saw many articles taking stock of research so far. Gartner (1988), for example, argued that the trait approach should be abandoned and entrepreneurship should be most usefully defined as creating an organization. There were no descriptions concerning the type of organization, growth ambitions, or the degree of innovation, because it is just too hard to pin down these concepts and they prove unproductive as research subjects. Instead, he argued for a behavioral approach: what do entrepreneurs do? He advocated defining and studying entrepreneurial activities instead of persons.

This leaves questions, however. First, entrepreneurial activities in Schumpeter's sense may be found even within existing organizations, or in activities that do not lead to a formal organization but that are nevertheless organizing[3]. Second, not drawing a line between entrepreneurship and small business management might tend to make the concept too wide to legitimate a special research field called entrepreneurship research as distinct from general management research. The "Schumpeterian dimension" might get lost altogether.

Gartner cited Yeats "How can we know the dancer from the dance" and advocated dance studies, but as Carland et al. (1988) responded, if we cannot know the dancer from the dance, the dancer should be just as interesting and they advocated continued – and refined – trait research. Since they envisioned behavior modification (e.g., encouraging people to start businesses) as a goal of entrepreneurship research, they argued that to modify a behavior, first one must know why an individual behaves in a particular manner. Inconclusive results should not be a stop sign, but rather a sign that the research methods need to be developed and refined.

But is it at all possible? Low & MacMillan, (1988:148), reviewing the field wrote, "…being innovators and idiosyncratic, entrepreneurs tend to defy aggregation. They tend to reside at the tails of population distributions, and though they may be expected to differ from the mean, the nature of these differences are not predictable. It seems that any attempt to profile the typical entrepreneurs is inherently futile". They go for the "creation of new enterprise" definition and advocate that entrepreneurship adopts "to explain and facilitate the role of new enterprise in furthering societal level economic growth" (ibid:141) as its main purpose.

Hornaday (1990) thought that the "E-word" should be dropped altogether from small business research, since it was developed as an "ideal type" in economics with little relevance for present small business research. Instead he advocated an owner-typology (craft, professional manager, and promoter) based on the owners' motivations and

---

3   At the end of his article, Gartner mentions internal start-ups, but it is not a main thrust of his argument.

intentions for the business (practicing a trade, building an organization, or pursuing personal wealth).

The term is a ghost that will not so easily be put to rest, however.
"For a field of social science to have usefulness, it must have a conceptual framework that explains and predicts a set of empirical phenomena not explained and predicted by conceptual frameworks already in
existence in other fields" wrote Shane & Ventakataraman, (2000:217).
The issue is both one of legitimacy, and one of a unique contribution
in the broader field of management research. Building on Schumpeter
and Kirzner, they argued that the phenomenon of entrepreneurship
must be studied, since it is the driving force in the economic change
process and the way inefficiencies in the market are remedied. It is also
the way society converts technical information into new products and
services.

They criticize both the focus on who the entrepreneur is and on
what this person does, saying that this presents a one-sided view of the
phenomenon since entrepreneurship "involves the nexus of two phenomena: the presence of lucrative opportunities and the presence of
enterprising individuals" (ibid:218). They define the field of entrepreneurship as "the scholarly examination of how, by whom, and with
what effects opportunities to create future goods and services are dis-
covered, evaluated and exploited".

The novelty is the attention to opportunities, as "objective phenomena that are not known to all parties at all times" (ibid:220). They
also distinguish between entrepreneurial opportunities and the larger
set of opportunities for profit, particularly those related to enhancing
the efficiency of existing goods, services, raw materials, and organizing
methods. The latter can be optimized through calculation but the former is unknown. The person is still important – some people see opportunities and others do not, depending on information and cognitive schema, and some act on them whereas others do not. They refer
to research indicating that those who exploit opportunities are
achievement oriented and optimistic. They have greater self-efficacy,
more internal locus of control, and a greater tolerance for ambiguity.

The main objection to this opportunity-based approach is the claim
about the existence of objective opportunities. They can only be identified after the fact, and how is it then possible to say that a number of
objective opportunities exist? The classic question in entrepreneurship
research "Who is an entrepreneur?" might now be replaced with
"What is an entrepreneurial opportunity?", notes Singh (2001:11).

Virtually all of the reviewed authors in economics, and most of the entrepreneurship research scholars reviewed here[4] envision entrepreneurship as something that takes place in a market, for profit. Non-profit organizations or activities are seldom discussed. Entrepreneurship as creating something new outside of a market context is not discussed either, leaving new things invented and applied in the public sector outside the field. Apart from this, there is little agreement.

Is it risk taking? Is it profit seeking? Is it wealth creation? Is it decisions in the face of uncertainty? Is it management? Is it being a capitalist? Is it the creation of a new organization? Is it the exploitation of opportunities? Is it making new combinations? Is it innovation? Is it growth? Is it breaking economic equilibriums, or is it bringing the economy back to equilibrium? Is it something requiring a special person, and what is then special about this person?

The quest for a definition continues. Meanwhile, empirical research on the phenomenon continues as well. Perhaps one might tell where the field is headed by examining the research that is done, instead of opting for an ex-ante definition? Two such attempts were presented at the 2001 Babson conference[5] in Jönköping. Grégoire et al. (2001), investigating co-citations in research articles published in Frontiers of Entrepreneurship Research from 1981 to 1999 concluded that five fields have attracted entrepreneurship scholars over time: personal characteristics of the entrepreneur, factors affecting new venture performance, venture capitalists' practices, social networks and research drawing from a resource-based perspective. Going beyond citations, Meeks et al. (2001) content-analyzed all articles in the three leading research journals in the field (Entrepreneurship Theory and Practice, Journal of Business Venturing and Journal of Small Business Management) from 1980 to 2000. They identified thirty conversations (topics) and classified each of the 1,624 articles accordingly. The three largest of the thirty conversations were small business management issues, international issues, and firm performance, but "contrary to hypotheses related to a Kuhnian progression of the field, results indicate no convergence in conversation, nor reduction in conversation regard-

---

4   The concept of non-profit entrepreneurship is not completely foreign to entrepreneurship research – some of the editions of "Frontiers of Entrepreneurship Research" which is the proceedings of the Babson entrepreneurship research conference (see footnote below) have an explicit section on this. However, it is extremely rare as a concept in the journals included in this study.

5   Formally the Babson College Kauffman Foundation Entrepreneurship Research Conference, an annual conference held to be the leading entrepreneurship research conference by entrepreneurship scholars. It is based in the USA but meets in Europe every other year.

ing fundamental definition and domain issues" concluded the authors (Meeks et al., 2001:1). The authors saw this as a problem, especially for issues of identity and legitimacy. "I want to know where to hang my hat", said Michael Meeks at the conference presentation.

In spite of a lack of a commonly accepted definition of entrepreneurship, there seems to be a general agreement among entrepreneurship researchers that *more* of it is desired, since entrepreneurship is associated with economic development and growth. Society needs more entrepreneurs, and more entrepreneurship – but some are better than others. You can be more or less entrepreneurial. Francis A. Walker, cited in the previous section, discussed it eloquently when he separated between four classes of entrepreneurs, from those rarely-gifted persons whose commercial dealings had the air of magic, down to those of checkered fortunes who sometimes did good but more often ill.

This thought has survived, both regarding the persons and their businesses. Much research has been devoted not only to finding differences between entrepreneurs and non-entrepreneurs, but also to scaling the same as more or less, using for example different demographic and personality/motivation measures. The scale for the businesses seems to involve both size and kind. Shane & Ventakamaran (2001) for example, reasoning from their opportunity-based view of entrepreneurship, thought it important and necessary to distinguish between opportunities for developing a cure for cancer and an opportunity to fill students' need for snacks at a local high school. This thought is present in many entrepreneurship texts, but that "big is better" is seldom further motivated, it is taken for granted. Size and/or growth measures for businesses (e.g., sales and employment), or profitability measures (e.g., profit, return on investment and the like) are frequently used in entrepreneurship research. To sum up, no one knows what this creature really is like, but most agree that it is a very good and useful one, and is to be kept and nourished.

A Feminist Deconstruction of Entrepreneurship

The discussions about the entrepreneur related above describe this person in words that lead the thought to a man, and not a woman. It is not only the frequent use of the male pronoun when referring to the entrepreneur (this was standard in science until the 1980s), but also the way he is described. I am not first to point out that entrepreneurship is a male gendered concept. It might be argued that this is because entrepreneurs have traditionally been men, but several authors hold that women entrepreneurs have been made invisible (Sundin, 1988; Sundin & Holmquist, 1989; Javefors Grauers, 1999; Stider, 1999). Other authors discuss male gendered measuring instruments (Moore, 1990; Stevenson, 1990), gendered attitudes to entrepreneurs (Nilsson, 1997), or male gendered theory (Reed, 1996; Mirchandani, 1999). But one needs only to read through the definitions of entrepreneurship to see that it is a male gendered concept. To make this point clear, I devote the remainder of this chapter to a feminist deconstruction of the entrepreneurship definitions discussed earlier.

A Short Note on Deconstruction

A basic idea of deconstruction is that a text says as much by what it does not say, as by what it says. The silences in a text can be said to hide, or make ideological assumptions appear neutral or absent. Analyzing them can make the devalued "other" visible. A deconstruction is of course always subject to further deconstruction – there is no end point where one has "revealed it all". Feminists have mixed feelings about it for this very reason. Some feminists favor positive knowledge claims on which to build political action. I agree with Joanne Martin, however. She writes that deconstruction is a powerful analytical tool, and "the risks are worth it" (Martin, 1990:211). Scholars using deconstruction employ a number of systematic strategies for analyzing the silences and the absences in a text.[6] The technique I have developed in this chapter is inspired by Saussure (1970), who said that one could only make sense of something by picturing what it is not. "Woman" is "not man", or "the opposite of man", and vice versa (Gherardi, 1995). Using my own literature review as analysis material, I went through the previous two sections of this chapter and underlined all words used to describe entrepreneur and entrepreneurship. Then I looked for their opposites, using an antonym dictionary. When the dictionary failed, I reached for inter-subjective agreements among knowledgeable colleagues. For the concept "entrepreneurship" I stayed here, but for "entrepreneur" I chose to compare the lists of words and their opposites to a widely used femininity/masculinity index in order to pinpoint its gendering. Through this deconstructive move, I take the review of entrepreneurship definitions one step further.

---

6   See Joanne Martin (1990) for an accessible introduction to and an application of deconstruction.

Deconstruction of "Entrepreneurship"

It was evident in the discussion that it is difficult to pinpoint, or at least agree on what entrepreneurship is. It might be easier to come to grips with it if looking at what it is not envisioned as. As mentioned, entrepreneurship in economic theory is discussed in conjunction with economic activity of some sort. One may thus count out new ideas and initiatives outside of a market context. If I invent and build a new gadget at home, for my own use, it is not entrepreneurship as discussed by the economists. Most of the economists also theorize the role of profit in entrepreneurship. The not-for-profit sector can thus be counted out. The public sector is also a not-for profit sector and could likewise be dismissed. Entrepreneurship in economic theory seems to be something taking place in the private business sector.

Opposites to some of the concepts (possibly) defining entrepreneurship are just the negation of it. "Not furnishing capital" would, for example be the opposite of the capitalist function. The opposite of wealth creation would also be the negation of it. Organizing or managing, likewise, would be not organizing and not managing. The latter might perhaps be seen as taking orders from someone else. For other concepts it is easier to envision meaningful opposites, for example for the concept "innovation". Entrepreneurship is discussed in terms of change and innovation. Innovation is also novelty, improvement and advancement according to my on-line dictionary. What would be the opposite? Status quo? Routine? Following traditions and old habits? The words risk, risk-taking, or risk bearing are also used. Safety and risk-avoidance would be the opposite of this. Likewise certainty would be the opposite of the uncertainty associated with risk. The opposite of perceiving new opportunities might be to think on old lines. Schumpeter saw entrepreneurship as a driving force in societal change, causing economic growth. Would there be something as a restraining force to counter this? Or is it just the absence of any force? And would the opposite of growth be standstill? Table 2.1 below summarizes the exercise.

Table 2.1: *Words Describing Entrepreneurship and Their Opposites.*

Entrepreneurship	Opposites
A market activity	Doing things that are not traded
For profit	Non-profit
Private sector	Public sector
Innovation, innovative	Routine, traditional, habit-like
Change	Stability
Risk	Safety
Risk-taking, risk-bearing	Risk-avoidance
Uncertainty	Certainty
Managing	Taking orders, or failing
Opportunity perception	Blindness to opportunity
Driving force	Restraining force
Growth	Stagnation, decay

I would guess that I am not alone to conclude that the second column is not very appealing. It conveys a feeling of a place where absolutely nothing happens and change is unthinkable. The conclusion I make of this, for the purposes of this study, is that entrepreneurship is constructed as something positive, associated with innovation, growth, and development. It seems as if entrepreneurship contributes to the "betterment of things", fitting nicely into the grand narrative of modernity where development is not only change, but also "progress", something that is both valued and seemingly inevitable (Foucault, 1969/1972; Lyotard, 1979/1984).

Deconstruction of "Entrepreneur"

Entrepreneurship is positioned here as a blessing for society. It follows that the entrepreneur would be a blessing as well, although sometimes misunderstood and unrecognized as Marshall and Schumpeter pointed out. What follows is an exercise similar to the one for the word "entrepreneur". The left hand side column lists the words the reviewed theorists have used to describe such a person, and on the right hand side column my suggestions for opposites can be found.

Table 2.2: *Words Describing Entrepreneur and Their Opposites.*

Entrepreneur	Opposites
Able	Unable
Intelligent	Stupid
Skilled at organizing	Disorganized, chaotic
Exercising sound judgment,	Making bad judgments,
Superior business talents	Inferior business talents
Astute	Gullible
Influential	Impressionable
Pilot of industrialism	Passenger (of industrialism)
Manager	Subordinate
Perceptive	Blind
Foresighted	Shortsighted
Courageous	Cowardly, cautious
Leading economic and moral progress	Following (economic and moral progress)
Strong willed	Weak
Unusually energetic	Plegmatic
Resolute	Iresolute
Firm in temper	Moody
Stick to a course	Wavering
Daring	Cowardly
Decisive in spite of uncertainty	Wishy-washy
Mentally free	Mentally constrained
Able to withstand opposition	Yielding
Self-centered	Selfless
Wants a private kingdom and a dynasty	No need to put a mark on the world
Seeks power	Avoids power
Independent	Dependent
Wants to fight and conquer	Avoids struggle and competition
Want to prove superiority	No need to prove oneself
Likes to create	Likes to copy
Seeks difficulty	Avoids difficulty
Visionary	Pragmatist
Active	Passive
Detached	Connected
Capacity for sustained effort	Feeble
Achievement oriented	Fatalist
Internal locus of control	External locus of control
Optimistic	Pessimistic
Self-efficacious	Self-doubting
Tolerance for ambiguity	Intolerance for ambiguity

The words in table 2.2 show a polarity between strong and weak, active and passive, leader and follower. These words resemble the dichotomy with which "masculine" and "feminine" are often described. Yvonne Hirdman has a list of quotes from thinkers throughout history that is very telling. An example is Philius from Alexandria who said, "The male is more complete and more dominant then the female, closer to action, because the female is incomplete, inferior and passive rather than active". Thomas of Aquino said "It is not likely that woman was created first. Because the philosopher (Aristotle) says that woman is a malformed man. Nothing malformed or incomplete could have been created first" (Hirdman 2001:19–20, my translations).

Going back to such thoughts makes it very explicit, but might perhaps be written off as outdated. Let me instead rest on Sandra Bem's (1981) research. Bem developed a sex-role inventory, widely used in American psychological research, and also quoted in some of the entrepreneurship research included in this study. The inventory, reproduced in table 2.3 below, captures what Americans, both men and women, generally considered typical masculine and feminine traits.

Masculinity and femininity is in Bem's research seen as two separate constructs – unlike table 2.2, table 2.3 should not be read from left to right. It is not a continuous scale with femininity on one side and masculinity on the other. An individual can score high or low on each construct. Bem devised a four by four matrix where people were masculine, feminine, androgynous (high on both dimensions) or undifferentiated (low on both dimensions). How people score on the test is not of interest here[7], the culturally accepted norms of what is masculine and feminine is.

One might expect that constructs of gender differ in different cultures. Comparing the USA and Sweden, Persson (1999) refers to Hofstede (1984) who found that Sweden scored lowest of all 39 participating countries on a masculinity index (6 for Sweden versus 62 for the USA and 87 for Japan). Persson tested and revised Bem's scale for use in a Swedish context. Several of the words did indeed have low face validity in Sweden.

As a result of his research, Persson deleted the words marked with an asterisk in the table below. He also pointed out that there might be other words that better yet capture the masculinity/femininity construct in Sweden and that were not included in Bem's list at all. Enough words remain, however, to make me conclude, by comparison to the previous list, that the construct entrepreneur, also in a Swedish context, is a male gendered construct. The words associated with entrepreneur in the table above are also the words associated with masculinity in the table below, and they are not the words associated with femininity.

---

7   Both Bem's American sample and Persson's Swedish sample turned out to be mostly undifferentiated or androgynous.

Table 2.3: *Bem's Scale of Masculinity and Femininity.*

Bem's Masculinity Scale	Bem's Femininity Scale
Self-reliant	Affectionate
Defends own beliefs	Loyal
Assertive	Feminine
Strong personality	Sympathetic
Forceful	Sensitive to the needs of others
Has leadership abilities	Understanding
Willing to take risks	Compassionate
Makes decisions easily	Eager to soothe hurt feelings
Self-sufficient	Soft spoken
Dominant	Warm
Masculine	Tender
Willing to take a stand	Gentle
Act as a leader	Loves children*
Individualistic*	Does not use harsh language*
Competitive*	Flatterable*
Ambitious*	Shy*
Independent*	Yielding*
Athletic*	Cheerful*
Analytical*	Gullible*
Aggressive*	Childlike*

Let me compare the lists more closely, and see if the conclusion holds. Below I have juxtaposed the words from Bem's masculinity scale and the words describing entrepreneur from table 2.2. I took away the word "masculine" since it is tautological. It turned out that, apart from "likes to create" and "tolerance for ambiguity", it was quite easy to associate the words describing the entrepreneur to corresponding words in the masculinity index. Some even appear in several places. The only masculinity-words for which I did not find a good fit were "athletic" and "aggressive". "Forceful" and "assertive" might cover aggressive quite well, however.

Table 2.4: *Masculinity Words Compared to Entrepreneur Words.*

Bem's Masculinity Scale	Entrepreneur
Self-reliant	Self-centered, Internal locus of control, Self-efficacious, Mentally free, Able
Defends own beliefs	Strong willed
Assertive	Able to withstand opposition
Strong personality	Resolute, Firm in temper
Forceful	Unusually energetic, Capacity for sustained effort, Active
Has leadership abilities	Skilled at organizing, Visionary
Willing to take risks	Seeks difficulty, Optimistic, Daring, Courageous
Makes decisions easily	Decisive in spite of uncertainty
Self-sufficient	Independent, Detached
Dominant	Influential, Seeks power, Wants a private kingdom and a dynasty
Willing to take a stand	Stick to a course
Act as a leader	Leading economic and moral progress, Pilot of industrialism, Manager
Individualistic*	Detached
Competitive*	Wants to fight and conquer, Wants to prove superiority
Ambitious*	Achievement oriented
Independent*	Independent, Mentally free
Athletic*	
Analytical*	Exercising sound judgment, Superior business talent, Foresighted, Astute, Perceptive, Intelligent
Aggressive*	
Leftovers	Tolerance for ambiguity, Likes to create

Finding a similar fit for the femininity scale is probably not as easy, since the lists are created in different ways. Bem wanted positive words on both lists so that no one would be hesitant to identify him/herself with them because of negative connotations. My list of opposites of the entrepreneur words in table 2.2 is constructed the other way – as negations of the entrepreneur words. Let me try anyway.

Table 2.5: *Femininity Words Compared to Opposites of Entrepreneur Words.*

Bem's Femininity Scale	Opposites of Entrepreneur Words
Affectionate	
Loyal	Follower, Dependent
Sympathetic	
Sensitive to the needs of others	Selfless, Connected
Understanding	
Compassionate	
Eager to soothe hurt feelings	
Soft spoken	
Warm	
Tender	
Gentle	Cautious
Loves children*	
Does not use harsh language*	
Flatterable*	
Shy*	Cowardly
Yielding*	Yielding, No need to put a mark on the world, Subordinate, Passenger, Irresolute, Following, Weak, Wavering, External locus of control, Fatalist, Wishy-washy, Uncommitted, Avoids power, Avoids struggle and competition, Self-doubting, No need to prove oneself
Cheerful*	
Gullible*	Gullible, Blind, Shortsighted, Impressionable, Making bad judgments, Unable, Mentally constrained, Stupid, Disorganized, Chaotic, Lack of business talent, Moody
Childlike*	
Leftovers	Phlegmatic, Stuck in old patterns of thinking, Likes to copy, Avoids difficulty, Feeble, Pessimistic, Pragmatist, Intolerance for ambiguity

The exercise proved interesting in spite of the difficulties. It turned out that the two femininity words most associated with the non-entrepreneur words were "yielding" and "gullible". Both words reinforce how language positions women as "less" than men and as subordinated men. Most of the positive words associated with womanhood in Bem's list – affectionate, sympathetic, understanding, compassionate, warm, tender, etc. – do not seem to be present in the discussion about entrepreneurship at all, neither as words describing the entrepreneur nor as their opposites. I think it is quite safe to conclude that the language used to describe entrepreneurship is male gendered. Entrepreneurship is thus a male gendered construct, it is not neutral.

That the description of the entrepreneur is male gendered should of course not be understood to mean that entrepreneurs (or men) are all those things used to describe them above. It is a particular, culturally constituted, and time and space bound version of masculinity[8] that is communicated, and which, through the theorization of the entrepreneur, is reproduced.

Not only is the construct male gendered, it also implies a gendered division of labor. Being an entrepreneur – strong-willed, determined, persistent, resolute, detached and self-centered – requires some time, effort and devotion to a task (well, energetic was also on the list), leaving little time for the caring of small children, cooking, cleaning and all the other chores necessary to survive. Performing entrepreneurship in the sense described above requires a particular gendered division of labor where it is assumed that a wife (or if unmarried, usually a woman anyway) does the unpaid, reproductive work associated with the private sphere. Perhaps not all of Schumpeter's entrepreneurs had a family, but founding a dynasty certainly required one.

Mulholland (1996) addressed this latter point in an ethnographic study of seventy of the richest entrepreneurial families in an English county. All but four were owned by a male head, who acted both as the family voice and gatekeeper, controlling access to female kin. She found that entrepreneurialism reinforced masculinity for the owners, while denying that men do emotional labor in the process of building their businesses. The respondents "denied male emotion – and yet their energies and passions were channeled into the creative process of accumulating capital, rationalized in building a business and reconstituting their masculine identities" (Mulholland, 1996:141). At the same time, it exonerated them from emotional labor within the family. They were seen as "family men", providing financially for their families, but this label hid that they spent hardly any time at home. The wives ran the family and the home, took all the responsibility for child rearing doing both mothering and fathering, fixed dinners for business associates, and acted as emotional nurturers and counselors for their hus-

---

8   Connel (1995:77) discusses the currently dominant version of masculinity as *hegemonic masculinity*. It is defined as "the configuration of gender practice which embodies the currently accepted answer to the problem of the legitimacy of patriarchy, which guarantees (or is taken to guarantee) the dominant position of men and the subordination of women". He stresses that few men embody it, sometimes not even members of the ruling classes but perhaps rather movie stars or sports stars, but that many men support it anyway (labeled *complicity*) since they gain from it – they "benefit from the patriarchal dividend, the advantage men in general gain from the overall subordination of women" (ibid:79). With hegemonic masculinity comes *subordinated* and *marginalized* forms of masculinity as well, as for example gays. Hegemonic masculinity is not static, it changes in time and context, but it cannot be ignored – it orders not only male/female relationships but also relationships among different men, embodying different masculinities. See Hearn (1999) and Nordberg (1999) for a critical discussion of the concept hegemonic masculinity.

bands. Some wives also filled Veblen's (1926) notion of "vicarious conspicuous consumption".[9]

Mulholland described a wife of a self-made man of the 1980's who, apart from her wifely duties, also joined the local English Speaking Society as a secretary and was the chair of the Conversation Society in the village, transmitting an upper middle class image essential to the construction of the husband's particular masculinity. The couple bought a small mansion, and this husband actually spent the weekends at home, not mowing the lawn, but rather playing tennis with his friends. Mulholland showed how the men in her study, by appropriating the labor of their wives, were able to claim their leisure time as their own. She also discussed this as a phenomenon not tied to class or money; it was as common among working class men as among the wealthy (Collinson, 1992).

In the early entrepreneurship literature, this arrangement is completely taken for granted, and in the later research it is very seldom problematized. As I will show in chapter seven, only when researching women entrepreneurs are childcare problems addressed. Entrepreneurship is researched as something disconnected from family and reproduction and gendered divisions of labor. The result is that the concept maintains an air of neutrality while hiding that it is highly male gendered. Reproductive work seems to be something that falls outside the sphere of entrepreneurship even when it is not carried out in the family. As discussed above, activities taking place in the public and the non-profit sectors are not discussed as entrepreneurship.

In many western countries, the bulk of the public sector consists of organizations such as pre-schools and schools, libraries, hospitals, primary care and eldercare, and the vast majority of the people who work there are women. Not only is a large part of the economy disregarded, the disregard itself seems to be gendered. Things that women do, things that can be seen to belong to the "reproductive" sphere whether done at home or in the public sector, do not count as entrepreneurship, contributing to making women's work invisible in the entrepreneurship literature.

---

9   According to Veblen, the leisure class (the idle rich) consumed to impress others, but when it became manly to work at the turn of the last century, the conspicuous consumption was handed over to the wives.

Summary

Revisiting the purpose, *to analyze the discursive construction of the female entrepreneur/female entrepreneurship in research texts from a feminist theory perspective*, this chapter has served to discuss the concepts of entrepreneur and entrepreneurship.

The first two sections of this chapter showed that there is no consensus as to what constructs "entrepreneurship", neither in economics nor in entrepreneurship research. The third section revealed that a few things are easy to agree on, however. First, entrepreneurship is constructed as something positive. Secondly, more of it is better than less, which is reflected in all of the different ways of measuring entrepreneurship. Thirdly, it is a male gendered concept with implications not only for individual entrepreneurs but also for the organization of society. Entrepreneurship as described in economics and in business research requires a particular gendered division of labor where it is assumed that a woman does the unpaid, reproductive work associated with the private sphere. It also disregards reproductive work carried out in the public sector.

As noted earlier, it is not the task of this study to define entrepreneurship. I believe however, that many of the thoughts in the various definitions discussed earlier will be present in, and important for, the discourse about women's entrepreneurship found in the research texts. The analysis above found the discourse on entrepreneurship in the economic literature to be male gendered. It is not gender neutral. Studying women's entrepreneurship implies that the concept "woman" is involved as well. There is a discourse on womanhood that is in conflict with the discourse on entrepreneurship. Being a woman and an entrepreneur at the same time means that one has to position oneself simultaneously in regard to two conflicting discourses. The two discourses will also be present in the framing of studies of women entrepreneurs. In later chapters I intend to find out how, and with what effects. This anticipates the discussion in the next chapter, which is devoted to the concept discourse.

3

Defining and Applying the Concept Discourse

In the previous chapters I discussed gender as socially constructed, and wrote about the implications of carrying out this analysis from a feminist perspective. I also discussed entrepreneurship as a male gendered concept. This might be rephrased as saying that the discourse on entrepreneurship is male gendered. This chapter introduces the concept discourse, which is something concerned both with what is said, and with the practices that make certain statements possible.

What is a discourse?

As discussed previously, a basic tenet of this work is that reality is socially constructed. Together, in social interaction, through the processes of externalization, objectification and internalization, humans construct their reality. Conversation is the most important vehicle of reality-maintenance, write Berger & Luckmann, (1966:172). Conversation can take many forms. Every-day talk is one of the most important, but conversation also takes place in for example the education system, in media, in governments, in boardrooms or, as in this particular study, a scientific community. Public conversation, or discourse, was of special interest to Foucault. He defined discourses as "practices which systematically form the object of which they speak" (Foucault, 1969/1972:49). Foucault made it clear that he referred not only to linguistic practices (or statements), but also the material and other practices that bring about a certain type of statements (Foucault, 1972). I will discuss both in this chapter, beginning with the former.

Borrowing from Foucault, discourse as a linguistic practice has been described as "a group of claims, ideas and terminologies that are historically and socially specific and that create truth effects" (Alvesson & Due Billing 1999:49), "a system of statements, which construct an object" (Parker, 1992:5), or "a set of meanings, metaphors, representations, images, stories, statements and so on that in some way together produce a particular version of events" (Burr 1995:48). What is common for these definitions is that discourses have some sort of effect. They are not neutral. Discourse analysis builds on the idea of language as constitutive as opposed to the idea of language as representational[1]. You can "do things with words" as pointed out by speech act theory (Austin 1965) where certain sentences, such as "I declare war on China", or "Beware of the dog" are acts in themselves. Things are also "done towards us" with words. Judith Butler, introducing the subject of linguistic vulnerability describes the constitutive aspect of language beautifully:

> When we claim to have been injured by language, what kind of claim do we make? We ascribe an agency to language, a power to injure, and position ourselves as the objects of its injurious trajectory. We claim that language acts, and acts against us, and the claim we make is a further instance of language, one which seeks to arrest the force of the prior instance. Thus, we exercise the force of language even as we seek to counter its force, caught up in a bind that no act of censorship can undo.

---

1 A common understanding of language is that it *represents* something "out there" and as such is a neutral device. The word "rock" refers to a physical phenomenon of a hard, immovable nature that everyone is familiar with and the word "rock" is then a handy invention to help us talk about it. This study uses a view of language as constitutive, where the coupling between the word and the referent could be described as loose, rather, and subject to constant renegotiation. This understanding is inspired by Ferdinand de Saussure (1970) who said that words and sentences must be understood not separately, but within a *system* of words. A language is such a system. Each word in the system has a meaning only because people agree that it has one (the meaning is socially constructed, to speak with Berger & Luckmann), but the actual word is arbitrary. Saussure called the concept that the word refers to (the idea of a rock in the example above) the *signified*. The word itself he called the *signifier*. One makes sense of the system of arbitrary signifiers through their difference from other signifiers, so language is only meaningful through difference. This goes for the signifieds as well. Puxty, (1993:123) writes, "each signified has its own conceptual space. Each signified inches out others when a space is required for it. Equally, in the absence of a signified, the conceptual space of signifieds closes in to fill the gap. However, signifieds are not 'things represented by the words'." "The concepts are purely differential and defined not by their positive content but negatively by their relations with the other terms of the system" (Saussure, quoted in Puxty, 1993:123). This means that not only is the signifier arbitrary, the way people have divided the world in signifieds is *also* arbitrary. The third party to this game, which is pretty much left out, is the *referent*. It is the actual physical rock in the example. Instead of a simple word-referent system, there is a system of words, which lives a life of its own with only a loose coupling to the referent. This becomes clearer if one substitutes "rock" with, for example "honesty". It is not as easy to point to a referent for this signifier as for "rock", but somewhat easier to define a signified.

Could language injure us if we were not, in some sense, linguistic beings, beings who require language in order to be? Is our vulnerability to language a consequence of our being constituted within its terms? If we are formed in language, then that formative power precedes and conditions any decision we might make about it, insulting us from the start, as it were, by its prior power (Butler, 1997:1).

Language circumscribes (and makes possible) what one can think and feel and imagine doing. It "typifies our experiences" to speak with Berger and Luckmann. Gergen (1991) writing on the socially constructed self says that if there is no word for a feeling we cannot have it, and exemplifies with cultures different from our own who have words for emotions that we lack. He concludes that it is the language of the Self, which constitutes the Self, not the other way around. People thus draw upon available discourses in the construction of their identity. A person may create many different identities depending on the circumstances he or she is in and depending on which discourses are around to be drawn upon. One is not totally free to fashion one's identity, since some discourses combine better than others. The available discourses on "white", "man", "father", "entrepreneur" and "industrial leader", for example, combine well. Journalists seldom ask the average Fortune 500 CEO about possible conflicts between the demands of work and family. Substitute "woman" for "man" and "mother" for "father" and the act is a bit harder to pull off. There are conflicting discourses of femininity that speak of caring, nurturing, motherhood, sensitivity, etc., that do not go as easily with the other ones. Why would we otherwise make "feminine leadership" into a special object? Or "female entrepreneurship"?

Viewing the self as socially and discursively constructed implies that the boundary between an internal, psychological existence and an outside world gets dissolved. It does not make sense to talk about "one" self, instead the self is regarded as "distributed" and "fragmented". This differs radically from the way the self is conceived of in most established social sciences at present, where the language of the self entails a view of the individual as an autonomous unit. In psychology, it is usual to talk about individual properties and characteristics. In sociology and business administration, knowledge is derived from the assumption that individuals have stable attitudes, which are mental dispositions that are thought to affect behavior. Most of economic theory is based on the assumption of the individual as a rational decision maker.

The language of the self in turn constitutes many of our social institutions, continues Gergen: "Without certain shared definitions of human selves, the institutions of justice, education, and democracy could scarcely be sustained. Without the language of the self – our internal states, processes, and characteristics – social life would be virtually unrecognizable" (Gergen 1991:6).

Discourses are thus not neutral. Foucault says that they have power[2] implications. Going back to the example from chapter one where the boys discussed how to conceive of the strange being in the stranded boat, they suggested a number of discourses, each portraying the object (or subject) differently, and each implying different things for the person in question. There was the "woman as a goddess" discourse, which might have implied being put on a pedestal, worshipped and indulged, but perhaps also isolated from a normal existence. The boys might have built a temple for her, and devised a fitting liturgy. Then there was the "woman as a slave" discourse portraying the woman in a totally different light and with different sorts of consequences for the woman. Contemporary discourses of women, such as "woman as the mother and housewife" or "woman as the co-breadwinner" also have different sorts of consequences for women.

---

2   Power is usually conceived of as *a resource*, as something one can possess and force upon others. American political scientist Robert Dahl claimed "A has power over B to the extent that he can get B to do something that B would not otherwise do" (Dahl, 1957:202–203). This makes power personal, tied to a powerful person, or a powerful position. Conflicts between articulated preferences are needed to empirically find out where power resides (Lukes, 1977). Power can also be seen as *agenda setting*. The people who control what is being discussed and what issues are raised – and not raised – have power. Issues that are never considered for decision making (nondecisions) become as interesting to study as decisions (Bachrach & Baratz, 1963). The idea of an overt or covert conflict to be able to locate power is still there. This ignores "... the crucial point that the most effective and insidious use of power is to prevent such conflict from arising in the first place" writes Lukes, (1977:23) and introduces a third way of conceiving of power which might be labeled ideological or *symbolic* – or the power of meaning. "The way we do it here", the norms and the rules in a given context decide what behavior is deemed good or bad. Also in Lukes' third definition, *someone* manages meaning. All three definitions are therefore concerned with the *locus* of power (Flyvbjerg, 1991). But "power is exercised rather than possessed," says Foucault (1995:26). In his view, power is exercised by drawing upon discourses that allow ones actions to be represented in an acceptable light, or by drawing upon discourses that define the world or a person in a way that allows one to do the things one wants. Power is therefore an effect of discourse, or knowledge. What Foucault calls knowledge is any version of events, any discourse that has received the stamp of truth. Knowledge brings with it "the potential for social practices, for acting in one way rather than another, and for marginalizing alternative ways of acting" writes Burr (1995:64). Power, seen in this way, is therefore not something that restricts, coerces, excludes, etc., but something that *is produced*, and the research focus shifts from "who, what and where" to "how". Drawing on a discourse produces and reproduces truth and power. Power therefore resides everywhere, and not in any particular group of people – but the more people who draw on the same discourse the more powerful a particular discourse becomes.

People draw upon available discourses in their reality construction. People drawing upon the discourse of woman as a mother might say things like "a woman's natural place is in the home", "there is nothing more important for children than a safe home with a caring mother", or "it ought to be possible to support a family on one salary". People drawing upon the discourse of woman as co-breadwinner might say that "women should be able to support themselves financially on equal terms with men", "an individual tax system is necessary in order not to discriminate women on the job market", or "women should be encouraged to start their own businesses".

Each discourse portrays the object (or subject) differently, and each discourse claims to say what it really is. The discourses thus have claims on knowledge and truth. Burr explains why a discourse analysis should be done: "...discourses are embedded in power relations, and therefore have political effects...To understand the power inequalities in society properly, we need to examine how discursive practices serve to create and uphold particular forms of social life. If some people can be said to be more powerful than others, then we need to examine the discourses and representations that uphold these inequalities" (Burr 1995:62–63).

The people producing the different discourses on women above make choices, but not all choices are available to all people at all times. Some things are not "thinkable" in some cultures, whereas other things come more easily to mind. Greimas & Courtés write, "the production of a discourse appears to be a continuous selection of possibilities, making its way through networks of constraints" (Greimas & Courtés, 1982:85). The selection of possibilities and the networks of constraints are, in a sense then, the study objects of this work.

What is a discursive practice?

If discourse as linguistic practice is mainly occupied with the "selection of possibilities", Foucault was equally concerned with the "networks of constraints". In his famous installation lecture to the College de France in 1970, "The Discourse on Language", (*L'ordre du discourse*), Foucault emphasized that a discourse is not only a group of statements, but also the practices that bring about a certain type of statements (Foucault, 1972). As mentioned above, he defined discourses as "practices which systematically form the object of which they speak". Foucault thus did not separate between discourse as content/exclusions from the content, and discourse as material and other practices. This is something that I do, to make it easier to explain what I am studying.

Foucault said that the production of discourses in each society is controlled, selected, organized and redistributed by certain procedures. The prohibition is the first and most obvious of the *exclusion procedures*, but Foucault does not refer to legal prohibitions as much as to the assumed understanding that you cannot speak about everything, you cannot say anything at anytime, and not everyone can speak about everything. The second exclusion procedure is the division of reason and folly and the neglect of the latter. The third is the 'will to truth', understood as the historically contingent manner in which false is demarcated from true, and what counts as knowledge. This is dependent on institutional support, such as schools and university systems, publishing systems, libraries, laboratories, and so on.

The above exclusion procedures are external to the discourse. The discourse tends to control itself as well. Foucault talks about *internal rules*, concerned with the principles of classification, ordering, and distribution. The first is the commentary. Each culture or discipline has a number of texts that are hailed as important and that are constantly commented upon. Whether the comments celebrate the original texts, try to explain them or criticize them, their role is "to say *finally*, what has silently been articulated *deep down*," writes Foucault, (1972:221) and in this way the discourse is repeated and reproduced. In the field of entrepreneurship research there are a number of such texts, the foremost being Schumpeter's "The Theory of Economic Development" and, indeed, I spent quite a few pages commenting on this in the previous chapter.

Another screening or sorting device is by author. Authors choose what they write, but not entirely freely, and once they have written one work, the next is expected to show at least some cohesion with the first. "What he writes and does not write, what he sketches out, even preliminary sketches for the work, and what he drops as simple mundane remarks, all this interplay of differences is prescribed by the author-function" (Foucault, 1972:222). Each epoch provides a certain author function and the author in turn reshapes it. This "author function" is particularly interesting in this research as the procedure of writing scientific articles is highly shaped and controlled.

Yet another restricting function is carried out by the disciplines, here in the sense of academic domains. The discipline regulates what is necessary for formulating new statements, through its "groups of objects, methods, their corpus of propositions considered to be true, the interplay of rules and definitions, of techniques and tools." (ibid:222). What counts and does not count as belonging to entrepreneurship research will be relevant here, as well as what counts as accepted methods for researching entrepreneurship.

Foucault discusses a third group of procedures enabling control over the discourses. It concerns a screening among the speaking subjects. "Here, we are no longer dealing with the mastery of the powers contained within discourse … it is more a question of determining the conditions under which it may be employed, of imposing a certain number of rules upon those individuals who employ it, thus denying access to everyone else" (ibid:224). Formal qualifications, expertise groupings or other means of excluding people are relevant, but also rituals about who can speak, how and when. The academic system abounds with such rules and rituals. The formal rules of thesis production and the ritualistic doctoral defense in Sweden are good examples.

Some philosophical themes about an ideal truth and an immanent rationality may further strengthen these limitations, continues Foucault. They serve to hide the notion of the discourse being produced through and restricted by the practices discussed earlier. Epistemological assumptions of a neutral and cumulative knowledge development in entrepreneurship research may be such a restriction.

What I here label discursive practices would be the rules and procedures as described above – first, the exclusion procedures, most important of which are assumptions that are taken for granted and the will to truth; second, the internal rules, particularly the role of the commentary, the author function, and the disciplinary restrictions; third, the procedures concerned with who is allowed to speak; and fourth, ideas about truth, that is, epistemological and ontological assumptions. These practices both enable and delimit the discourse. They systematically form the object of which they speak. Laying bare these restrictions is at the heart of Foucault's project. It is achieved through the following four principles, using Foucault's terminology:

- The principle of *reversal*: Instead of looking at what the discourse conveys, look for what it excludes. Instead of looking for its source and its origin, look for what is not there.

- The principle of *discontinuity*: Bear in mind that there is no "silent, continuous and repressed" discourse to be uncovered once the present discourse has been deconstructed. The discourse does not hide any unknown truth – a series of discourses, sometimes connected, sometimes not, is all there is. I interpret this to mean that a discourse analysis can only result in an alternative story, the value of which to be judged by ethical, moral or perhaps aesthetic standards.

- The principle of *specificity*: A particular discourse cannot be resolved by a prior system of meanings. "We should not imagine that the world presents us with a legible face, leaving us merely to decipher it", writes Foucault (ibid:229). Discourse must be understood as "practice imposed upon things" as opposed to things being rendered legible through discourse. If discourse shows regularity, it is not because of any inherent regularity, but because of the regularity in this practice. This is another way to say that there are no social laws and regularities to be uncovered by a study of language as representational of something, the social world is *created* through discourse. There is no "depth" *beyond* any "surface" (in fact, these two constructs are alien to discourse analysis). Regularities found are because people construct the same thing over and over again.

- The principle of *exteriority*: Do not burrow for any assumed hidden, inner essence or meaning of discourse, but look for its external conditions of existence. What circumstances make a certain discourse possible? How do these circumstances limit the discourse?

Foucault summarizes the four principles in four words: *event, series, regularity*, and the *possible conditions of existence* and contrasts these with the words *creation, unity, originality*, and *meaning*. The latter words have dominated the traditional history of ideas, "... by general agreement one sought the point of creation, the unity of a work, of a period or a theme, one looked also for the mark of individual originality and the infinite wealth of hidden meaning" (Foucault, 1972:230). Instead, chance and materiality must be introduced at the root of thinking, writes Foucault. He thus proposes a complete reversal of traditional conceptions of social science.

Proposing this as a scheme for his research at College de France, Foucault distinguishes between two camps – one being the "critical" group working mainly with the first principle – the principle of reversal and concentrating on studying "the will to truth". The other, "genealogical" camp would work mainly with the other three principles, looking at series of discourses over time. This research borrows from both camps. I study what the research discourse on women entrepreneurs conveys and what it excludes, but I also analyze the discursive practices with which it is produced.

Applying Foucault's Concept of Discourse

Applying Foucault's discussion on the principles and the discursive practices to my particular research project, I interpret it to imply that I should look for the following:

1. *Writing and publishing practices* delimiting the discourse.
2. *Rules and rituals* pertaining to who is allowed to speak.
3. The *institutional support* for entrepreneurship research: financing, university research centers and their status in the academic community, and so on.
4. *Founding fathers and foundational texts*, which I already commented on in a previous chapter.
5. The *content and the form:* How do the research texts position female entrepreneurs? What are they compared and contrasted to? How are they described? What aspects are chosen as relevant to study in the context of women's entrepreneurship?
6. The *exclusions:* What likely areas are excluded from the discussion? What is not chosen as relevant? What is not, and what cannot be said? Are there any *dissenting voices* indicating points of tension?
7. The stated, as well as the omitted, *reasons* for studying women's entrepreneurship.
8. *Ontological and epistemological premises* guiding, and limiting, the production of knowledge.
9. Disciplinary regulations, particularly the *research methods* used. What methods are legitimate to produce what counts as knowledge? And how does this limit the discourse? Are there other disciplinary procedures regulating what counts as knowledge?
10. *Ideas*, or assumptions, that are taken for granted about women, society, research, entrepreneurship, etc.

I translated Foucault's procedures and principles to points on my list as follows. The first point, concerning writing and publishing practices, is derived from Foucault's internal rules, particularly the author function, and the disciplinary restrictions. The second point, on who is allowed to speak, comes from Foucault's third group of procedures, the screening of the speaking subjects. The third point is derived from the first exclusion procedure, the will to truth, which according to Foucault is dependent on institutional support. The fourth point is the role of the commentary. Points five, six and seven are derived from

Foucault's first principle, that of reversal. To make conclusions on what is excluded one must of course first study what is included. Point eight is equivalent to Foucault's thoughts about the role of ideas about truth and rationality. Point nine is Foucault's disciplinary restrictions and point ten is the first of the exclusion procedures, i.e., assumptions that are taken for granted.

What is stated and included, I can of course report. As to what is not stated I can only be an informed speculator, guided by my feminist theory vantage point. This is quite all right according to Foucault since, according to the principle of discontinuity, I do not, and cannot, analyze the discourse on female entrepreneurship in order to present a truer picture – only perhaps point towards an alternative picture. Applied to this work, discourse analysis is thus about the text in scientific articles, and about the discursive practices that bring about these texts.

The list above says what to look for, but not how. The analysis methods will be briefly presented throughout the text. The interested reader will also find a more detailed report in the appendices, which contain a description of how I chose the texts, a short overview of text analytical methods, and a detailed report of the particular analysis methods used.

Summary

In this chapter I discussed the concept of discourse. The concept builds on a social constructionist perspective where language is seen as constitutive of social reality. Language is structured into discourses, which are ways of thinking about an object that construct this object. Discourses have power implications in that they structure what one holds as true and what one acts upon. Discourses on women entrepreneurs will thus have power implications for women entrepreneurs as a group. Discourses are furthermore often taken for granted; a discourse analysis may thus shed new light on that which is taken for granted and enable new and different ways of thinking about the object of study.

According to Foucault, "discourse" includes not only what is said and not said, but also the practices producing a discourse. The discussion resulted in a list of ten points pertaining to the content and the production of discourse to be used as a guide for the ensuing research.

Returning to the purpose of this research, *to analyze the discursive construction of the female entrepreneur/female entrepreneurship in research texts from a feminist theory perspective*, this chapter dealt with the first part of the purpose, "to analyze the discursive construction", but the discussion of discourses having power implications also shed more light on the merits of using a feminist theory perspective. A discourse analysis aims at questioning power relationships in society, and this particular discourse analysis aims at questioning gender relations as expressed in scientific texts about female entrepreneurs.

4
Writing and Publishing Practices

The following chapters are devoted to an analysis of 81 articles on women's entrepreneurship from a certain selection of scientific journals. This chapter introduces my selection, and discusses some of the discursive practices that produce these particular texts. In the previous chapter a list of ten points of what to look for in this discourse analysis are presented. This chapter covers the first three of these. The first point concerns the writing and publishing practices that delimit the discourse. The second point concerns the disciplinary regulations, and the rules and rituals pertaining to who is allowed to speak. The third point is about the institutional support for entrepreneurship research. It covers issues of financing and of university research centers and their status in the academic community.

The Selection of Research Texts

The leading research journals in the field of management and organization publish very little about entrepreneurship, and articles about women's entrepreneurship are extremely rare. There are, however, a great number of research journals specifically about entrepreneurship. I chose the four leading ones. These were Entrepreneurship Theory and Practice, Journal of Business Venturing, The Journal of Small Business Management and Entrepreneurship and Regional Development. There were 68 articles on women's entrepreneurship in these journals, published between 1982 (when the first one appeared) and 2000. Because of frequent citations in these articles, 13 more articles, published in other journals, were also included in the selection. A detailed report of the selection process can be found in appendix A, which also contains a list of the reviewed articles, in order of topic.

Discursive Practices in Research Article Production

As established earlier, not only the texts, but also the practices bringing them about constitute and delimit the discourse. Writing and publishing practices, disciplinary regulations and institutional support play significant roles in the shaping of research texts. The ensuing discussion is applicable to the selected journals, most of which are US based. I therefore build my discussion on sources written from a US horizon. Other journals, in other fields, may not necessarily embrace the same practices.

Academic writing is conversation, writes Huff (1999), but it is a conversation guided by many tacit rules and conventions, making conversation possible as well as simultaneously delimiting it. There are both internal and external rules, in Foucault's sense. In her excellent guide "Writing for scholarly publication" Anne Huff, an experienced and successful management and strategy professor, writer, editor and reviewer, advises to identify a few *conversants* – specific books or articles that have made a specific contribution to the canon of scholarly work in the field – before starting to write. Interacting references among these conversants indicate that one is on the right track – a conversation is going on. Joining the conversation, one should read before writing, connect with points already made, be polite towards the conversants and then say something this audience has not heard before. It is acceptable to include a new voice or two in the conversant list, but Huff advises to lean toward well-known work that a broad audience will recognize and find interesting.

The choice of conversation is important for your career, writes Huff. "The work you do now develops reputation and skills for the work you can most easily do next. Your list of publications and work in progress is a signal that others use to make decisions that can affect your career – sometimes you are not even aware that they are being made." (Huff, 1999:43). Drawing on more than one field of inquiry presents a problem, "… it is tempting to be side-tracked into thinking that you should publish a paper in field two, illustrating the application of their theory to the population you have studied …These thoughts are most often siren songs: they have tempted many to stray off course and dilute the potential impact of their work. My advice is simple: Identify conversants that will help you focus on your main field of scholarship!" (ibid:49).

It is easy to see Foucault's exclusion and limitation procedures at work here. The "function of the comment" is invoked, as new writers must connect with the canon in the field if they want to take part of the conversation.

Once a conversation is identified, the choice of publication outlet is often given. Academics write conference papers, research reports, books, book chapters but, foremost, articles in scientific journals. The journals have a special standing since they are peer reviewed in a blind review system and, particularly in the USA, tied to an academic's career development. American scholars are given tenure based, among other things, on the number of publications in recognized scientific journals. Money, prestige, autonomy, and quality of working life follow suit. All journals do not have the same standing, however, there is a tier system of A, B, C and D journals. Each university has its own such list, but Gaylen Chandler, one of the co-authors of Busenitz et al. (2003 forthcoming) informs me that none of the entrepreneurship journals are on the A-lists. Given this "publish or perish" system, scholars must compete for publication in the most prestigious journals, and of course it is wise to follow the publications' standards. Huff advises to read some recent articles in the journal of your choice to get the flavor of the journal and be able to adjust the writing to this. She says to look for established conventions, structure, tone, order of presentation, size of different components and use of examples. Even tense used and sentence length should be studied. The journals also supply presumptive authors detailed instructions on article length, structure, length of abstract, number of headings, font and font size, references, use of figures and tables, etc. that the author must conform to, thus streamlining the contributions submitted. The Journal of Small Business Management even postulates that the articles should use statistical techniques, openly dictating acceptable research methods.

Here Foucault's "author function" is at play, since both the unspoken writing conventions and the detailed instructions provided by each journal will guide what and how the author writes. The "disciplinary function" forces scholars to publish and therefore to follow these conventions, but it also regulates what is held to be the canon of the field and what are held to be acceptable methods. JSBM values statistical methods, the other journals analyzed in this study also have publishing preferences related to method as will be discussed in chapter five.

Not only are these conventions quite restrictive, the review process can also be a grueling experience. Jone Pearce comments in Huff, (1999:152) "Writing for the most competitive American scholarly journals is a brutal, humiliating business. Some reviewers are unkind, unfair, and just plain wrong! Many senior American scholars who have published enough in those journals to achieve tenure turn their attention to books (where the editors are nicer), to consulting, and to other activities that don't require so much anxiety and degradation." Why do it at all, then? She says that publishing in scientific journals is the only sure way to know that your ideas are of interest to others.

The "publish or perish" system is an American phenomenon, but it is spreading throughout the academic community, as it gets more internationalized. English is the international science language, and scholars from small language areas are forced to communicate in English if they want an audience outside of their own country says literary theorist John Swales (1990), who has analyzed writing conventions in scientific articles. This means that an increasingly larger audience is adhering to the US publishing conventions. Jone Pearce (cited in Huff, 1999:147) says on this topic "The real difficulty is that America and American journals overpower my field, due to size and early dominance. That means that American perspectives and standards domineer many conversations". She advices non-American scholars who want to (or have to) join the conversation, to do it the American way, to immerse oneself in exemplars, to seek help decoding and interpreting the material and to have American scholars passing by conduct a writing and publishing seminar. So the language barrier alone is a handicap to non-English writers, but the more subtle writing conventions may be an even harder knot to untie, thus reinforcing the dominance of native English speaking writers.

There is no formal restriction as to who can submit a manuscript to a scientific journal, but to be able to follow and take part of the conversation, a research education is often a necessity. One must be able to understand sentences like "Adding the product terms of strategy and gender to the equation significantly improves the fit of the model (Model chi-square improvement = $14.93; p<.002$)" (Carter & Rosa, 1998:138). This was a sentence taken haphazardly from my studied articles. The training and socialization that doctoral students receive at their universities is yet another form of mechanism simultaneously limiting and making the discourse possible. It is what Foucault referred to as the "rarefaction among the speaking subjects" (Foucault, 1972:224).

The rules and conventions of the conversation, the specialization of the journals, the US dominance and the training necessary to take part of the conversation indicate a conversation taking place among a limited number of people. This is further corroborated after studying the names in the editorial boards of the four main journals in my study. Being on the editorial board is an honorary task for a researcher, and it means that you belong to the group of a journal's main reviewers, setting the standard for the journal. The status of the members and the status of the journals mutually reinforce each other. The following statistics derived from the 2001 lists give a picture of the composition of the editorial boards:

Table 4.1: *Composition of Editorial Boards.*

Journal[1]	Size of board	Percent US based researchers	Percent women	Percent joint reviewers
ETP	41	78	27	39
JBV	50	92	12	30
JSBM	63	54	29	17
ERD	19	16	11	21

The first three are US based, and JSBM seems to be the only one of them that has made an effort to acquire a more international board – slightly less than half are from other countries, although 26% of the board are from other English speaking countries, making this at least a mainly Anglo-Saxon board. JBV's non-American members are from the UK and Canada. ETP displays the same pattern, with only two members from non-English speaking countries. ERD is European based and this is reflected in the board, with members from twelve different countries. The boards are male dominated, similar to other management research institutions. The last column is the most interesting, however. It turns out that some names appear on several lists. Ten people serve on both ETP and JBV, four on both ETP and JSBM, four on both JBV and JSBM, and of the people on ERD's list, two are also on JSBM's and one is on each on the other two. Then there is Jerome Katz who serves on all four boards. In addition to this, the editor of ERD and one of the editors of ETP are on the editorial board of JSBM. It is a small world.

I also compared these lists with the names of the editing group for the last four years (1996–1999) of *Frontiers of Entrepreneurship Research*, the proceedings of the Babson conference, and found that the editors were all on the advisory boards as well, most of them on more than

---

1   Acronym guide: ETP = Entrepreneurship, Theory and Practice, JBV = Journal of Business Venturing, JSBM = Journal of Small Business Management, ERD = Entrepreneurship and Regional Development.

one journal. The term "discourse community" (Swales, 1990) might be applicable. Swales holds that a discourse community is a community with a broadly agreed set of common public goals. It has mechanisms for interaction among its members that are used to provide information and feedback. It uses and owns one or more genres in the communicative furtherance of its aims. It has acquired some specific lexis. Finally, it has a threshold level of members with a suitable degree of relevant content and discoursal expertise. All requisites apply. Furthering entrepreneurship research may be the common goal. Scientific articles published in research journals are a mechanism of interaction and also make up a genre. Any one article in these journals will show the specific lexis used and as the analysis of the composition of the editorial boards showed, the community certainly has a threshold level of members with relevant content and discoursal expertise.

The people reviewing papers for publication are thus likely to know each other. The US reviewers, which constitute the majority in three of the four main journals in the selection, have a similar academic background. They have similar training, and there is a common standard for what constitutes good research. A submitted paper is typically returned once or twice with comments from the reviewers, and the author is asked to revise and re-submit. The final product may thus be quite different from the one first submitted. It might be closer to what the editor wants to publish in a particular journal than what the author wants to convey. In combination with the writing conventions and the publishing apparatus discussed earlier, this will shape the discourse in certain directions.

Institutional support in terms of research funding, research centers, and so on are also part of the discursive practices. It is beyond the scope of this work to give a detailed picture of this, but suffice to say that entrepreneurship is a rapidly growing field in academia. The last 20 to 30 years have seen a rapid expansion in terms of undergraduate entrepreneurship courses, research centers, and even universities devoted to entrepreneurship. The number of endowed entrepreneurship chairs is larger in the United States than the number of qualified and interested professors. In Sweden, my own university, founded in 1994, positioned itself as an international business school focusing on entrepreneurship. Since then, several more schools of entrepreneurship have been instituted at Swedish universities. Research financing is increasingly available from both private and public funds (Cooper et al., 2000). Governments (as well as the European Union) fund entrepreneurship research since it has been shown that employment increases come largely from new and small firms (Birch, 1979; Davidsson et al. 1994). Private funding is perhaps geared more towards performance issues. This pragmatic focus might explain the paradox that even though entrepreneurship is such a "hot" field, it still has not made it into the so-called A-journals on the grounds that it is "a-theoretical, undefined, fragmented and merely descriptive". In fact, one of the nicest words characterizing the theoretical status of the field I saw used in the many soul-searching articles I came across is probably "emerging" (Landström & Johannisson, 2001).

The preceding discussion described some of the discursive practices shaping the entrepreneurship discourse. I discussed how writing and publishing conventions, academic training, disciplinary regulations and research funding all help to shape the discourse. I also discussed the concept of a discourse community – how the practices form a certain community of people, who in their turn regulate the discourse. I paid special attention to the review process and the role of journals in promoting an academic career, making journals stand out as especially relevant and interesting – and also especially apt at regulating the discourse. This is the reason why I have chosen to concentrate on research journals as opposed to books and book chapters. The articles in the journals have received the discourse community's quality stamp. They adhere to the community's standards. Describing these practices may give some hints, but it does not reveal what they include in the discourse and nor, following Foucault, what they exclude, or where they draw the limit as to what belongs to the discourse and what does not. A discourse is defined more by what it is not than by what it is. I intend to show both what it includes and what it excludes in the analysis in the following three chapters.

Summary

This chapter presented my selection of texts. I selected 81 articles, most of which were from four entrepreneurship research journals, namely Entrepreneurship Theory and Practice, Journal of Business Venturing, The Journal of Small Business Management, and Entrepreneurship and Regional Development. These journals belong to a certain discourse community with certain discursive practices that perform a strong editing function of the texts. The writing and publishing practices of this community, including the blind review process and the disciplinary regulations on how to speak about entrepreneurship and on who is entitled to speak about it, have a regulative effect on the discourse. The effect is magnified because of another discursive practice, namely the publish-or-perish system. Researchers in entrepreneurship make a good career move if they publish in scientific journals, and to get published in scientific journals, one is wise to follow the other discursive practices. All of which impinges on the discourse.

5

Research Articles on Women Entrepreneurs: Methods and Findings

This chapter provides an overview of the articles. There are many options available when structuring such an overview, but since an overview already exists (Brush 1992) that is often quoted, I begin this chapter by following the same structure as Brush, for the purposes of comparison. I will therefore start with a presentation of theory bases, methods and samples[1].

Brush concluded that the methods used most often were cross-sectional surveys that used convenience samples and did not link the research to a theory base. One purpose of the overview is to see if this still is so, or if there has been a change. After this comes a summary of the articles' findings arranged according to topic[2]. Using the results from the previous sections, the chapter ends with a discussion and critique of the methodology as well as the epistemological departures in the reviewed texts.

Theory Bases, Methods and Samples

To facilitate comparison, this section begins by following Brush (1992) with an overview of the research designs, the samples, the theory bases, and the analysis techniques, using, as far as applicable, the same categories. However, I start by a table displaying the countries of origin.

---

1   See appendices B and C for details about my analysis methods.

2   The topics are: personal background and firm characteristics, attitudes to entrepreneurship or intentions to start, psychology, start-up processes, management practice and strategy, networking, family, access to capital, performance, and "other", which includes the conceptual papers. Appendix A presents the reviewed studies arranged in this order.

Table 5.1: *Countries of Origin.*

Country of Origin	Number	Percent
United States	52	64
United Kingdom	10	12
Canada	5	6
Norway	3	4
Sweden	3	4
Israel	1	1
New Zealand	1	1
Pakistan	1	1
Poland	1	1
Singapore	1	1
Multi-country (two New Zealand–Norway–UK and one US–Italy)	3	4
Total	**81**	**100**[3]

The USA heavily dominates the studies about women's entrepreneurship, published in the selected journals. Adding the other English-speaking countries makes a total of 83 % of the studies from the Anglo-Saxon sphere. Only three studies make cross-cultural comparisons, and all of the studies apart from one are from industrialized countries. The next table, 5.2, shows the distribution between empirical and conceptual studies.

Table 5.2: *Type of Study.*

Type of Study		Number	Percent
Empirical	descriptive/exploratory	37	46
	explanatory	36	44
Conceptual/review		8	10
Total		**81**	**100**

The majority of the studies in Brush's review were descriptive, reflecting the needs of early research to "map the territory". The last ten years of research show a trend towards more explanatory studies, such as the effect of education and experience on performance (Fischer et al., 1993) or the effect of strategy on discontinuance (Carter et al., 1997). The reviewed studies are divided about equally between descriptive and explanatory, and eight review or conceptual papers are also included. Several studies are basically descriptive, but compare men and women business owners. One might call these explanatory – gender as explanatory for any difference, but unless there is a clear hy-

---

3   The percentages are rounded up to make them easier to read. They add to 100 even if the whole numbers in the tables add to 99.

potheses about gender explaining, e.g., attitudes to growth, I have sorted these as descriptive.

Table 5.3: *Theory Base.*

Theory Base	Number	Percent
Not theory related	7	9
Refers to empirical results from previous research on women's entrepreneurship	29	36
Psychology (trait, psychoanalysis, etc.)	9	11
Sociology (i.e., networks, social learning)	13	16
Management theory/economics	6	7
Psychology and sociology	6	7
Psychology and management theory	4	5
Sociology and management/economics	3	4
Feminist theory	3	4
Institutional theory	1	1
Total	**81**	**100**

A third of the studies in Brush's review did not state any theory base at all. As table 5.3 shows, this figure is lower now, only nine percent, but it is very common to use only the empirical results of previous studies on women's entrepreneurship as a departure. These might in turn be based on some theory, but this is seldom discussed. Of the studies 45% could thus be characterized as being a-theoretical. One study is based on institutional theory. The rest use theories from psychology, sociology or management, or a combination thereof.

References to feminist theory – in any version – are absent from the majority of the papers. In my reading, 23 papers are influenced by some version of feminist theory, but only four explicitly say that they use feminist theory as their theoretical point of departure. However, in the other 19 papers, feminist theories or at least theories about women are commented on or may be inferred from the texts. In table 5.4 below, the result of such a reading is listed.

Table 5.4: *Feminist Theories.*

Feminist Theory	No.	Explicit Point of Departure	Inferred Use
Women in management	2		Fagenson, 1993; Miskin & Rose, 1990
Social feminism	4		Brush, 1992; Buttner, 2001; Buttner & Moore, 1997; Van Auken, Rittenburg, Doran, & Hsieh, 1994
Liberal and social feminism	9	Fischer et al. 1993 Cliff, 1998	Baker, Aldrich, & Liou, 1997; Brush, 1997; Carter & Allen, 1997; Carter et al., 1997; Dant, Brush, & Iniesta, 1996; Greene, Brush, Hart, & Saparito, 1999; Walker & Joyner, 1999
Socialist/Marxist	2		Goffee & Scase, 1983; Marlow, 1997
Social constructionist	6	Berg, 1997 Nilsson, 1997	Birley, 1989; Chell & Baines, 1998; Stevenson, 1990; Spilling & Berg, 2000
Total	**23**	**4**	**19**

Two papers in the early 1990s refer to the "women in management" literature, e.g., Kanter. I sorted four articles under "social feminism", as is understood in the USA. The main theoretical inspiration in these articles is Gilligan's (1982) "In a different voice" and Chodorow's (1988) writings about women's relational, nurturing, and caring styles. Van Auken et al. (1994) wrote about women's nurturing and communicative nature, referring to Tannen's (1990) research about communication styles.

Fischer, Reuber, & Dyke (1993) introduced liberal and social feminist theory as alternative theories, which could explain why women have achieved less than men, to entrepreneurship research. The article had an impact on other writers in the field. Cliff (1998) used this framework explicitly, and seven more papers refer to it implicitly, talking about women's "situational and dispositional barriers". Three of the papers under this heading concentrate on the dispositional barriers, building on Gilligan (1982). All of these papers, apart from one Canadian study, originate from the USA.

Two UK papers have an implicit socialist feminist perspective, referring to women's subordination, class, and patriarchy. I sorted six papers under the heading "social constructionist", meaning that they have a comprehension of gender compatible with the social constructionist/poststructuralist understanding. Berg (1997) and Nilsson (1997), both Scandinavian, use an explicit social constructionist understanding of gender, Spilling & Berg (2000) mention it as a dimension and the remaining have an implicit understanding as such.

The vast majority of the papers investigating women's entrepreneurship do not mention feminist thought at all. Those that do – particularly those papers from the USA – tend to stay away from the power dimension in feminism as will be discussed later. Having discussed countries of origin, types of studies, and theory bases, I now leave the conceptual papers aside, and turn to research design, methods, and samples of the 73 empirical papers.

Table 5.5: *Research Design.*

Research Design		Number	Percent
Cross sectional surveys (36 by mail, 5 personally)		41	53
Longitudinal (with structured questionnaire)		6	8
Repeated mail surveys	(4)		
Repeated phone interviews	(2)		
Personal face-to-face interview		15	19
Open or semi-structured	(9)		
With structured questionnaire	(6)		
Personal phone interview with structured questionnaire		3	4
Archival, database		4	5
Case studies		2	3
Experimental design		2	3
Focus groups		3	4
Observation		1	1
Total *(77 instead of 73, since four used a combined design)*		**77**	**100**

As shown in table 5.5, cross-sectional survey studies dominate. Half of the personal interviews employ a structured questionnaire, making it close to a survey study. Differences in the distribution of research designs as compared to Brush's review are marginal. Most notable is the increase of longitudinal studies from 2 to 6, and the use of focus groups and observations.

Table 5.6: *Analysis Techniques.*

Analysis Techniques	Number	Percent
Descriptive statistics	24	33
Descriptive and x2, or Correlation, or t-test	14	19
Multiple regression, Manova, Anova	14	19
Content analysis of text	8	11
Factor, cluster, discriminant analysis	7	10
Logit model	6	8
Total	**73**	**100**

Table 5.6 shows that only 11% use text analysis, the rest use statistical techniques. 33% are purely descriptive, with frequency tables, another 19% use descriptive analysis in combination with statistical tests and correlations. 37% of the studies use regression analysis, factor, cluster or discriminant techniques, which is a sharp increase as compared to ten years ago. Many of these latter studies use more than one technique, and they usually present the data in descriptive form first.

Table 5.7: *Sample Types.*

Sample Type	Number	Percent
Convenience sample	24	33
Stratified or systematic random sample	15	21
Random sample	14	19
Purposive sampling	10	14
Census or equivalent	4	5
Insufficient information	6	8
Total	**73**	**100**

Whereas earlier studies used convenience samples to a very large degree, the last decade has seen more advanced sampling procedures. A third of the studies still use convenience samples, but forty percent use random sampling procedures and fourteen percent a purposive sample. Five percent study an entire database that they say cover close to a whole population, the most comprehensive being a Norwegian census study (Spilling & Berg, 2000). In order to draw the correct conclusions from the studies using random sampling, however, it is necessary to look at the sampling frame. Some studies have created a frame representing, for example, female entrepreneurs from all over the United States, but many limit their frame to a certain industry, a certain membership list, or a certain region.

Table 5.8: *Samples.*

Samples		Number	Percent
Women business owners		18	25
Women business owners & other groups		3	4
Women managers	(1)		
Employed women	(2)		
Men and women business owners		30	41
Men and women business owners & other groups		5	7
Managers	(4)		
Copreneurs	(1)		
Copreneurs		2	3
Students		4	5
Nascent entrepreneurs (2 on women only)		3	4
Other samples			
(loan officers, family members, economic			
development organizations, counselors, media)		8	11
Total		**73**	**100**

Reflecting the change from purely descriptive to contingency studies, the number of studies using comparison groups has increased substantially. In Brush's review, half of the studies sampled only women, and 26% sampled both men and women. The figures are reversed in table 5.8–25% sample only women whereas 48% include men. Other comparison groups are used as well.

As can be seen in table 5.9 below, 62% of the studies compare men and women on some dimension, and 11% compare women entrepreneurs with other women entrepreneurs or with other categories. Comparative studies thus dominate the picture now. The rubric "men and women" in table 5.9 includes studies where the samples were men and women business owners, but also, for example, studies where attitudes towards men and business owners by loan officers were compared. This is the reason why table 5.8 does not coincide with table 5.9.

Table 5.9: *Use of Comparisons.*

Use of Comparisons	Number	Total	Percent
Men and women...		45	62
Men and women and/or their firms	(35)		
Men and women entrepreneurs by industrial sector	(4)		
Men and women entrepreneurs by country	(2)		
Men and women entrepreneurs and managers	(3)		
Men and women entrepreneurs and copreneurs	(1)		
Women and...		8	11
Women (and/or their firms) – within group comparison	(4)		
Women entrepreneurs and managers	(1)		
Women entrepreneurs and employees	(1)		
Women entrepreneurs by size of firm	(1)		
Women, by sex of superior	(1)		
Copreneurs and career couples	(1)	1	1
No comparison	(19)	19	26
Total	**(73)**	**73**	**100**

Table 5.10: *Sample Sizes.*

Sample Size – number of respondents	Number	Percent
5–19	4	5
20–49	5	7
50–99	9	12
100–199	16	22
200–499	14	19
500–999	9	12
1000–4999	10	14
5000 +	2	3
N/A or insufficient information	4	5
Total	**73**	**100**

Small samples dominated the early research, but the last decade has seen some very large studies. Of the studies 17% sample 1000 or more, 12% between 500–999 and 41% between 100–499. The large studies, however, usually divide their sample into several categories (men, women, by nationality, by industry, etc.) making the large size a necessity for statistical analysis.

Table 5.11: *Response Rates.*

Response Rates	Number	Percent
12–29%	10	14
30–49%	9	12
50–69%	9	12
70–90%	3	4
100% (case study, focus group)	2	3
Cohort or census studies	6	8
Unknown – only number of respondents stated	31	42
N/A or insufficient information	3	4
Total	**73**	**100**

Almost half of the studies do not give any information about the original size of the sample and the response rate. Only the number of respondents is stated, making any general conclusions about response rates hard to draw.

Brush observed ten years ago "the methodologies employed most often for research on women business owners have been cross-sectional surveys that used convenience samples, analyzed data with descriptive statistics, and frequently did not link the research to a theory base. In short, rigor is lacking in much of this work." (Brush, 1992:10). Seen from this perspective, things look a little brighter now. Cross-sectional surveys still dominate, but comparative studies, explanatory studies, more careful sampling procedures, and more advanced statistical analysis methods have become more prevalent. From a different perspective, methodological criticism may still be directed towards the studies, but before turning to this, the reader might be curious to know what has been found out about women entrepreneurs. What follows is a summary of the findings.

Findings from Research on Women Entrepreneurs

There is of course no way to do justice to so many studies in a short overview. Several studies investigate many different aspects of women's entrepreneurship. Comparing all studies on all aspects is not possible. I have therefore concentrated on the main research question or the main finding of each study in the discussion below. The discussion should be seen as a brief overview and an invitation to read further, rather than a complete report of findings on women entrepreneurs. The studies are arranged according to topic[4], and in chronological order within each topic.

Personal Background and Firm Characteristics

A number of studies are basically descriptive, and aim at giving a picture of women's participation in business life. Hisrish & Brush (1984) constructed a profile of the female entrepreneur in the USA and found that she was typically between 35 and 45 years old, middle class, married with children, well educated, and owned a small service or retail business. Scott (1986) had similar results from Georgia, USA, and also found that the same things – independence, challenges, and the opportunity to make more money – motivated male and female entrepreneurs. Birley et al. (1987) added that women were as well educated as men, and their results did not support the hypothesis that women needed any gender specific business training. Dolinsky (1993) found in a longitudinal study that the likelihood of entry, staying and reentry into business ownership increased by the level of educational attainment. This was found to be true for women as had been reported earlier on for men.

Carter et al. (1992) found that home-based businesses in Iowa tended to be predominantly female-owned, and that they were larger than the men's businesses but no more profitable. Rosa & Hamilton (1994) investigated ownership issues among British firms in three industrial sectors, suspecting previous studies for taking issues of co-ownership as well as sectoral and size differences too lightly. They found that co-ownership was more common than sole ownership for both sexes, and that women chose to start businesses in sectors that were dominated by small businesses.

---

4   This departs from Brush's (1992) organization. She used Gartner's (1985) framework for new venture creation to classify the articles. It identifies four components in venture creation: the individual, the organization, the environment and the new venture process. Brush found that over half of her articles dealt with the individual, the rest were divided equally between the organization and process, the latter mostly on networking. Only three papers fell under the environment heading, dealing with terms of credit and discrimination by bank loan officers. It can be debated if it is at all possible to isolate "process" as a variable disentangled from the actors, their context and the organization (Steyaert, 1995), and several papers were about more than one aspect which made this categorization less useful for me. For purposes of comparison, however, I did the same categorization as Brush anyway and found that the general tendency of focusing on the individual remained, with over half of the papers in this category. The rest were divided about equally between the other three headings, with "environment" (more bank papers but also other topics) receiving more attention than before.

Dant et al. (1996) investigated ownership structures of US franchise systems and found fewer women than in small business or at executive levels. This was also the case in "typically female" industries such as food retailing. Shabbir & Di Gregorio (1996) interviewed nascent entrepreneurs in Pakistan and found three categories – those who wanted freedom and independence, those who needed an income working from their home, and those who worked as entrepreneurs for their own personal satisfaction. Holmquist & Sundin (1990) found a subcategory on the rise among Swedish female entrepreneurs that was highly educated, professional, mostly single and lived in big cities. Married women in this study were overachievers, trying "to do it all", with both a family and a successful career.

The articles offer profiles of Polish, Hispanic, Singaporean and Norwegian women business owners. Polish men and women entrepreneurs were very similar concerning most psychological characteristics, motives and objectives, but the women were more interested in long-term growth and innovation than the men. Moreover, counter to men and women in the USA, they were more likely to have a technical or engineering educational background (Zapalska 1997). Hispanic male and female business owners were found to be similar on many different dimensions – education, sectors, profit margin, sales growth, employment, and company form (Shim & Eastlick 1998). The typical Singaporean female entrepreneur did not differ much from her counterparts in the USA, Canada or Australia (Maysami & Goby 1999). In Norway, 24% of the self-employed were women. They were found in agriculture, services and retail, and they were more likely to work part-time than their male counterparts. Of all recorded private enterprises in Norway 16% had a female CEO, but these firms accounted for only 7% of the total employment and only 5.3% of the total turnover of these firms, which lead the authors to conclude that Norwegian business is still heavily male dominated (Spilling & Berg 2000). Altogether, studies on personal background and firm characteristics show that the investigated women seemed to favor retail and service businesses, but this was not a pattern without exceptions.

Attitudes Towards and Interest in Starting a Business

Some authors concentrate on attitudes towards entrepreneurship or interest in starting a business. Fagenson & Marcus (1991) reasoned that conceptions of the traits of a successful entrepreneur would influence career choices. They asked a group of women what a successful entrepreneur must be like, and found that masculine traits were rated higher than feminine, but that women with female managers valued feminine traits a little higher than women with male managers. Matthews & Moser (1995) found among college graduates in business administration, that a family background in small business increased interest in starting a firm of one's own, and that males were slightly more interested than females. In a follow-up longitudinal study they concluded that the interest in starting a firm of one's own decreased over time, and more so for women (Matthews & Moser, 1996). Scherer et al. (1990) had a similar result – male students were slightly more interested in starting a business than females, and they also had a higher level of entrepreneurial self-efficacy. The authors speculated that men are socialized into entrepreneurship to a larger extent than women. Kourilsky & Walstad (1998), finally, found it alarming that only 62% of US schoolgirls wanted to start their own business, whereas 72% of the boys wanted to.

Psychology

Several studies attend to the psychological make-up of women entrepreneurs. Neider (1987) tested a small sample in Florida and found that women entrepreneurs were similar to men, with a high need for achievement, autonomy, dominance over others, energy and persistence. They liked to run their organizations lean and were reluctant to borrow, in order to maintain control. Masters & Meier (1988) found no difference in the risk-taking propensity between male and female entrepreneurs. Sexton & Bowman-Upton (1990) did two personality tests on male and female entrepreneurs and found that they scored similarly on conformity, interpersonal affect, social adroitness, harm avoidance and succorance. Men scored slightly higher on energy level and risk taking, women higher on autonomy and change. MacNabb et al. (1993) tested an instrument called ISA (identity structure analysis) on a group of nascent women entrepreneurs on Northern Ireland. They found some core values: need for achievement, independence and inner locus of control. However, some values were found that changed after a training program, for example the evaluation of risk and profit, affirming their assumption that values are not necessarily as stable as the literature suggested. Fagenson (1993) also examined values systems, and compared male and female entrepreneurs, and male and female managers. She found hardly any differences between the entrepreneurs, but great differences between entrepreneurs and managers, providing support for a situation-centered as opposed to a person-centered view.

Bellu (1993) tested whether or not female managers and entrepreneurs differed on task role motivation and attributional style. Entrepreneurs scored higher on self-achievement motivation than managers, as predicted, but four other tested motivations did not differ much. Entrepreneurs attributed failures to unstable external factors whereas managers were more prone to make internal attributions. Both categories attributed success to internal factors. The most noteworthy finding of the research on the psychology of women entrepreneurs is thus that it is similar to the psychology of male entrepreneurs.

The Start-up Process

Goffee & Scase (1983) interviewed 23 women business owners in Britain in an exploratory study and found that they started businesses in response to labor market or domestic subordination, to balance family and work or as a feminist move. They did not see entrepreneurship as a straight-forward solution to women's subordination, but concluded that it might offer heightened awareness, a sense of self-determination, independence and self-confidence. Pellegrino & Reece (1982) interviewed a small sample of female entrepreneurs in retail and service firms in Virginia to find out if women have more, or specific problems in starting a business, and found that they did not, except, perhaps, that they perceived lack of financial skills as a problem. Nelson (1987) found no evidence of women having unique start-up information needs. Shane et al. (1991) examined reasons leading to new firm foundation across country and gender in Britain, Norway and New Zealand and found only one cross-country, cross-gender reason: the desire for job freedom. Otherwise there were interaction effects and variations, suggesting contextual and situational models. A follow-up paper by the same authors investigated perceptions of the business start-up environment in terms of resource scarcity, turbulence, hostility and uncertainty. They found significant country differences but no gender differences or gender/country interactions, apart from females perceiving a slightly higher political uncertainty than males (Kolvereid, Shane, & Westhead, 1993).

Marlow (1997) interviewed a matched sample of male and female entrepreneurs in the service industry about the experience of starting and owning a small business and, again, found more similarities than differences. However, only women started businesses in order to be able to balance work and family. Alsos & Ljunggren (1998) questioned the rational for Scandinavian assistance to women entrepreneurs, which is based on the thought that women have particular problems during the start-up process. They identified nascent entrepreneurs in a randomly selected group of people and followed them over time. They found many more similarities than differences in the start-up process. The differences were that women wrote business plans to a lesser extent, started smaller businesses and borrowed later in the process – but there was no difference in the probability of succeeding. Summing up, the research on the start-up process found many more similarities than differences between male and female entrepreneurs.

Management Practice and Strategy

Chaganti (1986) differed between an entrepreneurial mode of strategic management and a feminine way and found through eight case studies that successful women entrepreneurs used the entrepreneurial mode, but their management styles were more feminine. Olson & Currie (1992) quoted a study, which had found a relationship between value systems and strategy for men, but the authors found no such correlation for women. The women in the sample represented all of four possible strategies, using the Miles-Snow typology, but they were all very similar on values. Van Auken et al. (1994) investigated advertising strategies. They found the same effectiveness rating for the strategies of both men and women, but women tended to rely more on referrals, the telephone directory, and community events. Analyzing the discussions in a focus group study, Buttner (2001) found women to rely mainly on relational practices as opposed to a command-and-control style of management.

Networking

Relational skills might suggest good networking skills. Several papers study women entrepreneurs' networking. Smeltzer & Fann (1989) studied if women in Kansas City and Phoenix networked optimally, or if choosing only their own sex held them back. They reasoned that the necessary instrumental knowledge and expertise is usually found with men. They found that women did indeed network with other women, but they were no worse off for that. They had the same growth rate as men. A comparable hypothesis is present in a study by Aldrich et al. (1989). They compared women and men entrepreneurs in the USA and Italy to find out if network composition, activity, and density differed by gender and/or country. There were no gender differences in activity and density – and only slight country differences. Women were likely to have men in their networks, but the contrary was not the case. Cromie & Birley (1992), using the same instrument as the previous authors, found similar results on Northern Ireland. Women's networks were as big and as diverse as men's, but they had fewer men and more women in their networks. Both studies saw this as a potential deficiency. Andre, (1992) found that American women business owners' participation in economic development organizations reflected their participation elsewhere in society – they represented small rather than large businesses, which were at the local rather than at the state level. Katz & Williams (1997) investigated weak-tie networking (churches, fraternities, political groups, sports clubs, etc.) among male and female entrepreneurs and managers, and found hardly any difference between the sexes – but significant differences between entrepreneurs and managers. The latter had, contrary to the hypothesis, more involvement in such organizations. The entrepreneurs had little or no weak-tie networking. All in all, networking differences between men and women were either absent or without consequence.

Role of Family

Some of the networking papers focus on the role of family. Family is here sometimes regarded as a potential support, sometimes as a detriment. Stoner et al. (1990) see husbands as essentially unhelpful and find that women entrepreneurs do experience work-home conflict. This was the case for young women in particular and those who ran new, not yet successful businesses. Marital status, the number of children, and the number of hours worked did not correlate with experience of conflict, however. Nelson (1989) asked women business owners in Texas if they used assistance from spouses or other kin, reasoning that they might not be the most qualified for such help. He found that women were quite pragmatic, turning for help to those who were the most qualified. Caputo & Dolinsky (1998) wondered if financial and human capital from household members makes it more likely for a woman to start her own business. They investigated the husbands' earnings and found a correlation only for those whose husbands were business owners themselves. They reasoned that role models, advice and encouragement were the most important.

There are few studies of family businesses with an explicit gender perspective in the entrepreneurship research journals, but one such study focused on how families integrated daughters into family business management. Dumas (1992) explored the issue in in-depth interviews with family members from 18 businesses. Among other things, she found that daughters were an untapped resource. They were not socialized into taking over and did not count until there was a crisis – the father became ill, or the son refused to take over. The daughters also experienced role conflicts towards both parents and employees as their role changed from daughter to manager.

Working couples in small business are identified as problematic by the literature, write Cox et al., (1984). However, they found in a survey of husband and wife teams in Texas no such report of problems, rather the situation was quite the contrary. Marshack (1994) compared copreneurs to dual-career couples and found that the copreneurs were more traditional. The wives did household work at home and traditional women's jobs at work. The dual career couples were less traditional in orientation. Altogether, these studies show that family plays a role for women entrepreneurs, but, interestingly, male entrepreneurs are not asked the same questions.

Access to Capital

The most frequently researched environmental constraint is access to capital and discrimination from bank loan officers. In an early study, Buttner & Rosen (1988) found that bank loan officers perceived men to be more "entrepreneurial" than women – men were rated higher on leadership, autonomy, risk-taking propensity, readiness for change, and endurance. Men were also perceived to be less emotional and to have a lower need for support, leading the authors to conclude that sex stereo-typing existed. The same authors found in a loan decision simulation a year later that gender did *not* influence bank loan officers' decisions (Buttner & Rosen, 1989).

Riding & Swift (1990) found in a large Canadian study that banks had higher collateral requirements for women. Interest rates did not differ. They also found that a lower percentage of women than men had a line of credit, leading them to conclude that the banking relationships seemed more difficult for women. Buttner & Rosen (1992), referring to their previous studies, noted that women often claimed to be discriminated against even though research did not fully support this. They hypothesized that there were gender differences in perceptions. They surveyed male and female entrepreneurs with a hypothetical situation in which they were denied a loan. They found no difference in estimates of the difficulty of getting a loan and no significant difference in the rankings of reasons for denial as a function of gender, age or experience. There were no significant differences in post-denial strategies either – women were actually more prone to seek venture capital.

Fay & Williams (1993) investigated the situation in New Zealand. They presented loan officers with a loan application and found no difference in chances for approval for university educated men and women, but women without a degree were rejected to a higher degree. Another very large Canadian study on loan refusals, requirements for co-signatures, interest rates, and the ratio of the amount asked for and the amount received, found no effect of gender when a host of background factors were controlled for. However, the factors that were associated with loan refusals (small size, low liquid assets, sales, and sales growth, etc) were strongly associated with women's businesses. Women were also unhappier with the inter-personal banking relationship (Fabowale, Orser, & Riding, 1995).

Carter & Rosa (1998) examined the financing of male and female-owned businesses in the United Kingdom and found more similarities than differences. Gender was not related to refusal, but men and women were refused for different reasons, which pertained to their businesses and personal backgrounds. Men had larger initial capitalization. Women used similar sources, but they were less prone to use overdrafts, bank loans and supplier credit.

Coleman (2000) found in a large US study that there was no differential access to credit because of gender, but rather because of the age of the firm as well as the size and type of business. As in the study by Fabowale et al. (1995), women's businesses were smaller, younger and more likely to be in services with low collateral – all things associated with risk by banks. However, women-owned firms paid higher interests rates for the most recent loan, and women were more likely to put up collateral, which led the author to conclude that women had similar access, but not as good terms.

The last study on this subject is about the venture capital industry. Greene et al. (1999) found a large disproportion between the number of women-owned businesses and the number of women-owned businesses financed by venture capital. Only 2.4% of venture capital financed businesses were women-owned. In conclusion, several studies report discrimination, but it seems to be related to structural factors rather than gender *per se*.

Performance

The subject of business performance and gender has received much attention over the last decade. Fischer et al. (1993) made a strong case for this. Why research gender differences if whether or not they matter is not researched as well? Most of the performance studies compare men and women, but a few study only women-owned businesses' performance or they compare different groups of women's businesses. An early paper by Cuba et al. (1983) studied management practices among a group of women retailers and found that delegation, education and prior work experience were positively related to financial success, whereas level of mental and physical effort and degree of participative management did not correlate. Lerner et al. (1997) tracked background factors (firm and owner demographics, network affiliations, goals and attitudes, etc.) among women entrepreneurs in Israel, and studied how these related to performance. They found that different things came to the surface than in the US studies, alerting the readers to the need to take culture into account. Important background factors were network affiliations (but only one of these), motivation, business skills, and previous industry experience. Previous start-up experience, education, and role models did not differentiate low performers from high performers.

Anna et al. (2000) compared women in traditional women's businesses (retail and sales) with those in non-traditional businesses and investigated if differences were related to sales. They used the venture efficacy construct as one of the independent variables. They found a few differences, but these were small and most examined parameters were very similar between the two groups. Different factors were correlated with sales in the different sectors, leading the authors to conclude that not all prospective women business owners should be viewed equally.

The majority of the performance studies, however, compare men and women. Women are by most authors found to have smaller and more slowly growing businesses, calling for an explanation. Chaganti & Parasuraman (1996), for example, studied gender differences in performance, goals, strategies and management practices. They found similar management practices, similar employment growth and return on assets, but women had smaller sales. Women rated both achievement goals and financial goals higher than men, and for strategy there were no differences except that women rated product quality a little higher. The authors draw no inferences as to cause and effect, but many other studies are explanatory. Miskin & Rose (1990) related a number of background variables to profitability. The only significant effect found was that previous ownership experience affected profitability positively for men. There was no such effect for women.

Kalleberg & Leicht (1991) published a large, often-cited study where they compared men and women in three industries and found that there was no gender difference in the probability of surviving, nor was there any difference in earnings growth by gender. Fischer et al. (1993) investigated the effect of relevant formal education and industry experience. They found few differences in education but some differences in experience – women had less experience in managing employees, working in similar firms, and helping to start other businesses. This correlated with their smaller firms, lower income growth, and lower sales per employee. There were, however, no differences on other, more important performance measures such as growth, productivity, and returns.

Rosa et al. (1994) surveyed male and female business owners in Britain in textile/clothing manufacturing, business services, and hotel and catering, using a variety of performance assessments. Females performed worse overall but the differences were inconsistent across sectors. The women were younger so age might also explain the performance difference. Their hypothesis that men were more likely to pursue growth and less likely to seek intrinsic rewards was not upheld.

Fasci & Valdez (1998) decided to hold industry constant to find out if women's firms were less profitable than men's. They concentrated on small accounting practices in a US nation-wide survey. They found that women had a slightly higher profit ratio, but much smaller gross revenue. When controlled for other factors, however, they found a higher ratio of profits to gross revenues when a man owned the firm. Also, home-based businesses and those started for family/flexibility reasons had lower profit ratios than those started for the challenge and related goals.

Chell & Baines (1998) investigated the relationship between gender and performance (sales and growth) in three industries in the business services sector in the UK. They also tested if women had a more integrative business life-style than men. They found no performance differences between male and female sole owners, but couples did not perform as well, most likely because the wife spent fewer hours with the business. Couples had a very traditional gender division of jobs both at work and at home. There was no support for the notion that women entrepreneurs had a more integrative life-style than men.

Kalleberg & Leicht, cited above, concluded that there were no differences in survival rates. Two other studies came to slightly different conclusions. Carter et al. (1997) studied if differences in resources and/or strategy between men and women affected the odds of discontinuance in retail firms. They reasoned that women have fewer resources, and that their different values systems may lead them to choose a strategy that draws on their relational skills and skills at juggling responsibilities. They found that women did in fact have a higher probability of discontinuing and some fewer resources, particularly prior business experience and start-up experience, however, resource deficiencies were more likely to affect *men's* odds of discontinuance. As for strategy – they differentiated between quality proponents, price competitors, niche purveyors and super achievers, they found that the woman who was a super achiever and competed in everything, including price, was the most successful.

Boden & Nucci (2000) studied the retail industry as well. They examined how individual differences between men and women entrepreneurs affected survival rates. Of the examined variables, they found that capital and work experience affected survival rates for both sexes, but management experience did not. Women had less capital, thus affecting their survival prospects. Several of the studies above point to women's performance as less than men's on one or several dimensions. DuRietz & Henrekson (2000) labeled this the "female underperformance hypothesis" and tested it in a rigorous manner. Controlling for firm size, industry and receiving sectors, they examined differences in sales, profitability, employment and orders in a sample of 4,200 Swedish entrepreneurs. There were systematic structural gender differences in the sample as a whole, but when disaggregated, only sales remained, and only in the 2–4 employees size category. Given different preferences for sales growth, there was thus no support for the underperformance hypothesis.

Cliff (1998) also questioned the female underperformance hypothesis. She did not question that women's businesses were generally smaller, but rather if women shared the research texts' conception of this as a problem. She did a both quantitative and qualitative study to explore gender differences in attitudes towards growth and size. The quantitative analysis concluded that women had fewer resources and placed less value on expansion, but there were no gender differences in growth intentions. The qualitative analysis said that both sexes set a limit to suitable size, and that this limit was affected by current size.

Women set this limit lower and they want to grow more slowly, maintaining control and taking fewer risks.

Buttner & Moore (1997) were also skeptical towards prevailing performance assessments and decided to ask how women themselves measured success. They inquired as to why female executives left their jobs and started businesses, and how their reasons correlated with self-reported measures of success. The most important measure of success was self-fulfillment and goal achievement, followed by profit and growth. Thereafter came balancing family and work, and at the far end making a social contribution. Those who left their old jobs for the challenge, rated self-fulfillment and profit first, and those who left for family concerns, rated balancing family and work as a success measure to a high degree. In conclusion, women's businesses seemed, on average, to perform less well than men's and with standard measurements, but when accounting for structural factors, there was little support for this statement[5].

Other Questions

Brush (1997) inquired into women's own opinions as well. She asked a group of eight female entrepreneurs in a focus group study what they perceived to be the obstacles and opportunities for women entrepreneurs. Being taken seriously, child and dependent care, access to growth capital, and lack of female role models in entrepreneurship education were the obstacles. Three opportunities were mentioned: modern genderless information technology, women's participative management style, and women's holistic employee policies.

Nilsson (1997), who is the only one of the reviewed authors that uses institutional theory, conducted a case study of a business counseling program directed towards female entrepreneurs in Sweden. She was struck by the legitimacy dilemmas involved for the counselors. The program was a government initiative. The regular counseling service, under which the program sorted administratively, did not perceive the women's program as fully legitimate and did not fully support it. The counselors had to seek legitimacy otherwise. They built it through tasks, procedures and through the target group; however, the program was never fully accepted.

---

5   Not included in the review is a new study by Watson (2002), who compared male- and female-controlled businesses. After controlling for industry, age of business, and the number of days a business operated he found no significant differences with respect to total income to total assets, the return on assets, or the return on equity. If removing the control variables, the female controlled businesses actually outperformed the male-controlled.

There are seven review papers or conceptual papers, apart from the earlier mentioned review concerning women entrepreneurs in Singapore (Maysami & Goby, 1999). Stevenson (1986) summed up the findings to date and concluded that many sex-based differences were actually related to structural factors. Birley (1989) also reflected on the findings and spoke for a contextual approach to researching women's entrepreneurship. Moore (1990) discussed the many different types of samples used in entrepreneurship research that make knowledge accumulation difficult and called for a common definition of entrepreneurship. She also advocated building solid statistical research bases and better methods, instruments and analyses. Stevenson (1990) discussed methodological problems – the exclusion of women in many studies, the use of instruments developed on men only on research on women, and the inadequacies of survey methodology. She asked for more qualitative, in-depth studies. Brush (1992) wrote the comprehensive and frequently cited review, which I used as the basis of comparison in the first section of this chapter. She concentrated on the differences found between men and women and suggested that women view their businesses as interconnected systems of relationships instead of separate economic units in the social world. Her standpoint is referred to as "the integrative perspective". Berg (1997) also employed the word relational but in a very different sense. She used constructionist, feminist theory and argued for seeing gender as a relational instead of an essential concept. Walker & Joyner (1999), finally, wrote a theoretical paper on the impact of Small Business Administration programs in eliminating discrimination. Among other things, they posited that the programs might actually increase pure gender discrimination through the resentment that results from programs targeted toward women.

By now the reader might be overwhelmed by the great amount of interest that women's entrepreneurship has received from the research community. Baker et al. (1997) presented sobering findings. The dramatic increase of women's entrepreneurship, one of the greatest changes in American business life according to the authors, was not reflected in mass media or in scholarly journals. The coverage of women business owners in periodicals actually decreased between 1982 and 1995. Two national newspapers mentioned women in about 4% of their articles on business owners. Of articles published in Entrepreneurship Theory and Practice and the Journal of Business Venturing 85% made no mention of women at all, and an analysis of these two plus Academy of Management Journal and Academy of Management Review between 1969 and 1994 counted only 22 out of 3,206 articles that featured women owners or entrepreneurs. The authors concluded that women are made invisible due to androcentrism, the taken-for-granted notion that the traditional male-centered business model is the neutral and normal model. This would not matter, they continued, if there were no beliefs that women would indeed make a different contribution and they posited that under looser institutional constraints, women's ownership behavior would indeed differ from men's.

Summary of Findings

The next logical step, had the research resulted in the hypothesized findings, would be to draw out the main results and present a clear, comprehensive picture of women entrepreneurs, their management ways, their businesses and their environments. Preferably a table, with one column for women and one for men. But how do you do this when the results are so full of mixed and contradictory results, and so many result in "null" findings? The only finding that is somewhat consistent across the studies is that women's businesses are concentrated in the retail and service sectors and, because of this, their businesses are smaller than the average male owned business.

Across a long range of psychological, attitudinal and other background factors, there are many more similarities between male and female entrepreneurs than there are differences. Differences are found within groups of female entrepreneurs, between different occupational groups as entrepreneurs and managers, and between entrepreneurs in different countries. A few studies point to women's relational management style, but the so called "integrative perspective" which posits that women see their businesses in a very different way from men is not supported. The "female underperformance hypothesis", while appearing in several studies, did not hold when put to rigorous tests accounting for structural factors. If differences in preferences are taken into account as well, there seems to be no support for such a hypothesis.

The start-up process is similar for men and women, and women appear to have no specific difficulties or information needs. Men's and women's networking are similar, except for the gender composition, which, however, has no bearing on the effectiveness of the network. Women seem to be discriminated against by banks in several studies, but the explanations appear to be mainly structural; they own the types of businesses that banks associate with higher risks. Balancing family and work is experienced as a problem for many women entrepreneurs, but the studies do not report if men have similar feelings. So personal characteristics, the process of starting and running a business and the investigated aspects of the environment appear to be similar for men and women entrepreneurs. The main difference is that the organization on average tends to be a little smaller for women, and it is often in retail or services.

Ways of Explaining the Few Differences Found

As noted above, many of the reviewed studies looked for differences between men and women entrepreneurs. They found very few, and in-group variation was typically much larger than between-group variation. The studies are full of falsified hypotheses about gender differences. This was disappointing to many, and in the next chapter, I will go into detail on how this "disappointment" was dealt with in the texts. However, several attempts have been made to explain the lack of differences from a methodological point of departure. I discuss these explanations below under three different headings: "lack of rigor", "insufficient measures and methods", and "essentialist assumptions". As the headings may indicate, the explanations come from different epistemological positions. The first is a "within-group" critique, i.e., differences may exist but they are not caught because of sloppy research designs. The second is a version of the first, but unlike the first, which sees research designs as at least potentially neutral (it is a matter of refinement), the second group of explanations recognizes that research instruments may be gendered. It still holds essential differences as likely, however. The third position rejects the assumption of essential differences between men and women and critiques the research questions instead.

Argument 1: "Lack of rigor"

Several authors have commented that research results about women entrepreneurs are contradictory or unsatisfying. Most common is methodological critique, with calls for "more rigor". Brush (1992) mentioned unsophisticated statistical methods, small sample sizes and convenience samples as problems. As discussed above, this has at least partly been remedied, but Moore's (1990) objection that the samples cannot always be compared still holds. As discussed in chapter two, entrepreneurship scholars have struggled with "entrepreneur" and found it a cumbersome, imprecise and hard to define construct. Using alternative concepts fitting the particular research questions such as "small business owner/managers, solo-entrepreneurs, fast-growth firms", etc., has been advocated (Hornaday, 1990). To allow knowledge accumulation, researchers should consequently report on how they define entrepreneurship and, particularly, on which criteria they selected their samples. However, researchers "have clustered businesses into a homogeneous group, despite differences in their size, growth potential, sector of the economy, charter, number of employees, revenue and mission, and type of ownership" writes Moore (1990:276). Even in those instances where single studies carefully report their selection criteria, this is often lost when the studies are referred to by later studies. Olson and Currie, for example, wrote, "Chaganti (1986) concluded that the gender of the entrepreneurs will cause management practices to differ" (Olson & Currie, 1992:50). This was indeed so, but Chaganti found these results from interviews with eight women entrepreneurs, seven in sales or personal/professional services, and one in a typical male-dominated industry (marine construction). Moreover, Chaganti postulated an "entrepreneurial" and a "feminine model" of strategic management and found the eight women to be "entrepreneurial" along most of the investigated seven dimensions, *except* for their managerial styles. Olson and Currie did not, I would claim, do full justice to their source. Knowledge built on very different types of samples is thus, through referral practices, generalized to hold for women entrepreneurs in general. It is even more questionable when results found for a group of women in the USA are generalized to hold for women in another country with a different set of norms and values and a different culture. The idea behind this sort of critique is that if research were only done rigorously, the results would not be so contradictory or so inconsistent with hypotheses. The critique assumes that gender differences are still there, they have only eluded researchers who did not look closely enough.

Argument 2: "Insufficient measures"

Another methodological objection, put forward by Stevenson (1990) is the use of male-centered notions of entrepreneurship to study female entrepreneurs. Early research on entrepreneurship was done on male samples and the body of knowledge on "entrepreneurs" was actually a body of knowledge on male entrepreneurs. Adding female entrepreneurs is an attempt to correct this, but the notion of what characterizes entrepreneurship and what questions are interesting and important to study are not gender neutral. Many of the measures used to assess female entrepreneurs, for example, were developed on male subjects. Stevenson (1990) noted that McClelland's (1961) work on the relationship between need for achievement and entrepreneurial motivation, which has been widely used in entrepreneurship research, was developed specifically and solely on the males within the societies studied. The women's job was, according to McClelland, to instill a high need for achievement in their sons through proper mothering (Herman, 1995).

Measures developed on males might not capture women's specific experiences and the effect is also that women are compared to a male norm, masked as neutral. "The question seems to be given what we know about men 'do women have what it takes to become entrepreneurs?' " writes Stevenson (1990:441). A related critique is the predominant use of cross-sectional survey studies. Of the empirical studies in this analysis, 56 (77%) used pre-formulated questionnaires. When pre-formulated questions, based on male centered notions of entrepreneurship are imposed on women entrepreneurs, there will be little chance to capture anything "different" about women entrepreneurs, only "more" or "less" of what is already imagined. This is an alternative explanation for the lack of differences found, but, as noted earlier, this critique still assumes that there *is* something essentially feminine to be measured.

Argument 3: "Essentialist assumptions"

A third objection concerns what is really there to be captured. It concerns assumptions about causal relationships related to psychological variables, and it concerns assumptions about the very existence of these variables. Many of the articles reviewed study innate psychological characteristics such as motivation, self-efficacy, risk-taking propensity, value systems etc., which are assumed to explain something else, for example performance. Psychology refers to this as "attitude research". Demonstrating causality is of course always a problem in cross-sectional studies, but the problem may be more than just the lack of a time dimension. Below I report on some critical voices from within the fields of psychology and economic psychology to show that it is not necessary to depart from a social constructionist position to question the value of attitude research. I will, of course, also discuss the topic from an explicit social constructionist viewpoint.

Psychology envisions an attitude as "predispositions to behave in a characteristic manner with respect to specified social objects or classes of such objects" (King & McGuinnies, 1972:8). It is conceived as a mental phenomenon, residing inside the skull of the individual and formed through socialization. A person's background and experiences thus are supposed to affect the attitudes, and the attitudes are in turn thought to affect behavior in some foreseeable manner. New information is thought to make up an intervening variable, causing changes in attitudes and, consequently, behavior. This construct has of course great appeal, since, if it would work, it would make it possible to control and change people's behavior by means of changing their attitudes through simply providing information, education, or propaganda. It probably also partly explains why psychology has gained such a prominent position in government (more on this in chapter seven).

The problem is that it does not seem to work. Psychologists themselves admit this, even if they often try to save the attitude/behavior construct anyway, by modifying the understanding of it. Wicker delivered an early critique. His review of 46 empirical studies of attitudinal-behavioral consistency was a big disappointment for scholars advocating causal relationships between attitudes and behavior. "Taken as a whole these studies suggest that it is considerably more likely that attitudes will be unrelated or only slightly related to overt behaviors than that attitudes will be closely related to action" (Wicker 1969:76). Abelson (1972) did another review. He found that people did not act as they said they would, and sometimes people behaved in ways they themselves found surprisingly contrary to their own assumed values. Further, there was no systematic relationship between how much a person learned through persuasive communication and how much the related attitude was found to change. He severely questioned whether information had any effect upon attitudes and whether attitudes had any effects on behavior. Foxall's review of the literature from 1970 to 1979 presented a more optimistic picture, but the difference was that the concept of "attitude" had been modified. Studies showing more consistency took other factors into account besides attitudes such as "*personal factors* which include other attitudes, competing motives, verbal, intellectual and social abilities, and *situational* factors such as the actual or assumed presence of certain people, normative prescription of proper behavior, alternative available behaviors … inspecificity of attitude objects, unforeseen extraneous events and the expected and/or actual consequences of various acts" (Foxall 1984:83).

The construct now includes things outside of a person's skull as well. "Since simple attitudinal-behavioural consistency, where it exists at all, is extremely weak, it is difficult to conclude other than that the notion of an underlying, 'true' attitude has been discredited and that social constraints explain behaviour successfully to a degree that makes ... any conception of pre-behavioral, mental processes inaccurate, untrustworthy and irrelevant", concluded Foxall (1984:83).

Behavioral decision researchers Payne, Bettman & Johnson (1992) question not only causality relationships, but also the very existence of stable inner attitudes and values. They write that preferences and beliefs about an object or event of any complexity are constructed, not merely revealed, in the generation of a response to a judgment or choice task. That is, when answering questions on a Likert scale, the attitudes are constructed in the very act of answering the question. It may even be argued that measures of behavioral intention reflect *past* behavior, and thus serve as a justification for actions taken in the past, more so than as a prediction for the future. If stable inner attitudes do not exist, and even if they do, they cannot explain behavior, it should be no surprise then that the studies taking this approach have inconclusive or unexpected results. As Abelson put it "We are very well trained and very good at finding reasons for what we do, but not very good at doing what we find reasons for ... People readily justify what they have done by accommodating their attitude statements accordingly. The reverse connection has proved more refractory." (Abelson, 1972:25).

Attitudes are inferred to exist. No one has ever seen one. The way they are "observed" are further, usually through reactions to items on a questionnaire or attitude scale. So, a researcher says that there is an attitude towards, for example, women in the military, which one can grade from one to seven, puts it down on paper, then asks a number of male teenagers to fill out the questionnaire and, lo and behold, they find that male teenagers have a negative attitude towards women in the military. Seen in this way, the procedures of psychologists are actually radically constructivist, i.e. nominalist.

Social constructionist writers also seriously question the idea of a causal relationship between behavior and some assumed inner state. Mary Douglas, building on Hume writes "in our experience we only find succession and frequency, no laws or necessity. It is we ourselves who attribute causality" (Douglas 1987, p 11). March & Olsen (1989) argue against the "logic of consequentiality" altogether. As they see it, people do not act according to some pre-defined values, motivations, or rational decisions. People act according to norms and rules, explicit or internalized. People do what they find suitable in the situation and what accords with their personal self-identity conception. March & Olsen (1989) call this the logic of appropriateness. The logic of consequentiality is invoked after the fact, as a way to justify and legitimize action. The logic of consequentiality should be seen as exactly this, and not as something having explanatory value for future behavior.

Assuming the existence of stable inner characteristics is an example of an essentialist position. The great majority of research on women entrepreneurs takes such an essentialist position towards gender – even some of the critics. Take the methodological criticism mentioned above for example. A call for more stringent sampling procedures is also a call for the elimination of confounding variables, so that one is more likely to uncover what "really" characterizes women entrepreneurs. A call for research notions that are not male-based implies that there really is something different about women's entrepreneurship that can be captured by better methods and different questions. An essentialist position entails that there is something real that makes you a man or a woman, above and apart from (or as a result of) the reproductive differences. There is a further belief that there is something innate in people that make them start and grow a company, and this something presumably differs by sex. One of the basic tenets of the constructionist theory that this work is based on is that reality is socially constructed in a process of externalizing your subjective experience as an objective fact and then internalizing the same thing as "reality". Previous generations' objectivations that are just "out there" to be internalized seem particularly objective, factual and unchangeable (Berger & Luckmann, 1966). These have become institutionalized. Following this line of thought, there are no special innate masculine or feminine essences. Whatever people call masculine or feminine is something of their own making. Things like courage, caring, listening skills, leadership ability, achievement orientation, family orientation, self-confidence, competitiveness, service-mindedness, persistence, self-efficacy and so on are socially constructed, and will differ from one person to another, one context to another, and from one point in time to another, irrespective of whether one is a man or a woman. From this point of view, the innate, stable characteristics that the female entrepreneurship research looks for are very elusive targets. The reviewed research on the internal characteristics of female entrepreneurs, may be looking for something that most likely does not exist, in order to explain something that cannot be explained by that non-existing entity anyway. This presumably explains the meager results. It is not, however, an innocent, but unfortunately as yet unproductive undertaking. Some things are accomplished. What is accomplished, on what grounds, and how, is the subject of the next chapter.

Summary

This chapter presented an overview of the selected articles. The studies covered topics such as personal background and firm characteristics, attitudes to entrepreneurship or intentions to start, psychology, start-up processes, management practice and strategy, networking, family, access to capital, and performance. The most common research question is related to differences between male and female entrepreneurs in these areas, but contrary to expectations, few such differences were found. Within-group variation was typically larger than between-groups variation. The results were also contradictory at times. Different explanations have been put forth as to the reasons for this. One explanation says that the research designs are unsatisfactory. Unsophisticated statistical methods, small sample sizes, and convenience samples in combination with insufficient sampling information and/or careless referral practices, may contribute to contradictory results. Another explanation holds that male gendered measuring instruments and pre-formulated questionnaires have been used, which makes it impossible to capture anything "differentially feminine" since only more or less of what is already imagined is measured. Both these critiques, however, assume that there is something female or male to be measured. The non-essentialist position questions the existence of stable inner psychological characteristics as well as the causal relationships assumed in much of the reviewed research. It holds that looking for something essentially female or male is to be looking for something in vain. The research, however unproductive in terms of finding differences, nonetheless produces something in the making and this is the topic of the next chapter.

6
How Articles Construct the Female Entrepreneur

This chapter goes in detail into the texts, and looks for arguments, underlying assumptions and the positioning of women. How do researchers argue for studying female entrepreneurship in the first place? Why is it important? Is it for furthering equality between men and women? Or are there other reasons? What are the research problems and hypotheses and how do these position women? The chapter also takes a closer look at some articles that are particularly unwilling to accept the "no-difference" finding, and looks at various ways of reasoning around this. I locate three strategies used to explain why women are different in spite of findings saying that they are not.

How Researchers Argue for Studying Women Entrepreneurs

As described in chapter four, scientific journal articles make up a separate literary genre with its own distinctive mark. The introduction section is the place to argue for the importance of your research. This is done in three steps: First, establish a territory by claiming the centrality or the importance of the research area. Second, establish a niche by indicating a research gap, making a counter claim or raising a question. Alternatively, indicate the continuance of a research tradition. Third, occupy the established niche. This is usually accomplished through the presentation of the work or its purpose and by announcing the principal findings (Swales 1990).

I analyzed how the first two steps were achieved in all articles[1] and found that the overwhelming majority argued that women's entrepre-

---

1   See appendix C for details.

neurship is an important research area because women's businesses have, or should have (depending on country and prevalence of female entrepreneurs) an important impact on the economy in terms of jobs, sales, innovation and economic growth and renewal. There is a startling absence of equality arguments. I conclude that instrumental reasons related to business and economic growth carry weight, and that equality arguments are either not interesting or not legitimate as reasons for studying the area. Below are the details of the analysis, followed by a summary table.

How Researchers Establish a Territory

One would think that articles about entrepreneurship published in journals catering to entrepreneurship scholars need not establish the centrality of entrepreneurship *per se*, and only a handful actually do. How they do it is interesting, however. Greene et al. (1999:168) cited above, made the point in one sentence only "Entrepreneurship is recognized as the engine of growth in the US economy" referring, as many others, to Birch (1979) who found that most of the new jobs were created in small businesses. Birley (1989:32) wrote "The entrepreneurial sector is now viewed as a significant factor in the design of strategies for economic recovery and growth in many nations". The claims are supported by statistics. A typical such statement is the following:

> Small businesses are an important source of economic growth and job creation. According to the U.S. Small Business Administration, there were over 22 million small businesses in 1994 employing 53 percent of the workforce ... Small firms account for 50 percent of the gross domestic product and the majority of new jobs created. In terms of innovation, it is estimated that small firms produce twice as many products innovations per employee as large firms, creating new products, services, lines of business, and industries (Coleman, 2000:37).

The authors stressed the importance of small business by mentioning the large number of firms and their impact on the economy in terms of employment, change, and renewal. While such circumstances are taken for granted in most papers, legitimating the study of *women's* entrepreneurship within this research community seem to need more of an effort. Quoting the US Department of Commerce statistics from 1972, an early paper started with the sad story of women's (lack of) entrepreneurship:

> The purpose of this research was to determine the reasons for the low level of success of a group of business owners which has a rather sad track record – American women. Though it is common knowledge that the average working woman earns about sixty percent of a man's pay for doing similar work, one would hope that a female could surmount the problem of sex/pay discrimination by creating her own business. Unfortunately, however, of the 400 000 women-owned businesses (approximately 3 percent of all small businesses), the female owner's share is only 0.3 percent of the total profits ... The statistics on women business owners are depressing, and the prognosis is not good (Cuba et al., 1983:40).

This depressing prognosis did not come true, however. I counted up to no less than 50 papers – six out of ten – that used statistics, updated over the years, which reflected the high start-up rate and ever increasing share of women's businesses to establish their research territory. It seemed almost like a formula. I quote a typical example:

> The United States is experiencing a sea change with respect to entrepreneurship. The rapid expansion of creative opportunity recognition and business venture development in recent years is viewed as the equivalent of an entrepreneurial revolution ... This revolution is having a profound effect on our nation's economic and social landscape as indicated by the significant contribution made by women. Between 1987 and 1996, the growth of women-owned businesses outpaced the overall growth of businesses by nearly two to one. These sales now total nearly $2.3 trillion – an increase of 236% between 1987 and 1996. Women-owned businesses employ one out of every four workers in the United States. This employment figure is likely to rise in future years because it is projected that half of all businesses will be owned by women by the year 2002 (Kourilsky & Walstad, 1998:78).

It is not yet the case that half of American businesses are women-owned, but close to 40% are (SBA, 1998), so the increase has indeed been large. Papers from other countries open with similar paragraphs, often comparing their figures with those from the United States.

> Levels of self-employment in the UK experienced unprecedented growth between 1979 and 1989 ... while male self-employment had risen by some 82% by Spring 1990, there had been a disproportionate rise in the number of female self-employed – the number of women in business in 1993 as two-and-a-half-times greater than in 1979 (Marlow, 1997:199).

Two more British papers cite corresponding figures, and so do papers from New Zealand, Canada, Poland, and Singapore. The Swedish and Norwegian papers also discuss figures, but slightly differently, since neither the share nor the growth rate of women's business ownership is as dramatic in these countries. Alsos & Ljunggren (1998) wrote:

> More men than women start businesses and become self-employed. This is the case for most countries. Recent statistics from Norway show that only 27% of the self-employed are women ... Studies from the Great Britain and the United States, however, indicate that the proportion of female entrepreneurs is increasing in these countries ... assuming that entrepreneurial abilities are evenly distributed across genders, the low rate of female entrepreneurs indicates that there is an under-utilized potential among women for business start-ups. Business start-ups are regarded as an important factor in the process of economic development ... Hence, utilization of the potential among women for business formation and growth is a significant policy issue, both at the regional and the national level (Alsos & Ljunggren, 1998:137).

The impact, or potential impact, of women-owned businesses on the economy thus seems to be how a majority of the authors establish the centrality of the research area. There were other strategies too, however. I created three basic categories, roughly equally popular among the remaining papers. For some authors, enough legitimacy was established from the observation that others had paid attention to the area. Some begin by a general statement like, "In recent years we have witnessed increased interest in female entrepreneurship" (Pellegrino & Reece, 1982); others specify where the interest comes from, like the following:

> Female entrepreneurs are getting a lot of positive attention in Sweden nowadays. Newspapers write feature articles about them, often concentrating on a single fortunate entrepreneur, and two magazines started during the past few years deal with this group and women business leaders. Government bills on Sweden's economic policy stress the economic importance of female entrepreneurs ... All over Sweden, educational courses and campaigns focus on women to encourage the establishment of new firms and the revitalization of existing ones. Female entrepreneurs have banded together to establish at least one nationwide organization. Many activities to this end are sponsored by regional or local authorities (Holmquist & Sundin, 1990:181).

Seven articles in this category refer to the increased interest from the research community such as Fischer et al. (1993:153) "Research on sex and gender differences in entrepreneurial characteristics and performance has received and continues to receive a considerable amount of attention". DuRietz & Henrekson (2000:1) observed, "In recent years the flow of research results regarding various aspects of entrepreneurship has grown into a veritable torrent."

A second, but related strategy of establishing a territory is to refer to a field of research and in the same move criticize it. This is similar to a move two in Swales scheme and, in fact, of the seven articles I put in this category, four began their article with move two, and had only a brief review of research items as move one, as the following examples indicate:

> Research on entrepreneurship within the field of economic geography as well as within economics or other social sciences is traditionally characterized by gender blindness (Berg, 1997:259).

> Previous studies into gender and business ownership have resulted in conflicting evidence about whether finance poses problems for women starting and running businesses (Carter & Rosa, 1998:225).

An odd, but interesting example is the following, where a certain configuration of research fields is first denounced and then immediately elevated as timely and relevant:

> Research in business, as in other disciplines, has been characterized by a certain trendiness in topics chosen for study. For instance, most publications today contain articles relating to (1) the critical role of strategy in the survival and success of business; (2) the influence of individual value systems, especially in small companies, on the functioning of an organization; and (3) the ever-increasing role of women-owned companies. While the past emphasis on these topics had not always reflected needs, studying these three facets is now both relevant and timely (Olson & Currie, 1992:49).

The third category, with eleven papers in my review, went straight to their particular research topic and/or method and frankly declared it important, as the following examples illustrate:

> Receiving assistance from trusted personal associates should be attractive to small business owners, since it is relatively cost free and potentially useful (Nelson, 1989:7).

> The formation and growth of new firms is a complex process and many
> factors associated with this process can only be identified by in-depth in-
> vestigation at the micro-level of the new firm and the new firm founder(s)
> (Shane et al., 1991:431).

How Researchers Establish a Niche

A study needs not only an important research area, but also a problem,
or something unknown. This is established through move two in
Swales' scheme. One of the steps in move two was labeled "indicating
a gap" and this is also the most common strategy among the reviewed
papers. Twenty studies indicated that women entrepreneurs as a group
were not well researched and offered to remedy this situation. Some
examples follow:

> Most of the available information about the nature, characteristics and
> performance of the small firm and its associated entrepreneur is based on
> studies conducted among predominantly, if not exclusively, male business
> owners/managers (Birley et al., 1987:27).

> One organizational property has been neglected by researchers: the sex of
> the owner (Chaganti, 1986:18).

> Few researchers have examined this highly trained group of women entre-
> preneurs who leave corporate environments to start businesses of their
> own (Buttner & Moore, 1997:34).

> In spite of this impressive growth, comparatively little is known about
> this population of business owners, and the obstacles and opportunities
> they fact in growing their businesses (Brush, 1997:1–2).

Another eighteen studies indicated the same sort of gap, but specified
it to a certain area within women's entrepreneurship, such as advertising, performance, or different groups of women. This category might
also be thought of as "ordinary research with a gender perspective
added" as the following examples suggest:

> Although the trends and projections show that women will play an in-
> creasingly important role in the entrepreneurial development of the econ-
> omy, little is known about what female youth either understand or think
> about entrepreneurship (Kourilsky & Walstad, 1998:78).

> Although more and more women are owning and managing small busi-
> nesses, research on women's networks is less prevalent than research on
> male-dominated networks (Smeltzer & Fann, 1989:25).

No entrepreneurial research has been conducted on the relationship between gender and career self-efficacy (Scherer et al., 1990:39).

Despite the tremendous growth in the number of women-owned enterprises and the increasing impact on society and the economy, there are
few studies discussing the relationship between women entrepreneurs
and advertising (Van Auken et al., 1994:11).

In view of the importance of this topic, it is surprising that there is little
empirical evidence on how gender differences affect organizational performance (Kalleberg & Leicht, 1991:137).

Almost half of the reviewed studies thus fall under a category that I
label "the under-researched woman". Another category might be
labeled "the mis-investigated woman". Here are some quotes from the
eighteen papers that point to methodological limitations of previous
studies or to mixed or inconclusive results of previous research:

While these studies have increased our knowledge, they suffer from limitations that handicap their *generalizability* ... (Dolinsky, 1993:43 emphasis in original).

There have been many attempts to identify the characteristics of the entrepreneurs and to predict the factors which influence business start-up
and growth, but for the most part the results have been inconclusive, un-
fruitful an fraught with methodological difficulties (MacNabb et al.,
1993:301).

The studies reported above dealt with restricted samples (Hisrish & Brush,
1984:31).

This retrospective technique, however, poses two problems: hindsight
might artificially clarify or change the description of the process; and the
retrospective procedure allows only an indirect comparison with those
who do not own businesses. There has been considerably less research
that examines business ownership in a prospective fashion (Matthews &
Moser, 1996:29).

As the number of women business owners has increased, questions of
whether or not WBO behave differently from their male counterparts, and
whether or not women receive any different treatment in the capital mar-
ketplace, remain unresolved (Riding & Swift, 1990:328).

Thus 56 papers indicate a research gap of some sort – either a gap of
research on women entrepreneurs as a whole, a gap in a specific area,

or a gap caused by insufficient methodology. Eight papers concentrate on the gap in women's performance instead. For example:

> Unfortunately, however, of the 400 000 women-owned businesses (approximately 3 percent of all small businesses), the female owner's share is only 0.3 percent of the total profits (Cuba et al., 1983:40, using statistics from 1972).

> Evidence suggests that women have more difficulty than men in gaining access to the support network necessary to successfully launch a new venture (Buttner & Rosen, 1988:250).

> However, there is evidence that businesses founded by women have not succeeded at the same rate as businesses founded by men. In 1985, women owned 28% of all sole proprietorships, yet received only 12% of revenues. One potential barrier to new business formation is access to startup capital (Buttner & Rosen, 1989:250).

> Despite this disproportionate growth, by 1987 women owned only one in three firms, and the economic scale of their businesses was substantially smaller than those owned by men ... Researchers now theorize that a collaborative or integrative approach that incorporates both perspectives offers a better explanation of gender-based differences (Carter et al., 1997:126).

A "gap-strategy" was thus the most common way of establishing a niche. Ten papers chose what Swales would call "counter-claiming" or "question raising" instead. They put forward an observed contradiction, between theory and empirical results or between two empirical phenomena as move two.

> Overall, it seems as if empirical evidence suggests that networking shows only a small, albeit consistent, gender-based difference, while there are some more theoretical arguments to the contrary. Why might this be? (Katz & Williams, 1997:183).

> However, as is shown in this paper, this phenomenal growth – this gender revolution in business ownership – has gone largely unnoticed by major US newspapers (Baker et al., 1997:221).

> However, defining women as resources does not always consider them as agents of development. Rather, it has been found that women entrepreneurs are needed for the sake of local development, rather than the other way around (Nilsson, 1997:239).

How can the inconsistency between female entrepreneurs' allegations and the results of this second study, which showed no differences in loan officer's funding recommendations, be explained? (Buttner & Rosen, 1992:59).

Seven studies (including the one which did not do a move two at all) chose not to indicate a particular gap, but offered to add to existing research, which Swales would label "continuing a tradition". Some examples include:

A multitude of factors can have an influence on the viability of a new venture but quite recently researchers have begun to focus on the importance of personal contact networks as an aid to business development (Cromie & Birley, 1992:239).

The effect of such barriers [of education and experience] might be expected to be greatest during the start-up phase, when knowledge of a vast array of topics is vital to the launching and survival of a venture (Nelson, 1987:38).

The Arguments for Studying Female Entrepreneurship in Summary

The following tables display the distribution of move 1 and 2 arguments in the papers. In the cases where there is overlap, that is, when a paper uses more than one of the alternative moves, I have made a judgment as to what constitutes the main argument by studying its position in the text and the amount of text devoted to it.

Table 6.1: *Move One – Establishing a Territory.*

Arguments used to establish centrality of research area	No. of papers	%
Entrepreneurship, and women's entrepreneurship is important for the economy	53	65
Women's entrepreneurship has received increased attention	11	14
Women's entrepreneurship has been researched but the research is flawed	7	9
My particular research area is important because I say so	10	12
	81	**100**

Table 6.2: *Move Two – Establishing a Niche.*

Arguments used to motivate the study	No. of papers	%
Women entrepreneurs have not been investigated as a group	20	25
Women entrepreneurs have not been investigated with regards to a particular research area	18	22
Women entrepreneurs are not researched in an adequate manner	18	22
Women entrepreneurs do not perform to standard	8	10
There is an observed contradiction regarding women's entrepreneurship	10	12
This adds to existing research	7	9
	81	**100**

The analysis suggests that women's entrepreneurship is important mainly for instrumental reasons, as illustrated by the quote "the engine of economic growth". The researchers write that their businesses have, or should have (depending on country and prevalence of female entrepreneurs) an important impact on the economy in terms of jobs, sales, innovation and economic growth and renewal.

The reasons given for why researchers have begun looking at women's entrepreneurship is, at least in the USA, that its magnitude is a new phenomenon. It is implicit that before, when the number of women entrepreneurs were fewer, they had no impact on the economy and were therefore not important. Since this is what motivated research in the first place, it is possible to interpret the second and third argument in table 6.1 above as derived from the first one. In a sense then, an overwhelming majority of the papers use instrumental arguments to establish the centrality of their territory. I note that equality arguments are absent and conclude that these are either not interesting, or not legitimate as reasons for studying women's entrepreneurship in the selected journals.

The arguments in table 6.2, "establishing a niche", follow logically from the instrumental arguments put forth. If women's entrepreneurship is important to the economy, it should be important to learn more about this group, or to improve upon or add to the existing research.

The fourth argument in table 6.2, that women do not perform to standard, indicates that women's entrepreneurship represents not only a golden opportunity for the economy, but also a problem. It seems that the instrument could use some fine-tuning. This is the topic of the following section.

Conceptions of the Female Entrepreneur as Problematic

Only one of the arguments in the previous analysis – the argument about their "substandard" business performance – posed women's entrepreneurship as a problem. Going beyond the introductions, however, "women as a problem" is a recurring pattern. I analyzed the research problems and hypotheses (which were not necessarily confirmed by the findings – often quite the contrary) to see how the authors envisioned the female entrepreneur at the start of their articles[2]. The result was that well beyond half of the articles focused explicitly on some sort of problem or proposed shortcoming associated with women. A recurring problem is of course the often-quoted small sizes and low growth rates of women's businesses (e.g. Hisrish & Brush, 1984; Kalleberg & Leicht, 1991; Rosa et.al, 1994; Fasci & Valdez, 1998). Explanations for this are often thought to reside within women themselves. Women are discussed as:

- Having a psychological make up that is less entrepreneurial, or at least different from a man's (Neider, 1987; Sexton & Bowman-Upton, 1990; Fagenson, 1993).
- Having less motivation for entrepreneurship or for growth of their businesses (Fischer et al., 1993; Buttner & Moore, 1997; Carter & Allen, 1997).
- Having insufficient education or experience (Boden & Nucci, 2000).
- Having less desire to start a business (Scherer et al., 1990; Matthews & Moser, 1996; Kourilsky & Walstad, 1998).
- Being risk-averse (Masters & Meier, 1988).
- Having unique start-up difficulties or training needs (Pellegrino & Reece, 1982; Birley et al., 1987; Nelson, 1987).
- Using less than optimal, or perhaps "feminine" management practices or strategies (Cuba et al., 1983; Chaganti, 1986; Olson & Currie, 1992; Van Auken et al., 1994; Carter et al., 1997).
- Behaving irrationally by turning to unqualified family members for help (Nelson, 1989).

---

2   The research questions are not always stated as formal hypotheses by the authors. Also, it is not *always* evident that the relationships as described here are those that the authors seek to prove. It could be that there is a statistical "null" hypothesis to be disproved in favor of an alternative. The discussions surrounding the formulations of the research questions lead me, however, to the contrary conclusion.

- Not networking optimally (Aldrich et al., 1989a; Smeltzer & Fann, 1989; Cromie & Birley, 1992; Katz & Williams, 1997).
- Perceiving other women as less cut for the role of entrepreneurship (Fagenson & Marcus, 1991).
- Attributing loan denials to gender bias instead of flaws in the business plan (Buttner & Rosen, 1992).

One might, as Zapalska (1997:76), question if women entrepreneurs do at all "possess the characteristics required for effective performance as entrepreneurs".

To give a taste of how the hypotheses may be formulated I give a few examples below:

Cromie & Birley, (1992:237–238)

1. Women will be less active networkers than men.
2. Women will have less dense networks than men.
3. Women will incline towards discussions with other women.
4. Family members will be the most important persons in the contact network of female owner-managers.

Fischer et al. (1993:158):

H1: Women will have less entrepreneurially relevant formal education than men, and their firms will therefore be less successful.

H2: Women will have less entrepreneurially relevant experience than men and their firms will therefore be less successful.

Carter et al. (1997:129):

H1: High levels of human capital and access to outside resources decrease odds of business discontinuing.

H2: Women-owned firms have lower levels of human resources and less access to financial recourses from outside sources than men-owned businesses, increasing the odds they will discontinue.

Smeltzer & Fann's (1989) study is a good example of how women's shortcomings are discussed. They studied women's networking and found in their literature review that just as men network with other men, women tend to network with other women.

> If the purpose of these networks were instrumental rather than social, women in men-dominated environments might obtain a greater variety of information if they networked with some men rather than all women (Smeltzer & Fann, 1989:26).

The idea of men obtaining a greater variety of information if networking with women is not put forward. They authors continue building their case:

> There has been a tendency for women to study non-business school subjects and to work as employees in "soft-sell" areas. As a result, the female small business owner/manager has a high need for technical information ... In addition, it has been found that females expressed a strong need for information and had difficulty locating sources of assistance ... The most common sources of formal information are bankers, accountants, lawyers, and specialty consultants – all occupations dominated by men. To be successful, it would seem that women must network with men rather than strictly with other women (ibid:27).

The women are positioned here as not only less knowledgeable than men, but also as not knowing their own best by turning to women instead of to men. The result of the study? Women were indeed found to be turning to other women, but they were no worse off for that. They had growth rates comparable to men's and the authors concluded "it appears that it may not be necessary for women to integrate networks dominated by men" (ibid:32).

Being a woman seems to be a potential shortcoming in and of itself, judging from the papers that investigate the impact of the variable gender on for example performance (Chaganti & Parasuraman, 1996; Chell & Baines, 1998; DuRietz & Henrekson, 2000), new firm foundation (Shane et al., 1991), firm ownership (Rosa & Hamilton, 1994), the start-up process (Alsos & Ljunggren, 1998), participation in economic development organizations (Andre, 1992), and access to capital (Carter & Rosa, 1998; Coleman, 2000) to mention some of the researched areas.

Some of these authors explicitly designed their studies to *contest* the idea that women were in some way inferior, but the struggle against this conception is very poignant in the texts. Below is a quote from a study investigating the start-up process in Norway, where male start-ups outnumber female, and where potential female entrepreneurs are thus positioned as an unexploited resource.

> ... female entrepreneurship has been in the focus of Scandinavian public debate, and various efforts are being made to promote it. The rationale behind projects encouraging female entrepreneurship seems to be that women have particular problems during the business start-up process. Typical initiatives are entrepreneurial training for women, business counseling agencies for women, and women network programs. These support efforts seem to be developed from an idea that women have less knowledge about how to start and run a business than men, and/or that they have a less developed network to utilize during the start-up process. However, this idea is to date not supported by research. All in all we know little about the mechanism leading to gender imbalance in business start-ups. Most studies on the gender aspect of entrepreneurship are conducted on small business owners or entrepreneurs who already have established a business ... At this stage the gender imbalance is already materialized, and the (male and female) respondents in the studies are only those who succeeded in setting up a business. The reason for the gender difference in the number of business start-ups, are therefore not explored by these studies (Alsos & Ljunggren, 1998:137–138).

The authors build their whole study on the common conception of women having greater start-up difficulties than men, and they must argue both against public policy ("this idea is to date not supported by research") and against previous research, which according to the authors *does* point to a number of problems for women but which, again according to the authors, is done on the wrong populations to draw such conclusions.

The conception of women as being *less* than something is thus prevalent in this research. Less than what? For the most part, "less than a man" is explicitly stated but sometimes authors write "less than entrepreneurs in general". Knowledge of the latter is, as discussed before, derived from research on males so for practical purposes the propositions are the same. The next section discusses conceptions of the man/the entrepreneur found in some of the research texts.

The Male Norm

The analysis of the introductions made what is highly valued very clear. Entrepreneurship is supposed to be the engine of economic growth. As such, a large firm is better than a small one. A firm with many employees is better than a firm with none or just a few employees. A quickly growing firm is better than a bread-and-butter firm. A profitable firm is better than one that just breaks even. Firms in high tech and manufacturing are better than those in retail and services because they are more likely to be big and growing, and those who lend money see them as better risks. Desiring to pursue growth is positioned as the norm, and those who do not choose to grow make up an exception to be explained, as Carter & Allen (1997) pointed out when finding that past research posited two explanations why women do not grow: they have either made a "life-style choice" and chosen to integrate work and family, or to contribute socially; or they face barriers in terms of lack of education, capital, or experience.

So, size, growth, profit and the industrial sector are ways to assess entrepreneurship. There are also ways to assess how entrepreneurial a business owner is, or how entrepreneurial he or she is perceived to be. Some of the articles in this review do exactly that, and this section looks more closely at some instruments used to measure a person's level of entrepreneurship.

Sexton & Bowman-Upton (1990) investigated psychological propensities of male and female entrepreneurs to find out if there was any real basis for sex role stereotyping. They administered an instrument based on the Jackson personal Inventory and the Personality Research Form-E test instrument. The descriptions of the variables measured describe how an entrepreneur is envisioned:

Conformity: A low scorer normally refuses to go along with the crowd, is unaffected and unswayed by others' opinions, and is independent in thought and action.

Energy level: A high scorer is active and spirited, possesses reserves of strength, does not tire easily, and is capable of intense work or recreational activity for long periods of time.

Interpersonal affect: A low scorer is emotionally aloof, prefers impersonal to personal relationships, displays little compassion for other people's problems, has trouble relating to people and is emotionally unresponsive to those around him/her.

Risk taking: A high scorer enjoys gambling and taking a chance, willingly exposes self to situations with uncertain outcomes, enjoys adventure having an element of peril, and is unconcerned with danger.

Social adroitness: A high scorer is skilful at persuading others to achieve a particular goal, is diplomatic but occasionally may be seen as manipulative of others, and is socially intelligent.

Autonomy: A high scorer tries to break away and may be rebellious when faced with restraints, confinement, or restrictions; enjoys being un-attached, free, and not tied to people, places or obligations.

Change: A high scorer likes new and different experiences, dislikes and avoids routine, may readily change opinions or values in different circumstances, and adapts readily to changes in the environment.

Harm avoidance: A low scorer enjoys exciting activities especially when danger is involved, risks bodily harm, and is not concerned with personal safety.

Succorance: A low scorer does not need the support nor frequently seeks the sympathy, protection, love, advice, or reassurance of other people and has difficulty confiding in others. (Sexton & Bowman-Upton, 1990:33).

An independent, active, uncompassionate, change oriented and danger seeking risk taker is portrayed. Do the opposite and envision a dependent, passive, compassionate, cautious risk avoider who seeks protection, love and advice. Who is the man and who is the woman? This is very clear in the next example, where two possible ways of management were postulated. One model assumed that men and women managed in an identical way. This model was called the "entrepreneurial" model. The other model assumed that "women behave differently as entrepreneurs and managers" (Chaganti 1986:19), and this model was labeled the "feminine" model. Already the labeling indicates that a feminine model is an exception, and the other one a norm. The author offered an elaborate table of the two models, which is worth quoting in full. Note the column headings.

Two models of strategic management in women-owned enterprises

Model 1: The Feminine Entrepreneur

1. *Shared Values for business:*
   Modest goals on profits.
   Primary interest is personal satisfaction.
   Prefers to remain small.
2. *Strategies for business:*
   Marketing: sells only products which need personalized service; enters and remains in small, local market niches.
   Finance: enters low-capital businesses; always able to invest only limited capital.
3. *Structures and Systems:*
   Structure would remain informal, decentralized and small.
   Motivation systems would depend on personalized and non-monetary rewards.
   Operations control remains weak and systematic record keeping is limited to non-existent.
4. *Staff and Skills:*
   Staff size would remain small, would not hire trained personnel or use expert advice.
   Prefers to hire female employees.
   Firm remains weak in management particularly in finance and planning.
5. *Styles of Leadership:*
   Friendly, personalized team-oriented and informal style. Firm stays small to ensure staff satisfaction.
   Entrepreneur is low in assertiveness and sense of power.
   Intuitive and emotional approach to decisions.
6. *Performance:*
   Profits and growth remain low.

Model 2: The Successful Entrepreneur

1. *Shared Values for business:*
   Aggressive goals for profit.
   Interest in continuing growth.
   Interest in profit greater than interest in personal satisfaction.
2. *Strategies for business:*
   Marketing: markets diverse products; niche approach is used initially, but seeks large markets with growth.
   Finance: relies on equity in the beginning, but borrows extensively with growth.
3. *Structures and Systems:*
   Structure would be informal but centralized initially, but more formal as firm expands.
   Motivation systems use both monetary and non-monetary rewards, but stresses monetary rewards.
   Operations control is weak at first, but systematic procedures are introduced with growth.
4. *Staff and Skills:*
   Staff size grows with business, would hire trained staff as firm expands.
   Hires mostly men for reasons of expertise and experience.
   Firm is initially weak in management skills, but acquires them with growth, beginning with finance and planning.
5. *Styles of Leadership:*
   Style is personal and informal but autocratic in the beginning. Grows more professionalized and delegative with expansion.
   Entrepreneur is bold, decisive and result-oriented.
   Decision-making is intuitive initially, but more rational with growth.
6. *Performance:*
   Profits and growth initially low but increase over time (Chaganti, 1986:20).

The table tells the story of the successful entrepreneur (who is not feminine), who is detached, rational, calculative, bold, decisive, aggressive, and result-oriented. The feminine model is the opposite of that. One is modest in goals, weak in expertise, irrational (does not use experts or hire trained personnel), unassertive, and emotional. The two papers above investigated the psychological characteristics of entrepreneurs, and the finding did in most aspects refute that women entrepreneurs were particularly "feminine", but the idea that there is a weaker side prevails.

Some authors study other people' perceptions of entrepreneurs or entrepreneurship instead. Fagenson & Marcus, (1991) researched women's perceptions of the characteristics needed to succeed in the entrepreneurial world thinking that if entrepreneurship was male stereotyped it may deter women from choosing an entrepreneurship career. They used Spence and Helmreich's Personal Attributes Questionnaire which was selected for "its proven reliability and validity in measuring the sex-role stereotypic traits of men and women" (Fagenson & Marcus, 1991:38). The instrument had a masculine and a feminine scale comprised of the following items:

Masculine	Feminine
Competitive	Emotional
Active	Understanding
Independent	Warm
Able to make decisions	Able to devote oneself completely to others
Does not give up easily	Gentle
Feels very superior	Helpful to others
Self confident	Kind
Stands up well under pressure	Aware of others' feelings

The words in the left column are the ones associated with outer success, and the ones in the right hand column are all associated with care. Not surprisingly, the left column was the one that was identified as the "entrepreneurial one" by the respondents, also by the ones who had female managers. The authors thought that female role models would influence the respondents to value the feminine side more, but this was only marginally the case.

Buttner & Rosen (1988) investigated bank loan officers' perceptions of the characteristics of men, women, and successful entrepreneurs. In this study, the authors surveyed the literature on entrepreneurs to find out what they were like and found that "entrepreneurs have been found to possess a set of leadership skills and attributes that include an ability to inspire others, autonomy, and a high level of endurance. Entrepreneurs demonstrate a propensity to take risks and are ready for change. Entrepreneurs also possess social skills such as persuasiveness, low need for support, low conformity, and lack of emotionalism" (Buttner & Rosen, 1988:251). Based on this they designed an instrument that measured the following:

Leadership: self-confidence, demonstrated leadership ability, ability to inspire others, intelligence, forcefulness, and assertiveness.

Autonomy: self-reliance, independence and dominance.

Propensity to take risk: ability to handle risk, ability to evaluate risk, copes well with uncertainty, enjoys taking risks, willingness to take chances, and enjoys gambling.

Readiness for change: adapts readily to change, unafraid of new and different experiences, and easily bored by routine.

Endurance: high energy level, capable of sustained effort, persistent, and does not tire easily.

Lack of emotionalism: not aware of others' feelings, not emotional, and not compassionate.

Low need for support: low need for reassurance, low need for support, low need for sympathy, does not desire close friendships, and does not confide in others.

Low conformity: does not go along with the crowd, and not easily influenced by others' opinion.

Persuasiveness: persuasive and manipulative (Buttner & Rosen, 1988: 252).

The list is very similar to the ones previously discussed. Again, men were perceived to be more "entrepreneurial" than women. Women were rated lower on leadership, autonomy, risk-taking propensity, readiness for change, endurance, and a low need for support. They were rated as more emotional as well.

The last two studies confirm that there is an idea of what women are like, and an idea of what entrepreneurs are like, and that these ideas are different. The feminine side is in this context consistently valued as less cut for entrepreneurship than the "entrepreneurial". The two studies previously discussed largely refuted that women entrepreneurs were more feminine, but the idea prevails that these two, opposite and mutually exclusive ways of being and behaving exist. It is as if the problems and shortcomings associated with female entrepreneurs could be explained by them being and behaving in a more "feminine" and less instrumental way. To put it succinctly, it is as if the problem with women might be explained by the fact that they are women. The reviewed authors seldom succeed at this, however. This is the topic of the next section.

Three Strategies for Explaining the Meager Results

There seems to be reluctance among entrepreneurship researchers to report falsified hypotheses about gender differences. Most of the findings refuted the idea of men and women being different, or treated differently. While some accepted this at face value, several authors were not willing to give up the idea of differences that easily. The discussion sections of the papers are particularly revealing. I found three different, and sometimes overlapping strategies present. I call them "making a mountain out of a mole-hill", "the self-selected woman", and "the good mother" strategies. Below is a discussion of each strategy, with citations from the texts to show how I came to these conclusions.

Making a Mountain out of a Mole-hill

The first strategy is to overemphasize the few differences that are actually found. Usually, authors report statistically significant differences, dropping the word "statistically", and portraying them as socially significant, which they seldom are (McCloskey, 1998). Most surveys – which are the majority of the studies in this review – use Likert type scales. An example is Anna et al. (2000) who used a seven point Likert scale to measure venture efficacy for women in "traditional" (retail and sales) versus "non-traditional" (male dominated) industries. A result of the study was that women in traditional industries had significantly higher career expectations of life balance and security. The difference between the groups was actually only 0.39 and 0.54 respectively. How important is a 0.39 difference on a seven-point scale? And does it matter? The standard deviations were 1.07 and 1.54 respectively. The overlaps between the two groups seem to be more significant than the differences, but the discussion is seldom geared towards this, but rather towards stressing the few differences found[3].

Miskin & Rose (1990:28), building on Nina Colwill (1982:12–15), warn that research designs based on the search for differences "tend to favor a focus on differences rather than similarities which often results in the publishing of studies that find significant differences but not reporting similar studies where no significant differences are found.

---

3   Davidsson (1995) discusses how little it takes to produce a statistically significant result. In a study comparing values between populations in two cities (230 respondents in one city, 216 in the other) he found a statistically significant difference of 0.38 on a scale with a possible variation between 4 and 16. To achieve such a results, writes Davidsson, it only takes that 20 respondents from one of the cities fill in an answer on the four questions related to this factor that is one scale step more "entrepreneurial" than 20 respondents from the other city, while the mean for all the others is identical in the two cities.

This can lead to inferences from published research of differences larger than actually might exist." This warning is quite applicable in the gender-and-entrepreneurship research field.

Olson & Currie (1992) who looked at the correlation between value systems and strategy for women contractors offer an artful example of how "findings" of gender differences along several dimensions were discursively constructed, and measured against a male norm. They studied correlations between values and strategies for women owning construction businesses. They compared the results to the results of an earlier study, which focused on male minorities, also in construction. Contrary to the results for the men, they found no correlation between value systems and four possible strategies for the women. The women in the sample were "remarkably" similar on values, but displayed all four strategies. The authors were so surprised that they tested the hypothesis a second time, with another statistical method, but the results were the same. How can this be explained?

> The results of this research and its comparison to studies investigating male entrepreneurs in the same industry raise numerous issues. First, there may be a pre-selection process that determines the occupations women enter. The fact that all the women surveyed here prioritized their values in a similar order suggests that their personal beliefs may have led them all into the same profession. Their *values* could have had a greater influence on their *career choice* than on the *strategies* they use within their line of work (Olson & Currie, 1992:55).

Here values are still seen as instrumental, but they apparently work differently for men than for women. Interestingly, all women rated family security as the most important, consistent with, write the authors " a recent study that states that female entrepreneurs generally possess shared values for business which tend to reflect themselves in an orientation toward conservatism and survival rather than high growth and profit" (Olson & Currie, 1992:54). Valuing family security and conservatism thus led these women to become contractors, which is a somewhat unusual conclusion. But how does one explain the differences in women's strategies if not connected to values? Below is a second quote from this study. I have partitioned it into four sections for clarity, but it is actually one continuous quote.

> If female entrepreneurs' values are leading them into certain professions, then other factors must be affecting the types of business strategies they use in operating their firms. Given that no correlation surfaced between

> value sets and business strategies, some women may adopt business prac-
> tices which are inconsistent with their own values.

The first two sentences imply that the correlation found between values and strategies for men is the norm. Women do it wrong, since they
"adopt practices inconsistent with their own values".

> If so, are they putting the survival of their companies ahead of their per-
> sonal beliefs? Can this situation be a potential cause of dysfunctional
> conflict? In the long run, does this conflict contribute to hindering an
> enterprise's growth or even causing it to fail?

Adopting practices inconsistent with their own values is thus posited as
a serious mistake, possibly having detrimental effects on their businesses, causing a "dysfunctional conflict", "hindering growth" and
even "causing it to fail".

> Because the women in this study operate in a male-dominated industry,
> they may believe in one thing but act differently because they feel that a
> certain type of behavior is expected of them, and is necessary for their
> company's survival. The outcome of this investigation implies that women
> in male-dominated fields of work may feel forced into allowing external
> factors (customers, suppliers, environments, etc.) to totally dictate their
> strategies, regardless of their personal values. In contrast, their male
> counterparts' strategies mirror personal values.

They are further bereft of their own initiative and "forced into allowing external factors totally dictate their strategies" while men go ahead
as usual, maintaining their inner locus of control. This mirrors the
idea of the entrepreneur as someone pursuing his own vision regardless of others, and the woman as the one who adapts to the needs of
others.

> This investigation further establishes what earlier research has implied –
> that there is a difference in the manner in which men and women pursue
> their businesses (Olson & Currie, 1992:55).

The authors, who did not really study differences in strategies between
men and women, but correlations values/strategies, nevertheless manage to conclude that the research "establishes that there is a difference
in the manner in which men and women pursue their businesses".

A similar strategy is used by Kolvereid et al. (1993) who investigated men and women entrepreneurs' perceptions of the environment in

three different countries. They hypothesized that female entrepreneurs in all countries would perceive their business start-up environment to be characterized by a higher degree of resource scarcity, turbulence, and hostility than would male entrepreneurs. They found country differences, but no gender differences on the nine investigated items, except that women perceived higher political uncertainty than men (a difference of 0.3–0.5 on a six-point Likert scale), which they explain as follows:

> The political uncertainty item, the only item to which male and female entrepreneurs scored differently, is probably the item containing the strongest evaluative/affective flavor. A possible explanation may be that men and women do not perceive the environment very differently but tend to evaluate it differently. This effect may be due to differences in the value systems of men and women" (Kolvereid et al., 1993:49).

This formulation implies that there is something objective called "perception" and then something more subjective, containing an "affective flavor" which women are more prone to be subjected to. This finding implies, according to the authors, that women have different value systems. The authors conclude in the abstract; "the results support the notion that male and female entrepreneurs perceive their business start-up environment differently" (ibid:2). A minor difference on only one of nine items thus led to the conclusion that men and women do indeed differ.

The Self-selected Woman

The second strategy is to explain the lack of differences by stressing that women entrepreneurs are different from ordinary women. I call it the "self-selected woman" strategy. Buttner & Rosen (1989:251) noted:

> Research evidence suggests that male and female entrepreneurs do not differ on attributes associated with entrepreneurial success. Research by DiCarlo and Lyons (1979)[4] showed that female entrepreneurs differed significantly from women in the general population on the entrepreneurial attributes: need for achievement, independence, leadership, autonomy, aggressiveness and (lack of) conformity.

---

4   Since the authors have missed including this reference in their reference list and I did not find it on ABI/inform it is unfortunately not included in my reference list either.

Cromie & Birley (1992:248), researched networking by female entrepreneurs in Northern Ireland and found that "the profile of their personal contact network were remarkably similar to those of the men in the sample".

> Contrary to our expectations, female personal contact networks are not particularly narrow. They are as diverse as those of their male colleagues both in terms of the nature of their employment and of the nature of the relationship. Thus, the women are no more likely to consult family and friends than are men ... The results described above are particularly interesting when the cross-ties are analyzed. Clearly, the females tend to rely heavily upon a male colleague as their prime contact, but then revert to their own sex for the rest. On the surface, this is not particularly surprising, since the men do the same. However, whether the relationships are based upon professional or social foundations, it is clear that the women contacts have jobs, and jobs that would appear to be both useful and relevant ... How might we explain this outcome? While women could well be at a disadvantage before launching their businesses, it is plausible that they do make a sustained effort to develop their networks in the early years of managing their venture ... Women may well recognize their deficiencies in this area of network contacts and proceed to develop them vigorously (Cromie & Birley, 1992:248–249).

The women were found to revert to their own sex. The dictionary in Microsoft Word tells me that the word revert means "relapse, regress, or slip back". Synonyms for these latter words are "deteriorate, degenerate, and loose headway". Clearly not a recommendable thing. Surprisingly, they were no worse off for that – they found (unusually?) useful women to network with. But the authors are unwilling to give up their idea of the disadvantaged women. The women in their study have "recognized their deficiencies", made a "sustained effort" and "proceeded to develop them vigorously". They have seemingly made up for their deficiencies by hard work. Or by acting like "entrepreneurs" as the words describing such ("active, high energy level, endurance", etc.) in the previous section indicated. By making a concerted effort to behave like a man, they have overcome the deficiencies associated with being a woman.

Aldrich et al. (1989b:354) looked at networking behavior in the USA and in Italy. They reasoned that women have less access to useful contacts than men, which might be an impediment to the current rise of female entrepreneurship. They found, to their surprise, no gender differences in activity and density of the networks. They noted, however,

> ... the women in the American sample were members of a very male-dominated group ... and the women in the Italian sample were taking courses at a male-dominated institution. Thus, we cannot necessarily infer from our results that the gap between 'male' and 'female' worlds is closing (Aldrich et al., 1989b:354).

The authors say that they cannot rule out the possibility of a closing between the male and female world, which is a valid and correctly cautious conclusion. It assumes, however, the existence of such a gap. Regarding the studied women as unusual women implies the existence of other, more ordinary women.

Masters & Meier (1988), however, do see a closing of the gap and attribute it to the women's movement. They investigated differences in risk-taking propensity between men and women entrepreneurs and found none. They speculated that the women's movement has perhaps created a new breed of women:

> It appears that the women's movement has had an impact on the behavior of women in the business environment. The closing of the gap between men and women with respect to risk-taking propensity may be one such influence (Masters & Meier, 1988:34).

Bellu (1993:341) found that women "bring into the performance of their roles a propensity for taking *greater* (my italics) risks than their male counterparts". How could this possibly be explained?

> The fact that, for a variety of reasons, women continued to face more hostile and prejudicial environments (e.g., exclusion from and/or low participation in networks and information-gathering systems) would, indeed, suggest that the only way they can confront their [relevant external environment] is audaciously, with a willingness to accept a greater degree of [perceived environmental uncertainty] and consequently of risk. Clearly, this is an important issue which, in view of its obvious consequences (e.g., greater probability of business failure) ought to be further investigated (Bellu, 1993:341).

This is yet a version of the "women entrepreneurs are unusual women" strategy. The women are found to be unusual compared to expectations – they take even greater risks than males. This is not accepted at face value. Instead, factors in the environment are thought to explain it, just as in the study by Olson & Currie discussed above. Moreover, it is a behavior best avoided, since, according to the quote above, it may ultimately lead to business failures.

Yet another version of the "self-selected woman" strategy is to distinguish between "normal" women entrepreneurs, and those who display a pattern more associated with success, such as running a large business or one in manufacturing. The study by Anna et al. (2000) discussed earlier differed between women entrepreneurs in traditional women's businesses (retail and sales) and non-traditional (high technology, construction, manufacturing). The former were described as small, partly due to competitive pressures in the sector, and the latter as having greater growth potential. Some women do choose to start non-traditional businesses. Could these women be different? The authors found some (small) differences in venture efficacy, career expectations and social support. The traditional businesswomen had higher venture efficacy for opportunity recognition, higher career expectations of life balance and security and financial support from others were more important than for the non-traditional, all of which are associated with caring for the family, financially or otherwise. The non-traditional businesswomen had higher career expectations for money and wealth and higher venture efficacy for planning, which was associated with financial success.

Carter & Allen (1997) pursued a similar track, looking for differences between women with small and large businesses. They found few differences. Structural factors, like financial resources were more important than life-style choices. The underlying idea in both studies, however, is to see if there are differences between the woman entrepreneur who behaves like a regular woman entrepreneur, and the one who is more successful, that is, not like a regular woman.

The examples above are ways of saying that there are regular women and there are women entrepreneurs, alternatively, regular women entrepreneurs and more *entrepreneurial* women entrepreneurs. In both cases, the former is associated with the idea of womanhood and some sort of weakness, and the latter is an exception. It is as if the idea of women's essential difference must be saved.

The Good Mother

The third strategy, which I call the "good mother" strategy, is to cherish the small differences found and from these, combined with general knowledge on women and women's life situations, mold an alternative, female entrepreneur model. Brush (1992) is the most cited author on this. She found (as I did) more similarities than gender differences on personality factors and motivation in her review, but stressed that the instruments were developed on males and thus "may not fully explain the personality traits of female entrepreneurs" (ibid:12). Demographic characteristics were also similar; except that women entrepreneurs seemed to be unmarried to a larger extent, and if married they were less likely than men to have a non-working partner at home.

However, she referred to studies showing differences too. These indicated, for example, that women's background experience and education was less suited for an entrepreneurship career than men's, that women felt that social adroitness were their strongest assets and lack of financial skills a liability, and that men were being pulled into entrepreneurship whereas women were being pushed out of a need to balance work and family. Finally, she referred to a study, which proposed that interest in helping others was a key motivator for women to become business owners.

As for women's organizations, she found them to be small, young, and service-oriented. Management styles were participative, informal, and "feminine". (A study finding women to be structured, formal and well planned was written off as done on women real-estate owners with firms averaging 15 years of age – the exception again). Stressing social goals such as customer satisfaction was reported, and mentioned problems were those of managing conflict between personal and work responsibilities as well as women's difficulties in penetrating informal financial networks. She referred to studies of women networking with women for both social and instrumental support. Leaning on Gilligan (1982), Brush asserts that

> ... women's 'reality' is characterized by connectedness and relationships ... rather than the autonomy and logic more typical of men's reality. This stream of literature further argues that women's social orientations are directed towards cultivating strong relationships rather than achieving independence (separateness) and position ... A woman's identity is defined in the context of a relationship with decisions situationally determined. Women's personal reality is 'web-like', connecting family, work and community relationships. Men's reality is seen as separate and autonomous, with decision making being logical and rule-based (Brush, 1992:17).

This led Brush to conclude that women perceive and approach business ownership differently than men. She proposed the "integrated" perspective, explained as follows:

> This paper suggests that women perceive their businesses as 'cooperative networks of relationships' rather than separate economic units. In this conception, business relationships are integrated rather than separated from family, societal, and personal relationships. The business is 'integrated' into the woman business owner's life (Brush, 1992:16).

A dichotomized picture is painted here, very much alike the dichotomized ways of measuring entrepreneurship as discussed above under "the male norm". The difference is that the "feminine" column is still different, but not necessarily "in lack". Rather, it is complementary.

This idea is carried forth by several authors. Carter et al. (1997), investigating the influence of initial recourses, strategy and gender on discontinuance among new firms in retail, suggest that women made up for their deficiencies in initial resources (which they were found to have) by drawing on their service skills and relational skills:

> By choosing a founding strategy that fit their particular competencies, women appear to manage their businesses in ways different from men and with different outcomes ... Unexpected was the finding that the most beneficial strategy for women-owned businesses in retail appears to be the super achievers strategy. It may be that the effectiveness of the super achievers strategy reflects the fact that women are particularly adept at 'scrambling' to give the customers whatever they want whenever they want it. By emphasizing multiple strategy foci simultaneously and 'being all things to all people', businesses headed by women may be able to ward off discontinuance ... Alternatively, it might be argued that the effectiveness of the generalists strategy reflects women's relational orientation. Women were seen as emphasizing cooperative networks among family, society and person. The ability to juggle expectations from many quarters may be the underpinning of effectively executing the super achiever strategy (Carter et al., 1997:141).

They expected women to be niche providers, but found something else. To explain this, they drew on ideas of women as relational, cooperative and good at being all things to all people, that is, service-minded. Their womanly character did thus explain why they were super-achievers – but one might just as well have reasoned that they were smart, cunning, goal-oriented, calculating, cold-blooded strategists.

Nowhere is the idea of women as relational as clear as in Buttner, (2001:253). She uses a "relational frame", drawing heavily on Gilligan (1982) and other authors in the same vein, proposing, "Understanding how women run their businesses may provide an alternative paradigm to the traditional, male-dominated, hierarchical, command and control approach common in many business organizations." The author summarizes the contributions of the cited authors in statements like the following:

> Females develop a sense of connection based on their original relationship with their mother
> ... an inner sense of connection is a central organizing dimension of development, particularly for women.
> ... Women tend to define power in terms of care for others
> ... Females' social development includes evolution of an ethic of care in making decisions involving others (Buttner, 2001:257).

The author did content analysis of transcriptions from focus groups discussions with 117 successful female entrepreneurs using four categories derived from relational theory as a sorting device. She found that the role expectations of mothering carried over to the business setting for many, and that women tended to lead in a participative and democratic manner. Additionally, the participants "often defined professional growth in terms of growth of others" (ibid:264). Self-fulfillment and profit were the most important goals, as was the case for men, but the author suggested that women tend to go about it in a different way than men. "The good mother" strategy turns women's proposed differential disadvantages into advantages, but it does not challenge the dichotomized and gendered understanding of entrepreneurship. It still presents a very polarized picture where the "male way" is still a norm, albeit not as positive as in the earlier versions.

The conception of the woman entrepreneur as the "good alternative" is not unchallenged. Chell & Baines (1998) commented Brush as follows:

> While maintaining that gender is socially constructed, an interpretation of Brush's theoretical position is that, taking her arguments to their logical conclusion, she appears to assume a fundamental difference between men and women in respect of their ways of doing and their ways of being which is biologically determined. However, this also assumes a homogeneity of men's and women's socio-economic behaviour that studies of male business ownership do not appear to justify (Chell & Baines 1998:120).

Chell & Baines (1998) tested Brush's notion of women's integrative life-style and found no support for this in their sample. Only a few voluntary integrated the business into their family or domestic lives and it was as likely for men as for women to want this. Therefore:

> ... the idea that men and women have a totally different and distinctive orientation to their business, that is, that men prefer (by implication) to keep their business and domestic lives separate while women prefer to integrate their business and domestic lives, does not stand up to empirical examination (Chell & Baines 1998:132).

Marlow (1997) discusses the fact that working women, whether wage workers or business owners, are still performing double shifts – one at home and one at work. An "integrated life-style" is thus necessity rather than choice. She describes this experience of women as basically negative, and "tainted by patriarchal expectations" (ibid:208). The critical authors cited above are from the UK, where the discussion of women's entrepreneurship has a distinctly different flavor than the US discussion, which is one of the topics of the next chapter.

Summary

This chapter showed that the primary argument for researching women's entrepreneurship in the selected texts was instrumental. The actual or potential impact of women's businesses on economic growth is the *raison d'être* for this research. Equality arguments are largely absent. A majority of the texts position women as a problem in this equation. Either they do not do it right, or they are not right. What is 'right' can be seen as male gendered: pursuing growth, size, profit and selecting high tech or manufacturing industries where this is more likely to be achieved than in service and retail. Women who do the opposite are said to have made a "life-style choice". The scales measuring how "entrepreneurial" an entrepreneur is, are also male gendered – the words with a masculine connotation are equated with entrepreneurship and the words with feminine connotations are associated with weakness.

This idea of a strong and a weak side correlating with male and female bodies seems to be difficult to release. I found three kinds of arguments explaining why men and women are different in spite of research findings indicating the contrary. One strategy was to focus on some small difference found while ignoring the similarities. Another was to declare women entrepreneurs as exceptions compared to regular women. A third was to mould an alternative, motherly entrepreneur where all the "female" traits were upgraded. A polarized picture is still presented, however, with the male way as the norm.

7

How Articles Construct Work and Family

When research focuses on women entrepreneurs, it becomes apparent that life consists not only of work, but also of home, family, and children. This chapter examines the various ways of how this is dealt with in the research texts. Some articles contest the dominant way of constructing the private sphere of life, therefore this chapter also discusses differences in conceptions of the individual and his/her place in the social world.

The Division between Work and Family and between a Public and a Private Sphere of Life

The division of life between a public and a private sphere and between work and family is an assumption, which is taken for granted and goes mostly unquestioned in most of the reviewed studies. Consequently, what sorts under "family" and "private" is also seen as an individual and not a collective responsibility. The division is very clear in the literature. Below are a few examples to illustrate how this is achieved.

Cox, Moore, & Van Auken, (1984) studied working couples in small business. They began with an extensive literature review and found that the literature suggested major problems for such couples, summarized in the following quotes:

... the biggest problem faced by couples who work together is keeping work-related problems isolated from their personal lives

... competition between spouses and too much togetherness [are] potential sources of marital strife

... potential marital problems aris[e] from the lack of an emotional outlet for couples who work together

> ... coordinated career couples have no 'hiding place' at home and no opportunity to be alone
>
> ... the inevitability of conflict (both positive and negative) between couples who work together, with serious ramifications for small business profitability
>
> ... yet another potential marital problem ... stems from the common expectation of husbands that the working wife should handle homemaking and child-rearing responsibilities in addition to job responsibilities
>
> ... six major areas of potential trouble for couples who work together: (1) strife caused by restricted job mobility; (2) excessive demands on each spouse's time and energy; (3) inability to separate professional and personal problems; (4) role conflicts; (5) spouse competitiveness; and (6) bringing home work-related problems (Cox, Moore, & Van Auken, 1984:24–25).

This list of problems suggests a number of things. The first sentence indicates that work-related problems should be kept separate from personal life. These two spheres are distinct and different and not to be mixed. The second says that competition is something that belongs to the work life. Spouses should not compete. The third and fourth sentences say that a working person needs an emotional outlet. This outlet should be at home, and preferably provided by someone one does not work with and who can provide a safe hiding place. Emotions are something private, they are not public or work-associated.

The proposed lack of opportunity to be alone is curious – I would assume that the chance of finding a moment alone is the same if your partner works with you or not, but aloneness seems to be envisioned differently here. Can being with your non-working partner be interpreted as being "alone", whereas being with you co-owner is "not being alone"? This would imply that your non-working partner does not count as a person. What counts is work. The fifth sentence suggests that if for no other reason, mixing private life and business life should be avoided since it causes conflicts and in the end (here comes the heavy argument) has serious ramifications for the business's profitability. The sixth sentence corroborates the idea that homemaking and child rearing is thought to be the wife's responsibility.

The authors also found some good points about co-ownership in their literature review, for example improved communication, an enhanced sense of intimacy, and business and managerial stability, but these seemed to be pleasant outcomes to lighten a burden of necessity. The literature review suggested that the three main reasons for working together were the following: financial/business necessity, to reduce employee theft, and to avoid retirement. There was no mention of positive reasons for working together. In their empirical study, Cox et al. (1984) actually surprised their readers by finding none of these postulated problems. They rather found a long list of advantages – a sense of equity, shared housekeeping chores, and a good marriage. However, their literature review provides an example of the stronghold that the public/private divide has.

This is also evident in Stoner, Hartman, & Arora (1990) who explored work-home role conflict in female owners of small businesses. The title alone suggests, first, a division of the two spheres and, second, difficulties in combining them. They begin their article as follows:

> A critical problem faced by female entrepreneurs is the tension that exists between their personal lives and career pursuits. This tension may be viewed as a form of interrole conflict in which the role pressures from the work and home domain are incompatible. In short, involvement in one role becomes more difficult because of involvement in the other role. The social and psychological significance of this topic is enhanced by the continued growth of female-owned firms (Stoner et al., 1990:30).

This opening paragraph reinforces the idea of two incompatible spheres, and also suggests that it is a problem faced by females. Males are not mentioned in this discussion. Because of the rise of female entrepreneurship, the problems may multiply and even reach a "sociological significance". Their literature review expands on the problems, identifying areas such as time pressures, family size, and availability of support from family members as potentially affecting the level of role conflict. They found that female business owners did experience "significant interference or conflict" between work and home roles. They came home from work "too tired to do the things they would like to do, felt that the demands from business took away form their personal interests … and made it difficult to relax at home". However, the older ones, with successful businesses, experienced less of this conflict, leading the authors to conclude that "this finding indicates that there is considerable crossover among the business and personal dimensions of life for female business owners" (ibid:36).

Words like "interference, conflict, crossover" confirm the idea of the two spheres. The article further suggests that the problem is particularly female, just as the considerable crossover is a particularly female phenomenon. Females cross boundaries, and this is proposed as potentially troublesome.

Nowhere is the division as poignant as in a study by Caputo & Dolinsky (1998). They studied the effect of household and family composition on women's choice of self-employment. Like most other studies, they begin by noticing the increase of women's entrepreneurship in the USA as a reason to expand research efforts on this, and they note that the impact of household members' (partners, children and relatives) financial and human capital on women's choice of self-employment is not well researched. Their literature review departs in labor economics, which says that the cost of childcare diminishes the likelihood of females participating in the labor force. Self-employment would be a way to solve this problem:

> One way mothers may begin to overcome child care cost considerations is by pursuing self-employment. As self-employment typically permits a more flexible work schedule, it more readily enables mothers to care for their own children, thus reducing if not eliminating the cost of child care (ibid:9).

Childcare seems to be mainly the mother's responsibility in the view of these authors. They postulate that the time the father makes available for childcare would have an effect on this equation (increase chances of woman seeking self-employment), by noting that:

> One viable means for a working woman to adapt her work schedule around that of her husband so that he can be available to contribute child care is through self-employment (ibid:10).

However,

> Regarding the effect of the time a husband makes available for other house-hold chores on a woman's employment choice, no effect is expected a priori. In contrast to a child's need for supervision, which often requires an immediate response, most routine household chores can be completed when time becomes available in the woman's schedule (ibid:10).

So, necessity might have it that husbands help with children, but other routine household chores seem most definitely to be the wife's responsibility. Having established that self-employment for women is a good thing, since it has the benefits of allowing flexibility so they can care for their own children, they go on to investigate factors that increase the likelihood of this. They found that the husband's level of income mattered, but only if he was also himself self-employed. They explain the results as follow:

> ... these findings may suggest that entrepreneurial husbands, particularly when successful, offer their wives confidence in the pursuit of entrepreneurship. Accordingly, entrepreneurial husbands appear to serve as role models in influencing women's choice to pursue entrepreneurship (ibid:15).

The authors apparently presume that the men started their businesses before their wives did, and so can serve as role models. They further presume that women are less confident and that their husbands can offer them confidence. It is a patriarchal model where men and men's work is an unquestioned standard, and women, in addition to counting less, are seen as the flexible resource that makes things work. According to the authors, this is quite in order and should be encouraged:

> Quality care, when provided outside the household, can be difficult to find and is often financially draining. In 1993, for example, the Federal government spent nearly $2.5 billion on taxpayers who needed dependent care in order to accept or maintain employment ... To the extent to which it is a societal objective to minimize such costs and maximize the quality of care, married mothers with children appear to be the most attractive segment to target for programs fostering entrepreneurship, as the flexibility of self-employment makes home-based care most feasible (ibid:16).

The authors further note that limited capital is also a factor reducing chances of self-employment.

> ... To increase such opportunities for these women, government officials may consider further underwriting private sector efforts such as community-based micro-loan funds that make start-up capital available (ibid:16).

This paints a picture of a society where family and childcare is a fully private responsibility. It also paints a picture of a society where the man is the breadwinner who does things on his terms, and the woman the loyal and flexible adapter who takes responsibility for the children. The problem of combining work and childcare is to be solved by women's self-employment. For a Scandinavian, this sounds very odd and not very pro-woman. I see the woman in this scenario working constantly. The most evident solution to me is not micro-loans, but public childcare, in which case men and women can participate in the labor force and provide childcare and perform "other routine household chores" on equal terms. This seems to be an unusual model, though. In most of the texts in this review, the family and the public are regarded as two different spheres. The text cited above sees public day care only as an expense for taxpayers, not as a gain for society.

Likewise Kourilsky & Walstad (1998), instead of speaking for public, free of charge, quality education for everyone, advocate mother-daughter entrepreneurship training programs, so that they can start a business together to save for their daughters' college education. They present such a program as follows:

> MADE-IT is an experience-based entrepreneurship curriculum targeted for female youth and their mothers. It develops in mother and daughter teams the knowledge and skills to identify a business opportunity, create a business feasibility plan, and initiate a business venture – whose profits are intended for the daughter's college education (Kourilsky & Walstad 1998).

Carter & Allen (1997) hypothesized that a reason why women's businesses are smaller is because they have made a so-called life-style choice and decided to allot time to family and community involvement. This hypothesis was not confirmed, in fact quite the contrary proved to be the case. The authors found that deterrents to growth were not the number of children or the level of community involvement, but rather the lack of financial resources. The authors called for dispelling gender stereotypes about women-owned businesses, but at the same time, they did not question the gender stereotypes about men's businesses. Size and growth is the unquestioned norm for "entrepreneurship". Yet choosing to grow is also a choice. It might be labeled as much a life-style choice as not wanting to grow, for both men and women.

Assumptions about the Individual and the Individual in the Social World

Just as the world may be divided into public and private, it may also be regarded from an individualist versus a collective, or societal perspective. The studies discussed so far take a mainly individualist perspective of entrepreneurship. It is the individual entrepreneur and her business that is in focus and contextual or historical variables affecting the business such as legislation are seldom discussed. Some investigate what they call structural factors such as women's level of education and previous business experience. These include Carter & Allen (1997) discussed above, and also Scott (1986), Carter, Van Auken, & Harms (1992), Fischer et al. (1993), Dolinsky (1993), Stevenson (1986), and Greene et al. (1999) to mention a few.

The underlying idea in these studies is that it is not the way individual women are constituted that is problematic and a possible deterrent to growth, but rather their lower access to relevant business education and managerial or entrepreneurial experience. Having a family might also be regarded as a structural factor. The results are, as mentioned before, inconclusive, but what strikes me is that even if these so called structural factors are put forward as explanations, the remedy is envisioned as individual. Either individual women are advised to get the right education, or policy makers are advised to arrange entrepreneurship training for women. I would label this as individual adaptation to existing structures, not structural change.

There is a corresponding trend in how feminist theory is discussed, in the few cases when it *is* discussed. Fischer et al. (1993) introduced feminist thought in this literature by discussing liberal and social feminism. They explained liberal feminist theory as saying that men and women are essentially equal since they have the same capacity for rational thought, and the reason why women have achieved less is because they are deprived of vital resources like business education and experience. There is a power perspective in this line of thought, even if it is not explicitly mentioned in the article. Of course, there is, as discussed earlier also a male norm. If women were not deprived of these resources, the reasoning goes, they would behave as men behave. Social feminist thought, the authors explained, suggests that men and women *are* – and will remain – different, not necessarily because they were born so but because they were socialized differently. According to the first thought, women would want to start and succeed with businesses as much as men if they only could, and according to the second thought, they might have different desires.

Accordingly, they studied educational background and previous experience, as well as value systems. This way of structuring research on women entrepreneurs has had some impact on the following studies. It was taken up explicitly by Cliff (1998) but later studies using it (Brush, 1997; Carter et al., 1997; Greene et al., 1999; Walker & Joyner, 1999) have done away with the word "feminism" with its implicit power perspective and instead talked about "situational and dispositional barriers".

This tends to make feminist thought and action into an individual undertaking. The collective dimension is lost. A woman might even use one of these "barriers" to compensate for the other according to Carter et al., (1997:127) who wrote, "We test whether dispositional characteristics can be used to overcome or moderate deficiencies that arise from situational differences". The idea was that a woman could draw on her relational skills (a result of the dispositional barriers) and use a founding strategy with a competitive advantage compared to those without such skills, which would compensate for her lack of education or experience, i.e., the situational barriers. In this line of thinking, even structural factors become an individual responsibility.

The section usually called "implications for public policy" is most revealing as to whether the researchers take an individual or collective perspective. Hisrish & Brush's (1984:37) list of advice is a clear example. Apart from a call for the elimination of stereotypes "so as to increase acceptance of women in the business world" they advocate "more visible role models for young women so that they can see how women can be successful in business and in various professions" and "changes in women's own attitudes and goals, including a willingness to learn finance". Women should also be encouraged to study technical and managerial fields, they should be trained in finance, cash-flow management, marketing, etc., and they should "avail themselves of all of the information services now available". If they do all of this "their chances for success in the business environment should increase significantly".

All in all, even if structural circumstances are taken into account, the research emphasis is clearly on the individual level and suggested recommendations for change are also on the individual level. Individuals are advised to adapt to existing structures. Existing structures are seldom questioned, and macro-level structural changes are not called for. Entrepreneurship researchers are not revolutionaries. The tendency to focus on individual explanations and remedies is prevalent among the vast majority of the reviewed studies, and it is particularly evident in the US studies. It is congruent with the "psychologization" of America as Ellen Herman (1995) explains in *The Romance of American Psychology*. She describes, in painstaking detail, the growth of psychology from a marginal academic field to its current status where societal concerns like racial politics, economic progress, issues of poverty and unemployment, third world revolutions, "civilization", and even warfare are perceived in terms of the self, and where, consequently, the personal self has been made a legitimate area for government policy and intervention. Racial unrest was said to occur because the black male "could not support his normal desire for dominance" (ibid:192). The lack of entrepreneurial initiatives was attributed to mothers who did not instill enough need for achievement in their sons. Psychological theory, whether right or wrong, writes Herman, served to legitimate policy initiatives, and psychological language offered a convenient way to camouflage clear political purposes as neutral methods of scientific discovery or therapeutic treatment, and to avoid the mentioning of capitalism, communism, or socialism.

I found, however, some dissenting voices, all of them British. The clearest example is an early article by Goffee & Scase (1983) in *The Sociological Review*. The title alone, "Business ownership and women's subordination: a preliminary study of female proprietors", suggests a sociological interest rather than one of business performance. They ground their research in feminist theory and class theory, beginning the article with a thorough theoretical discussion of female proprietorship and the women's movement and the need for collective action by women if society is to be restructured for greater gender equality. Their interest in proprietorship is to see if it may, perhaps, offer an *individual* solution to women's subordination in society. They concluded from in-depth studies of a small sample of female entrepreneurs that women start businesses in response to labor market or domestic subordination, to balance family or work, or as a feminist move. They did not find entrepreneurship to be a straight-forward solution to women's subordination, but said that it can offer heightened awareness, a sense of self-determination and independence, and self-confidence.

> ... it would seem that the reality of business proprietorship rarely conforms to women's expectations. Although they often seek independence from men they can become dependent upon them for finance and various technical and professional services. Striving for self-determination, they can become even more burdened with domestic and business responsibilities (Goffee & Scase, 1983:641).

However, business proprietorship can offer unanticipated benefits. For example, "the prejudices they encounter from men can exaggerate their trading difficulties, but, at the same time, contribute to the development of a feminist consciousness" (ibid:642). The authors concluded:

... proprietorship can heighten the awareness of women's subordination and, in this manner, query existing structures to a greater extent than is commonly assumed. As a result, the material and ideological effects of male and female proprietorship are somewhat different: whereas the former sustains, the latter questions the dominant structure of gender relationships in society (ibid:644).

This strikingly different perspective may be a result of this being the only one of the reviewed articles, which was not published in a business administration or management journal (which further highlights the individualist doxa in entrepreneurship research). However, there are some more exceptions, also British. Birley (1989), for example, argues for studying structural labor market changes in conjunction with the study of entrepreneurship:

... the mere fact that many large firms have substantially reduced their employee base, and that management at all levels can no longer look to the large firm as a source of long-term security, has meant that many have sought self-reliance through the ownership of their own firms (Birley 1989:35–36).

Acknowledging macro-level societal changes is very different from discussing so called "push-factors" at the individual level, such as reaching the "glass ceiling" as a reason for the increase of women's entrepreneurship. Birley writes on women's choices of industry:

For any 'minority' group, its position in society will be a significant factor in determining individual attitudes to entrepreneurial activity. Until very recently, the major role of women was seen in most Western economies by both men and women to be that of wife and mother. Indeed, even should they take employment, this was almost always in addition to their role as homemaker. It is not surprising, therefore, that the market-entry choices of female entrepreneurs differ from those of men (Birley 1989:37).

Explaining women's choices by institutional circumstances as the labor market or the family is very different from explaining them by essential differences between men and women or by women's "life-style" choices. Chell & Baines (1998:120) argue that " ... the family is fundamental to any understanding of women's participation in enterprise and this is irrespective of whether the woman is married and/or has a family". These, and other, institutional factors circumscribe women's choices. According to Chell & Baines, we must:

... recognize the importance of structuring factors in society: extant institutional arrangements – the family, industrial, educational, financial, socio-legal, political and cultural, for example. Such structures, it is argued, shape expectations and create limits and intangible barriers as to what is in fact possible ... An even stronger position than this is that taken by the Marxist feminist view which, briefly, is to argue that overlaying the institutional structures are the class structure, a gendered labour market and gendered occupations. Such factors militate greatly against the opportunities for women to make a full economic contribution in an occupation of their choice (Chell & Baines, 1998:118).

Marlow (1997) argues that women's subordination in the labor market carries over in self-employment:

... there is clear evidence of gender discrimination throughout the labour market with empirical studies offering stark evidence that women are largely concentrated in low status, low paid work ... self-employment ... is far from being the solution to problems of subordination, patriarchy and labour market discrimination, which they may wish it to be ... In terms of sectoral argument it is well documented ... that female self-employment is concentrated in the personal service sector, where start-up costs are low ... Reflected in low start-up costs, however, are low profits and poor growth potential, creating a volatile sector highly sensitive to external pressures. To survive, the firm demands a high level of commitment from the owner to 'make ends meet'. Thus, the low paid, low status, tenuous nature of employment is converted through self-employment to low profit, highly-competitive areas of business ownership for women. The enterprise culture is not heralding new choices or offering escape from subordination for the majority of female small firm owners. Meanwhile, those who choose the self-employment option in order to accommodate the demands of domestic labour are, by definition, still undertaking a dual role, and no more likely than those in paid employment to gain assistance from other family members with domestic tasks (Marlow, 1997:200–202).

This is essentially the same story as Brush (1992) tells with the "integrated perspective" where women see their businesses as "co-operative networks of relationship", but the latter view is a much cheerier version focusing on the individual where women's responsibility for family is turned into an individual choice as well as a strategic advantage, than Marlow's, which acknowledges patriarchal pressures and labor market changes that are not to the benefit of women. The cited stud-

155

ies also have methodological objections concerning the focus on the individual. Rosa & Hamilton (1994) held:

> The emphasis on the individual "female entrepreneur" in much of the small business literature in the last decade disguises the fact that many women in business ownership are in partnership with others, usually with men (Rosa & Hamilton (1994:11).

Chell & Baines (1998:318) added:

> Simply excluding mixed co-ownership can facilitate direct comparisons between aspects of male and female experiences, attitudes and behaviours but this is achieved at the very high cost of masking the real-life complexity of gender and small business ownership.

Rosa, Hamilton, Carter, & Burns (1994) explicitly noted the overlap between male and female groups that was not given due attention in some of the articles reviewed earlier. They found, for example, that men were more likely to be refused bank loans, most respondents, irrespective of sex, got along well with their bank manager, and many wives contributed significantly to the management of their husband's business, and vice versa. Regardless of the sex of owner, many businesses would not have started without the foundation provided by the full-time employment of the spouse, many of whom were in professional public sector employment. They comment on their results as follows:

> The rarity of fundamental dichotomous differences contrasts to the large numbers of significant differences where an attribute is well represented in both sexes, but differs in its incidence ... In this sense, gender differences should be interpreted as occurring within a framework of underlying commonality (Rosa et al., 1994:26).

The advice for future research is accordingly:

> Future studies should study gender within and across categories of ownership and co-ownership rather than on a straight dichotomy of female and male. This would mean grounding theoretical frameworks much more on gender theory, rather than on ideological assumptions of entrepreneurial individualism and success (Rosa et al., 1994:30).

> ... simply 'adding women in' is insufficient ... What is often needed is a revision of the theory. The question then becomes: does the theory become 'gendered' i.e. highlight gender differences between males and

females, or does the theory become conceptually richer and different because, having a mixed sample of male and female respondents, different
questions are asked and issues raised with both? (Chell & Baines,
1998:132).

Why is there this difference in focus between most of the US and
some of the British studies? Rosa & Hamilton suggest:

> This preoccupation with the female entrepreneur is rooted in the debate
> of whether proprietorship represents an opportunity of liberation for
> women, or whether it is yet another form of subordination of women in an
> exploitative capitalist system ... A researcher's views on this debate may
> be fundamental to the way in which 'ownership' is treated in a study. A
> belief in the benefits of proprietorship for women tends to stress 'individ-
> uality' ... if a researcher takes a less unidimensional view of proprietor-
> ship, then the concept of the 'lone female entrepreneur' is perhaps too
> limited. A woman in business is not an island, even if a sole legal owner,
> and cannot 'escape' from the wider society. The social conditions that re-
> inforce gender inequalities may impinge on her business and personal life
> at several levels (Rosa & Hamilton, 1994:11–12).

However, even this idea of the existence of two views – women's entrepreneurship as an opportunity of liberation or yet another form of
subordination – is a phenomenon seldom found in the US texts where
words such as "subordination, patriarchy, liberation, capitalism, etc."
are not found. It is as if the debate that Rosa & Hamilton refer to is a
British debate. The view on entrepreneurship in the US texts lends
more towards the universally positive.

At this point, I can only speculate about the reasons. One reason
might be the predominance of a psychological understanding of social
issues in the US as described by Herman (1995). European sociological thought never "made it" in the United States. Another reason may
be found in the different political scenes of the USA and Britain. The
former has a political system where private ownership has never been
questioned and an ideology of every man's equal chance to make it in
this world. The latter has a long history of labor parties in rule, socialized (and then again privatized) industries, and explicit class struggles.
There are different ideas of how the "social" is constituted in the two
countries. However, they are alike in one aspect. Both countries view
childcare as being a private responsibility.

Marlow (1997) found when comparing a matched sample of men
and women entrepreneurs that only women found it difficult to com-

bine work and family. As for suggestions of how to remedy the situation, men had few such, and the women offered only "privatized" solutions to what was in fact, as Marlow puts it, group subordination. The women suggested for example hard work, visible financial success and sharing domestic responsibility with the family.

> ... if women are utilizing self-employment as a solution to dual demands of domestic and waged labour, then the experiences of self-employment is tainted by patriarchal expectations. Moreover, if women perceive that the solutions to such issues lie in privatized, individual effort or merit to achieve within existing scales of judgement, small firm ownership will reflect the subordination evident in other areas of women's lives (Marlow, 1997:208).

The researcher noted that the suggestions were "privatized", but the respondents had no such reflections. They adapted to a society where childcare is a private responsibility. This is not the case in Sweden where public daycare is available for every child upon the age of one, and where either parent get paid parental leave before that time. Would the experience of entrepreneurship differ for Swedish women because of this?

Hildegard Theobald (2002) made a comparative study of middle-level female managers' coping-strategies in Germany and Sweden. Germany also has a "privatized" or, in Theobald's terms "conservative" state family policy with a strong emphasis on motherly care for small children. Sweden, on the other hand, has a well-established and acknowledged equality policy. She found that the Swedish women, apart from being better represented at managerial levels than in Germany, were more positive towards affirmative action, women's networks and an open debate on gender policy as a way to improve promotion chances of women. They were also more willing to attribute a higher rate of influence on their career development to their gender. The German women opted for improving their chances for promotion on an individual basis, being afraid of otherwise being put off as "women's libbers". Public family and gender policy seems to be related to employed women's career strategies.

What about women entrepreneurs? The two Swedish studies in this review do not address the question directly, but a census study by Sundin & Holmquist (1989) revealed that Swedish women entrepreneurs, unlike those in the United States and Britain, did not seem to have to choose between having a family and running a company since they tended to be married and have children to a larger extent than the non-entrepreneurs. The discussion about entrepreneurship as a solution to childcare problems is also absent in Sweden. I will return to this issue in the final chapters. For now, suffice to say is that most of the reviewed studies take an individualist perspective on entrepreneurship, taking the family's, and particularly the woman's primary responsibility for childcare for granted. They do not question institutional arrangements but suggest for women to adapt.

Summary

Most of the reviewed studies have an implicit understanding that there is a public sphere and a private sphere that are separate from each other, work belonging to the former and home, family and children to the latter. What is classified as "private" is also seen as an individual and not a collective responsibility. There is also a gendering of the two spheres. Men's place in the public sphere is unquestioned. It is the woman who is thought to adapt to her husband's fixed schedule. The caring for small children is regarded as the woman's responsibility. The studies do not ask men how they are able to combine entrepreneurship and childcare. Women's entrepreneurship is then positioned either as a difficult challenge since it is hard to do both jobs, or as an opportunity, i.e., family and work can be combined since entrepreneurship may allow more flexible hours. Public childcare is not discussed at all.

Entrepreneurship is almost universally positioned as positive. Few studies question the double burdens put on women. Few studies question men's privileged status and women's subordinate position. Women's difficulties or shortcomings are seen as something they should do something about themselves. Institutional arrangement are not questioned, instead women are advised to adapt by changing themselves.

8
The Scientific Reproduction of Gender Inequality

According to Foucault's theory as discussed in chapter three, discourses consist both of what is included and what is excluded. Certain practices also exist, which make for the repetition and recreation of a certain discourse. Discourse structures knowledge, and knowledge structures what people hold as true and act upon. Discourses are thus not innocent representations of the social world; discourses create the social world and they have effects on power relations between people.

This chapter summarizes the book within this framework. By discussing the inclusions and the exclusions in the discourse on women's entrepreneurship, I draw out underlying assumptions and discuss their effect on the positioning of the female entrepreneur. The underlying assumptions are part of the mechanism recreating the discourse, but so are the writing and publishing practices. Since a feminist viewpoint entails an interest in the change of such practices, I conclude the chapter with a discussion of the implications of this analysis for research on women's entrepreneurship.

The Discourse in the Analyzed Research Texts

This section discusses the discourse on women's entrepreneurship in the reviewed articles. I discuss it as one discourse. There are of course variations, possible subcategories, and exceptions. All articles do not encompass all of the elements of this discourse. The articles that deviate from the discourse I describe do this, however, in opposition to a dominant model. An article that questions an assumption that is taken for granted does this explicitly, as the analysis in chapter seven demonstrated. It organizes its critique around this assumption. This leads me to formulate one discourse as a dominant one and I discuss exceptions as they are related to the dominant discourse.

The analysis of the research texts showed several assumptions or constructs that were taken for granted – about women, men, businesses and the social world – that from a feminist point of view merit a discussion. I have organized the following discussion around four basic assumptions, which have relevance for the positioning of women, that are present in the great majority of the articles. The first, and almost universal assumption, is that entrepreneurship is a good thing. The second such assumption is that men and women are different. The third is a certain division between a public and a private sphere of life, and the fourth is individualism.

These four constructs are related to each other, and each of them is also related to other constructs. "Entrepreneurship is good" is for example related to "economic growth is good". This "package" of assumptions about the world enters the research process, where it is reproduced and refined and sent out again in the form of research articles. In a summary of my findings, I discuss these four constructs and their effects through a "prototypical" article.

First Construct: "Entrepreneurship is good"

As described in chapter six, the prototypical article begins with a statement that entrepreneurship is good for society because it contributes to economic growth. The relationship between these two constructs rests on studies showing that most new jobs are created in new businesses. That economic growth is good is not questioned, and it is not even commented upon. It acts as a silent backdrop that is completely taken for granted.

A proposed societal gain in terms of economic growth is thus established as the legitimate base for research on entrepreneurship in the reviewed articles. What is then the argument for researching women's entrepreneurship? As discussed earlier, the designation "female" entrepreneurship or "women's" entrepreneurship already suggests that it is an exception to a norm. The suggestion that women's entrepreneurship should be researched separately is somewhat peculiar. There must be something about it that merits special attention. But what might this be?

The most obvious reason is that what was known about entrepreneurs was known about male entrepreneurs. The early research used samples dominated by men (e.g., Smith, 1967). Researching women's entrepreneurship is thus a way to correct the record, a work that is carried out in many other subjects, for example art and literature. There are now encyclopedias available on women artists and writers who were previously ignored. The above reason is only occasionally stated, however, and when it is, it is not stated alone.

Another possible reason is that of injustice. In most western societies, there are fewer female than male entrepreneurs, and the proportion of women business owners diminishes by increasing size of the business. One might thus argue that women are given unequal access to economic power in society and this should merit a closer look at women's entrepreneurship. This is, however, not a common argument in the reviewed articles.

Instead, the typical article carries on with the economic growth argument. It states that women's entrepreneurship has (or should have, depending on country and prevalence of women entrepreneurs) an important impact on the economy in terms of economic growth. So hard currency arguments count as a reason to do research, while simple equality does not. Women's entrepreneurship is positioned as a resource for the economy. This is particularly plain in the many US studies that point to the recent rise in the number of women entrepreneurs (and their impact on the economy) as the reason to study them. It is implicit that before, when women entrepreneurs were fewer in number and had no impact on the economy, there was no reason to study them. If researchers rested on equality arguments, a small, or even diminishing proportion of women entrepreneurs should make a greater case for research interest.

The stated reason to study women's entrepreneurship is thus essentially the same reason as stated for the study of entrepreneurship – it is instrumental for economic growth. If this is so, and if equality arguments and arguments of correcting the record are irrelevant, it may be that the studies assume that women contribute to the economy in a way that differs from men. This brings me to the second basic construct in the typical article, that of essential differences between men and women.

Second Construct: "Men and women are different"

The typical assumption of male/female differences hinges on another assumption, namely that of the existence of an "essence", of stable inner individual characteristics, which is a highly questionable assumption as discussed in detail in chapter five. It is assumed that

163

essences exist, however, and the search for them in "difference research" becomes a search for a dualistic essence that lies behind empirical observations, and the results (where overlaps are bigger than mean differences) are interpreted through this dualistic frame in a sort of circular reasoning. The categories determine the results, so to speak.

The prototypical study looks for differences between male and female entrepreneurs. Women are thought to have different values, attitudes and ambitions. Women are thought to prioritize differently, network differently and pursue different strategies.

Different from what? There is no "neutral" standard according to which men and women are supposed to deviate in opposite directions. Instead there is an "entrepreneurial" model against which men and women are measured, and this entrepreneurial model is based on research on men and it is based on entrepreneurship as a male gendered concept as discussed in chapter two.

This is evident in the choice of independent and dependent variables in the research designs. When the dependent variable is performance, it is usually measured as size, profit, sales growth, or employment growth. Women are found to start smaller businesses, grow their businesses more slowly than men, and to be less profitable, which is not surprising since they favor retail and service businesses which are labor intensive and have a local and highly competitive market. They will almost, by definition, come out on the weak side. They do indeed contribute to the economy in a way that differs from men, in that they contribute less, measured by standard measurements. This is then constructed as a problem. The relevance of the performance measure, as defined, is seldom questioned. Size, growth and profit are the assumed standards, and why women's businesses do not perform as men's in these regards and what policies to recommend in order to amend this situation, seem to be central questions in the research about women entrepreneurs. This shows how an assumed performance norm is imposed on women, rendering them inadequate. Taking the performance measure for granted excludes a discussion of its relevance, and it renders women secondary. The result is doubly oppressive, since the majority of men's businesses actually come out on the same weak side as women's in terms of size, growth and profit, but this point is seldom made in the research texts. Davidsson (1989:209) writes that most existing small firms do not grow to any considerable extent; neither do they have an interest in growth. This is true for male as well as for female entrepreneurs. The very few firms that do grow quickly happen to be mostly male owned and will therefore cause the means in measures such as size, growth rate, etc., for male businesses on the whole to be larger than for those of females.

So, provided that lack of growth is a problem, it is a problem pertaining to the majority of all firms, irrespective of the sex of the owner; however, the reviewed research texts construct it as a female problem. The rhetorical effect is very peculiar. Somehow all men get to be free riders on their few growth-oriented fellow businessmen in these texts, while the women are marked out as the non-growers. Why some men grow their businesses is not explained by how men are, but, surprisingly, it seems perfectly all right to try to explain it by how women are not.

The choice of independent variables might also illustrate how a male gendered norm is applied. The early entrepreneurship research produced a picture of the entrepreneur as a person with a high need for achievement, a high need for independence and a certain configuration of his value system, a picture which has carried over into the research on female entrepreneurs. The research producing this picture was conducted on men, and the measurements were developed on men. McClelland's (1961) work on need for achievement, for example, which has been very influential in the entrepreneurship literature, focused explicitly on men. He claimed that economic growth would be automatically achieved if mothers instilled enough of the need for achievement in their sons. Daughters were not discussed. Stevenson (1990) reports an early study, which explicitly excluded the female survey responses since they might contaminate the results. The resulting construction of the entrepreneur is the stereotypical independent self-made man. This is not an image that fits most women (nor indeed many men) very well, so women are by implication already rendered insufficient by the research design.

The prototypical study envisions an entrepreneurial (male gendered) way of being and doing, and a feminine way, which is the antithesis to the former. The prototypical study, however, finds very few, and if so, very small, differences between men and women. The study does *not* confirm the existence of a masculine and a feminine way. Overlaps are much larger than differences. For a researcher who is concerned about women unjustifiably being rendered the weaker sex, unconfirmed hypotheses about women's weaknesses should be very good news. But it seems as if it is not. I found three ways of rationalizing the lack of differences.

One common strategy of dealing with the "bad news" is to ignore the similarities and the great overlaps between men and women and instead tout any small difference that is found. "Statistically significant" gets translated to "significant", even if it is not. Attention is then put on differences. In chapter six, I called this strategy "making a mountain out of a molehill".

Another strategy is to proclaim women entrepreneurs as exceptions to regular women – even if the study has no data on "regular women". They are said to be "self-selected". The result is that the idea of women as different from men is saved. It posits that there are regular, feminine women, and then there are those self-selected women entrepreneurs who are different from the regular ones. A version of this is to distinguish between ordinary women entrepreneurs (who are feminine and have small, low-performing businesses) and extraordinary women entrepreneurs who display a pattern associated with the image of the typical male entrepreneur. Both versions serve to maintain the construction of male and female as a binary opposition, a construction that researchers do not seem to be willing to let go of in spite of research results to the contrary. It is as if the idea of what makes "woman" must be saved.

Related to the above constructs is the "good mother" strategy, where findings about women entrepreneurs combined with theories about women as relational, caring and mothering result in the construction of an entrepreneurial model and in which all feminine traits are valued. Instead of weaknesses, feminine characteristics are seen as strengths. This is a good try at enhancing women's status, but it fails, since by assigning all the good (nurturing, relational, democratic, ethical, etc.) traits to women, it leaves the male/female dichotomy intact and does not seriously question the dominant construction of the entrepreneur. Rather, the female model becomes a compliment to the male norm.

There is a discourse similar to the "good mother" in leadership, as discussed by Wahl (1996a). The "business case" for more women managers says that companies should promote women to top management since they are good at listening to personnel and to customers, they have more empathy than men and they are good, democratic and relational leaders. As such, they complement the tougher, insensitive male style. The problem for women of flesh and blood is that to be eligible for top positions, they must first compete with men through the ranks, and this competitive game does not reward a feminine style. Once at the top, the woman is suddenly supposed to become feminine. It is a "Catch-22" situation. A "feminine" woman will not be seen as a "real leader", and a woman leader who behaves like leaders normally do, will not be seen as a "real woman" but be slotted in the "bitch" and "iron lady" categories. This is because "leader", as "entrepreneur" is a male gendered concept. The idea of a feminine style reinforces, rather than challenges the construction. A feminine style will only be accepted as long as it is a complement, and secondary, to the norm, only as long as it does not challenge the norm. Advocating traits that are missing in the male model is a worthy cause, but by assigning the traits to gendered bodies, the power relationships between male and female goes unchallenged. I would claim that from a feminist point of view, this is a dead end rather than a step forward.

For leaders as well as entrepreneurs, constructing an alternative, feminine model embodied by women also implies that both men and women are given a very limited repertoire at their disposal. The feminine model is an alternative stereotype to the independent self-made man, but it is just a different sort of straightjacket, for women as well as for men.

These three strategies show the stronghold of the assumption that men and women are different by nature. It is so powerful that it acts as blinders. Some researchers hold on to it in spite of having themselves produced evidence to the contrary. The assumption excludes a discussion of similarities between men and women, it precludes a discussion of the meaningfulness of investigating gender differences, and it prevents a questioning of the usefulness and consequences of gendered norms for humans of either sex.

Third Construct: "The division between a public and a private sphere of life"

The existence of a line dividing a public sphere of work from a private sphere of home, family and children is also taken for granted in the entrepreneurship literature. In the mainstream literature, the private sphere is not even mentioned. Entrepreneurship is something that takes place in the public sphere. The line does not become visible until women enter the literature as research objects, and it is then made visible in several different ways.

The most common approach is to see it as a problem. Combining the two spheres is posited as a potential problem and drawback for women (but not for men). It is said to be a source of tension for women – interrole conflict is supposed to arise. Women entrepreneurs (but not men) are asked how they are able to combine work and family – and at least in the USA, they often chose not to, since a larger proportion of female entrepreneurs were single and childless than women at large (Brush, 1992).

But it can also be constructed as a solution. Those who do combine a family and a business are said to have made a "life-style" choice. They settle for smaller businesses, or they go into business to add to the family income, or they choose entrepreneurship before employment because it allows flexible work hours and a better opportunity to care for small children. Here women's entrepreneurship is perceived as the flexible resource that makes the work/family equation add up.

The private sphere is in most texts perceived as an obstacle to women, but it is sometimes constructed as a source of inspiration and a benefit to business life as well as to individual women entrepreneurs. Researchers that use the "good mother" argument and speak for the benefits of a feminine way of conducting business rely on psychological texts speaking about women's unique characteristics that have been developed through the experience of mothering as well as through the experience of being a daughter. According to these theories (Gilligan, 1982; Chodorow, 1988) a daughter, unlike a son, does not have to severe the bonds to the mother in order to acquire a sense of self. She stays "relational" whereas the son becomes "independent". When women go into business they are supposed to carry these traits with them and enrich business in general as well as their own personal careers. The previous chapter showed that there is very little empirical support for this notion, but the idea is appealing to many and survives.

In these ways, the public/private divide is made visible in the research texts. The "private" is a messy world populated by women and children, with household chores and social responsibilities, with child bearing and child rearing and with caring and community involvement. "Family" is also in the private sphere, and so is leisure. Men and work populate the public sphere. It is a clinical place where children and home do not obstruct rational planning.

The institution of marriage ties the two spheres together, but by labeling one as "husband" and the other as "wife" it simultaneously divides them again into the two categories of public and private. What sorts under private is seen as the wife's responsibility and what sorts under public (including the breadwinning role) is the husband's responsibility. Women's entrepreneurship does not change this construction in the typical article. It makes it visible, but it is not questioned and is taken for granted.

Fourth Construct: "Individualism"

The prototypical study has a strong, unquestioned individualist assumption. Only a few studies, such as those quoted in chapter seven for example, question it. The typical study focuses on individuals, and on individual businesses. The performance of an individual business is supposed to be related to what an individual entrepreneur is and/or does, or, in the case of bank discrimination studies, how individual loan officers treat individual women. Networking studies, which clearly study something social, also cast their studies in terms of how an individual builds up and uses a network. It is the individual who is right or wrong, and the success of the business hinges on the individual. Family, housekeeping and childcare is cast as a fully individual responsibility. There is no concept of such tasks being solved on a communal basis.

Even if structural factors, such as women's unequal access to business education, are accounted for, suggested remedies for such things are still on the individual level. Individual women are advised to get more business education, a better network, more management experience, etc. Institutional arrangements are not questioned, instead individuals are advised to adapt.

It is almost as if the social world does not exist. The typical study sees the entrepreneur as a lone island, completely in charge of her own success. Yet people are not lone islands. No one can start and run a business without other people involved. One needs suppliers and customers, co-workers, employees, partners, advisors, lawyers, accountants and most people have a family. Legislation, public services, infrastructure, the labor market, business cycles, politics, etc., are all, in a sense, part of the business. As discussed in chapter one, it is not only men and women who are gendered, but jobs as well. Women may be pushed into entrepreneurship through changes in a gendered labor market, and they start gendered businesses. Such topics are seldom discussed, and when they are, they are discussed in terms of individual choice.

This may be a result of the psychologization of the social as discussed earlier in chapter seven, but it could also be a result of the favored research methodology. I would suspect that the two interact. The psychologization of the social, where social circumstances and issues of social change are perceived through the self, lends itself to value research methods aimed at studying individuals and the "self", as discussed in chapter five. The focus on individuals is also reflected in the theories used by entrepreneurship researchers. As the review in chapter five showed, only one of eighty-one studies used institutional theory, which explicitly theorizes institutional aspects as well as institutionalization processes.

The result of this neglect of social aspects is that the power perspective is lost. Issues of women's subordination to men are not touched upon in the typical study. The results of entrepreneurship in terms of possible changes of women's subordination also go untouched with only a few exceptions. If the social world is neglected, changes taking place in this world are also neglected. Shortcomings become individual women's responsibility in terms of adaptation to an existing institutional order; there is seldom a discussion about changing that order. There is no talk about women's collective action to change gender inequalities. The individualist assumption is thus an ideological assumption in favor of the status quo of the current political/economic arrangement. By implication, it does not challenge the current state of women's subordination to men.

The focus on individuals and individual businesses thus serves to exclude a discussion of how the social world is arranged and of possible changes in this arrangement. An entrepreneurship researcher might of course object, and say that the entrepreneurship discipline is *supposed* to study individuals and individual businesses, while leaving the rest to macroeconomics, sociology, and political science. Along with other social constructionist writers, I think that this idea has had its day. It is less meaningful to look at the individual apart from her social world. Even the individual is constructed socially, as discussed in the first chapter.

What does the discourse exclude?

Foucault said to use the principle of *reversal*, i.e., instead of looking at what a discourse conveys, look at what it excludes. If the previous discussion centered on what was present in the discourse and the assumptions that brought this about, this section explicates what is omitted, neglected, disregarded, or avoided, but the absence of which is still present between the lines.

A universal assumption that economic growth is good effectively excludes discussions based on the contrary point of view, or the point of view that economic growth has both pros and cons. Few would question the use of new jobs, or the idea that increased wealth makes for a better standard of living, but many question that economic growth is unequivocally good. These voices may be concerned with issues such as environmental pollution, depletion of the earth's resources, an increasingly uneven income distribution between people or between rich and poor countries, the extortion of cheap labor, negative effects of increased competition on people's health resulting in stress, burn-out, and escalating health care costs. This is just to mention a few objections to the blessings of untamed economic growth. These voices are seldom heard in the entrepreneurship literature. The assumption of economic growth as only positive serves to exclude such critical perspectives.

Likewise, the unquestioned construction of entrepreneurship as good serves to preclude critical perspectives on entrepreneurship. One might, for example, see the promotion of entrepreneurship through research as a political move, promoting a neo-liberal market ideology while covering up the dismantling of a welfare system, and have objections to that. One might see it as a false promise (since many new businesses fail within the first few years) leading to failed expectations and a lessened quality of life, or one might see it as something running counter to egalitarianism and therefore leading to social injustice[1]. One might perhaps see attempts to make women who have become unemployed through cut-downs in the public sector start their own business, as unfair policy, arguing that it would be better for women with a large public sector. One might be concerned about the construction of women's life-style entrepreneurship as a convenient way to make the work/family equation add up without questioning prevailing gender roles. These voices are not heard in the reviewed literature either. One might of course also argue for entrepreneurship because it can allow an individual to make a fortune. This is common in the popular press about entrepreneurship, but such displays of covetousness are not *comme-il-faut* in the research literature. This is still present, however, in that business performance is one of the most researched themes, yet this is argued in the name of contributions to business renewal and economic growth.

The limitation of performance measures to size and growth measures of the individual business limits the discussion of the role of the business. Taking alternative measures into account, one would get a more full-fledged comprehension of the business and its role in the social world. One might, for example, consider long-term duration, liquidation rates or perhaps tax frauds, which should be equally impor-

---

1   See Erkkilä (2000) for a discussion of critical voices in debates about entrepreneurial education in the USA, the UK, and Finland.

tant from a social perspective. The list could be expanded to include contributions to the public good by taxes paid, the level of environmental pollution, the use of limited sources of energy, the health of the employees, the health and happiness of the owner, and so on. Expanding the notion of performance to include a count of the value of women's unpaid work at home might even have turned the comparison between men's and women's contributions upside down.

The persistent conception that men and women should be different serves to prevent a discussion of the observation that they seem to be more similar than different, or that within-sex variation is larger than between-sex variation. If one took such results seriously, there would be good reasons for questioning current gendered arrangements, which are often based on assumptions of difference.

The instrumental focus in research on women's entrepreneurship seems to exclude equality perspectives. Power relations between men and women and issues of women's subordination to men are untouched by most authors. The idea that women should have primary responsibility for child care is not questioned, which excludes a discussion of alternative arrangements. The instrumental/individualist focus and the avoidance of power issues further serves to delimit researchers' use of feminist analysis. This is peculiar. Since the studies explicitly focused on gender one would think that the richness of feminist theory would be an asset to be used for analysis. However, apart from the cited articles in chapter seven, feminist theory is absent, or watered down to something only concerning individuals. As discussed in chapters five and seven, liberal and social feminist theory was translated to "women's situational and dispositional barriers" and presented as something women should do something about on an individual basis. Feminism is about power relationships, collective interests, collective action, and social change. In the research discourse on women's entrepreneurship, parts of feminist theory have been co-opted by the individualist discourse and turned into something individual, while for example socialist and Marxist, or for that matter post-structuralist feminist theory is largely absent.

The silent areas are all concerned with how the social world is constructed. If one were to pinpoint what the discourse on women's entrepreneurship excludes, it would be this. Discourses create the social world – and this particular discourse seems to create a social world, which is "not social", but perceived through the individual. It makes the individual the locus for social change, much as Herman (1995) described. She says, "psychological experts … extended the reach of government and the purposes of public policy to include the subjectivity and emotional realities of power" (ibid:237). The effect is that individuals are to be blamed or, even worse, to blame themselves for all the problems in the world, while institutional arrangements remain largely unquestioned. Berger & Luckmann (1966) described the social construction of reality as a two-way street. Individuals construct the social world, but they are in turn constructed by it. The reviewed research focuses on the first but neglects important aspects of the latter.

The individualist canon in the research on women's entrepreneurship takes current social and institutional arrangements for granted while focusing on the single individual and her business. This produces an incomplete picture, since what one conceives as an individual cannot be separated from how one conceives of the individual in the social world. It further serves to legitimate the current social order since it excludes a discussion of alternative arrangements.

How does the discourse position women?

Throughout the studies I reviewed, women entrepreneurs were thought of as "something else", i.e., something else compared to male entrepreneurs. They were the exception to be explained. The mechanism foremost behind this result was the polarization of male and female, against a background of entrepreneurship as a male gendered construct. Most of the research on entrepreneurs up until the mid 1980s was done on samples of entrepreneurs that were all or almost all male. Knowledge about entrepreneurs was thus derived from research on men. Yet the conception of entrepreneurship, from which the research questions were formulated, was also male gendered from the beginning, as discussed in chapter two. One cannot claim that the entrepreneurship models were male gendered just because the research subjects were men. Indeed, the male gendered entrepreneurship concept was imposed on them just as it was imposed on women. As mentioned in chapter two, it is a particular construct of masculinity that not all men may encompass.

With the advent of the increase of women entrepreneurs, however, the tests were repeated, using the same constructs and variables for comparison. The construction of independent variables was based on the stereotypical independent, self-made man with a high need for achievement, and a value system associated with the "rugged individualist". This is a notion, which makes a woman entrepreneur an anomaly from the beginning.

The dependent variables centering on performance and calculated by size and growth measures, construct women as the weaker sex in two ways. Women entrepreneurs are concentrated in small retail and personal service businesses with a local, limited, and highly competitive market. Entry and exit are easy. Not controlling for these factors, which the studies do not always do, will automatically make women come out on the weak side compared to men. One might also claim that the measures favor men because the measures as such are too restricted. As discussed in the previous section, performance could be measured in so many different ways other than size and growth measures. Some of these might favor women more than the traditional measures.

One might also discuss the relevance of these measures for men. As discussed earlier, most men do not live up to the standards either. The performance measures limit the conception of a business and its role in society, but they also impose a standard upon men, which they may not desire. The same goes for the picture of the achieving individual. This is a cultural construct which many men may find oppressive, frustrating, or just distasteful. It certainly limits the choices for individuals. Men who want to do something against this idea of masculinity (where it prevails) must do this in constant opposition, if they want to maintain an identity as a "man". However, such issues are not discussed in the reviewed research. The performance norm and performance measures are taken for granted, just as the construct "entrepreneur" is taken for granted and perceived as something neutral. The effect is that female entrepreneurs are positioned as deviations from the norm. They are cast as the "Other" (de Beauvoir 1949; 1986).

Results pointing in the other direction – that women are in fact very similar to men – are shied away from. Either one makes a big fuss about small differences while ignoring similarities, or one proclaims women entrepreneurs to be self-selected, to be exceptions to regular women. The idea of "regular women" is just an idea, an assumed notion about what regular women are like. It seems to be a treasured idea, however. The strategies used here serve to save it, but they simultaneously preserve the idea of the woman as "the Other".

Constructing women's entrepreneurship as a positive alternative by stressing their relational and ethical strengths (the "good mother" argument), is a response to a male norm which does not adequately describe many women's experiences. However, the attempts at redeeming women's role as Other are bound to fail, since they are a direct response to the male norm. Without The One there would be no need to construct The Better Other. The One is in the background, firmly established in the position as primary. The "good mother" argument preserves the male/female dichotomy and is a dead end from a feminist perspective.

The division between a public and a private sphere also puts women entrepreneurs in a secondary position. The way the discourse draws the line implies a gendered division of labor where the man is the primary breadwinner and the woman the primary caretaker. The research asks women how they are able to combine work and family, but men are seldom asked the same question. Women are thought to have a choice between family and work (or an obligation to do both) whereas men have not. In the case of the "life-style" entrepreneurs, their businesses are seen as a complement to the husband's income.

Women might feel this in very tangible ways. Having to carry the load of household work in combination with running a business means that they cannot attend to the business as much as a male entrepreneur who is not subject to such expectations. A further effect, perhaps mostly a result of the construction of the husband as the primary breadwinner, is that male entrepreneurs can expect support from a housewife, but the opposite is uncommon.

As a consequence, men and women entrepreneurs do not compete on equal terms. Not only must women work longer hours to do both jobs, the fact that they are thought to take full responsibility for the household in addition to work means that bankers, customers, etc., expect the same, which may put women at a disadvantage compared to men. Single women and women who do not cook and clean may be subject to such stereotyping as well.

The caretaker discourse carries over in the discourse of women's entrepreneurship. Women's entrepreneurship is positioned as a "life-style", as a solution to childcare problems, as the flexible resource that makes it possible to support a family without challenging the man's right to a career. Sometimes it is positioned as a solution to the glass-ceiling phenomenon. In these ways, women are asked to adapt, as individuals, to a social order that discriminates women compared to men.

The discourse encourages individual adaptation, while mentioning little about the possibility of collective action. Research about women's entrepreneurship construct women's "shortcomings" and make their amendment an individual responsibility. The existing social order is not questioned. One might, for example, envision an alternative social order where men and women share household work and the care for small children on equal terms, and where both share the responsibility for providing for the family. This would require alternative solutions for childcare, for example public childcare centers available for everyone, which would in turn require a re-conceptualization of childcare as an entirely individual responsibility. Yet the discourse seems to exclude such discussions. I would claim that this discourse, while talked about in enthusiastic terms, does women a disfavor. The entrepreneurship discourse is not a vehicle for women's liberation. It is a tool that maintains the status quo in terms of women's position in society, and it preserves the present power relationships between men and women.

Through an uncritical acceptance of entrepreneurship as something unequivocally positive, through the assumption that men and women are essentially different, through taking a certain construction of the public/private dichotomy for granted where women are given responsibility for children and household work, and through the individualist canon in entrepreneurship research, attention is turned away from structural and institutional arrangements. The result is the loss of a discussion of institutional factors relevant for women's entrepreneurship, the loss of a power perspective, and an acceptance of the current state of women's subordination to men. So, while researchers celebrate that women break established gender barriers and start businesses in record numbers, the academic study of them is framed in such a way as to put them safely back into place in a secondary position.

Does someone benefit from this discourse?

The previous section should leave no doubt concerning the fact that women as a group do not benefit from the discourse on women's entrepreneurship. This is not to say that individual women business owners are not pleased with their lives and their businesses, but this is a different topic. The research discourse most definitely positions women as secondary to men.

Do men benefit from the discourse? Yes and no. The discourse sustains a social order, which benefits men as a group compared to women as a group. The proclamation of women entrepreneurs as unusual women sustains the idea of the masculine entrepreneur and maintains "entrepreneurship" as a male gendered dominion. Women's entrepreneurship as a "life-style", confirms men's primary right to a career and their primary right to housekeeping services from a woman. It suggests that they are not the first ones counted on to change diapers or to shoulder the double burden of gainful work and household work. Women's entrepreneurship as a solution to the glass-ceiling problem reinforces a social order where men support men in a homo-social pattern and acknowledges the discrimination of women in the corporate ladders.

Yet, this is not necessarily desirable for individual men. Having to take full financial responsibility for a family is a heavy burden, particularly if one lives within an economy like the USA, with its lack of public daycare, where schools and universities charge tuition, and where health care is not free. Living in such a culture, where one is measured by one's achievements counted in prestige or money, limits life choices. Missing out on time with small children can be a great loss. Feeling that one must live up to the ideal of a man (as put forward in the entrepreneurship discourse) can be debilitating. It puts strict limits on what a person may be like to be a "man", leaving all the "feminine" traits out of reach. The male gendered norm may be as troublesome for men as for women. The research that compared men and women on personal characteristics showed that both lived up to the norm to the same extent – so it is not that men automatically score high on the desired attributes just because they are men. This may, incidentally, be a reason why some men do not see the validity of the feminist struggle. It is hard to identify with being an "oppressor" when feeling oppressed oneself, by other men or by male norms that one does not embody.

There is one group, however, that benefits directly from the discourse of women entrepreneurs as being weaker than men and as having special needs, namely those who work to support women's entrepreneurship. To raise funds for programs aimed at forwarding women's entrepreneurship, one needs a discourse that legitimates it, but this discourse may simultaneously keep women entrepreneurs in place. This is paradoxical.

In Sweden, liberal feminist arguments of women's unequal access to economic power are used to motivate efforts to support women entrepreneurs in the first place, but the "women as an unused economic resource" argument can also be found. Women in the rural areas of Sweden are, for example, supposed to solve their own unemployment problems (caused by cut-backs in the public sector) by starting a business, and by the same token they are to keep the depopulated rural areas alive (Ahl, 2002; Proposition, 1993/94:140).

When it comes to designing programs for this aim, however, arguments of gender difference are used. The Swedish government started a special business counseling system for women where the counselors were also women, reasoning that women would hesitate to contact men counselors. Swedish women were also given access to special women's loans and additional start-up benefits. The women's loans were instituted since it was assumed that women have greater difficulties getting a bank loan than men. Unemployed women in Sweden are eligible for one year of start-up support as compared to half a year for men. The Swedish government also instituted 144 special resource centers for women with advisory services, and there is a program to encourage women innovators. The European Union social fund looks positively at applications for projects specifically aimed at supporting women entrepreneurs. These may take the form of special support groups, assertiveness training, women's empowerment networks, and so on (Ahl & Samuelsson, 2000).

These programs build on the idea of women as the weaker sex while simultaneously reproducing that idea. The measures that are intended to help actually define the helpless. They produce a picture of women being in greater need of assistance, that is, having less ability than men to successfully get a business going. Built into the discourse on enhancing women's entrepreneurship is therefore a construction of women entrepreneurs as the Other, as someone in need of special assistance. Nilsson (1997) found, for example, that both women and men tended to discount the advice given in the special advisory program mentioned earlier. It was as if the advice given in an advisory system without men involved counted for less. The established gender regime is thus recreated instead of changed, and equality is not accomplished. But however unproductive in terms of results, the discourse is a valuable resource for the people running these programs, and for the consultants who obtain project money from the European Social Fund. Even the women entrepreneurs who seek project money can capitalize on their own supposed weaknesses.

This poses a dilemma for the people involved in such support programs. Arguments are needed to raise funds for programs for women entrepreneurs. Arguments about women's weaknesses reproduce women as secondary to men – but these may also be the same arguments that produce money. This raises the question as to whether or not such programs are worth the price, or if they could be argued and designed in a way that does not reinforce the dominant discourse. One might, for example, claim that using equality arguments only should be sufficient. If equality arguments are *not* sufficient, however, there is serious reason to question how the support practices position women.

Other actors can also use the discourse on women's entrepreneurship. An interesting example is a study by Beyer (1996), commissioned by 'Företagarnas Riksorganisation' (the Swedish small business owners organization) entitled *The Female Entrepreneur Profile*. Beyer surveyed a number of women entrepreneurs to find out what their needs were. The not-so-surprising result was that nothing would help women entrepreneurs more than lower taxes. Lower taxes are what this organization, which is basically a lobby organization, has always worked for. Using 'female' in the title was a new angle, and they were able to attract some fifteen members of parliament to a breakfast meeting when they presented the study. I interpret this as an example of how an organization has co-opted the discourse on women entrepreneurs, and used it for its own purposes.

The discourse on women's entrepreneurship is marginal in the academic community, and in the entrepreneurship research community as well, as discussed earlier. One of the basic assumptions in research on women's entrepreneurship, namely that of entrepreneurship's contribution to economic growth and renewal, and its ability to alleviate unemployment is, however, paramount to the entrepreneurship research community. It attracts research funding from both governments and private research foundations, and it is probably the basic reason why entrepreneurship research has grown so quickly over the last few decades. So the community thrives on one of the assumptions that, in combination with other assumptions, construct women entrepreneurs as secondary. One cannot claim that the research community benefits from a discourse of women entrepreneurs as the Other, but it is possible to conclude that something that the community *does* benefit from, *produces* a picture of women entrepreneurs a secondary. The research community does not have the incentive to question the growth-is-good assumption and may therefore also be reluctant to question the discourse on women's entrepreneurship in its current shape.

This discussion has concluded that women, by and large, do not benefit from the discourse; men do not necessarily benefit from it; the support system for women's businesses most definitely benefits; and researchers themselves may, if not benefit directly, have incentives not to change it. It would seem, however, that these interests would not be strong enough to resist the challenge of a discourse, which produces women as secondary. Why is it then so persistent? Why is it being reproduced? Why does it not crumble and fall?

I turn to historian Yvonne Hirdman (1992) whom I quoted in chapter one, for an explanation. She said that the gender regime is the base for all other orders, social, economical as well as political. A change in

the power relation between the sexes would change other power centers as well, and other power centers would quite naturally resist this.

> A change of relationships between men and women is therefore always a
> revolutionary change. And as we know, societies do not tolerate revolu-
> tions (Hirdman, 1992, p. 230 my translation).

The real benefactor of the discourse is an abstract entity, namely "the
current social order". The current gender regime, the current political
and economical arrangements, and the current power relationships
between men and women produce this discourse and are in turn produced by it. If this is, in a sense, an overriding mechanism upholding
the discourse, I now turn to the particular discursive practices that
enable it.

What discursive practices uphold the discourse?

As discussed in chapter three, Foucault emphasized that a discourse is
not only the "selection of possibilities" but also the "networks of constraints", that is, the discursive practices that bring about a certain type
of discourse.

The most important discursive practices are the things that are
taken for granted. Taking something (or most things) for granted is of
course unavoidable. Anything that is problematized is questioned
against the background of something that is not problematized (Berger & Luckmann, 1966). Things taken for granted in the reviewed research on women's entrepreneurship are, as detailed earlier, assumptions of entrepreneurship and economic growth as good, the existence
of essential gender differences, a certain, gendered division between a
public and a private sphere, and an individualist focus. I believe it is
easier to see, and question, these assumptions, for somebody living in a
society where different things are taken for granted. This was clear in
the dissenting voices in the British articles cited in chapter seven.

From a Scandinavian perspective, with yet another public/private
divide and a somewhat less individualistic focus, it seems like the assumptions in the research are very much tied to a US institutional order. A Swedish researcher would be less likely to write about women's
entrepreneurship as a solution to childcare problems, since Sweden
has low-cost, public daycare (available to all children upon the age of
one) which most Swedes take for granted. A Swedish researcher would
also question the assumption of women's entrepreneurship as "addi-

tional" family income, since the Swedish social order builds on a dual breadwinner system. Men and women participate in the work force almost to the same extent and only two per cent of Swedish women are housewives (Statistics Sweden, 2000). Since Swedish parents get a year of paid parental leave[2], paid by tax money, and time off to care for sick children, it is probably easier to combine a job and a family than it is to combine a business and a family. These are examples of how problems of childcare, which in the USA are fully within the private sphere, can instead be organized in a collective manner. Such alternative arrangements are however completely outside the discourse studied. The assumptions about men, women, work, and family, which are taken for granted, exclude such discussions.

As noted in chapter seven, the analysis reviewed a tension between the mainstream articles that were largely from the USA, and some British articles, which did indeed account for a power perspective in gender relations. The British articles protested, in a sense, against the dominant discourse. To make their point, they had to position their text *against*, for example, the dominant individualist assumption (see e.g. Chell & Baines, 1998) or the assumption of gender differences (Rosa et al., 1994). This is another way to say that the US discourse on women's entrepreneurship has the dominant position in the particular discourse community that I studied.

Writing and publishing practices are also part of the discursive practices. Three out of the four main journals I studied are US based. They have an editorial board consisting largely of Americans and many of the reviewers work for more than one of the journals. This means that they will attract research that reflects the same assumptions (Foucault's "author function") and reject studies based on different ones. Scholars departing from other assumptions are likely to turn elsewhere, or they might modify their texts to fit the dominant discourse. Articles may also be rewritten during the "revise-and-resubmit" process to better fit the dominant model. The use of feminist theory seems to have met this fate. Why would otherwise Marxist and socialist feminist theory be avoided, and liberal and social feminist theory turned into women's "situational and dispositional barriers"?

Foucault also talked about the discipline as regulating what is necessary for formulating new statements, through its "groups of objects, methods, their corpus of propositions considered to be true, the interplay of rules and definitions, of techniques and tools." (Foucault,

---

2   Both are entitled to a year off work, but only one gets paid. The parents may share this benefit as they wish, but one month is reserved for either parent.

1972:222). All this both enables and restricts the discourse. The reviewed research focused on individuals and individual businesses, ignoring legislation, labor market changes, political changes, power relations between men and women, etc. It favored survey methods, which in combination with objectivist assumptions and assumptions of gender differences, constructed women as secondary.

Women entrepreneurs are investigated in other disciplines as well, with other disciplinary regulations, other discursive practices, forming the discourse differently. My selection of articles targeted those journals that label themselves specifically as entrepreneurship research journals, and only the "leading ones" at that. It covered certain journals, dominated by a certain country, and a certain time period. If looking at research about entrepreneurs in other disciplines, such as history, economic history, sociology, cultural geography or anthropology, a different picture emerges. Some of these disciplines have a much stronger focus on structure than on individuals (see for example Bladh, 1991; Allen & Truman, 1993; Kovalainen, 1995; Berg & Foss, forthcoming).

To produce a different picture in entrepreneurship research, however, some of the disciplinary regulations may need to be changed. This may not be happening. As discussed in chapter four, the publishing of articles in academic journals is a prerequisite for an academic career in the USA, and even if questioned, this practice is spreading throughout Europe. Anne Huff (1999) advised non-American scholars who want to join the scientific conversation to do it the American way. If Europeans import the rating system as well (with US based journals ranked highest), this means that the field will become increasingly dominated by the USA.

At present, critical researchers do not seem to bother too much about the entrepreneurship journals. Critical or feminist studies about women's entrepreneurship, if at all available, are more likely to be published in feminist journals, (Mirchandani, 1999; Sundin, 1988), in organization/sociology journals (Goffee & Scase, 1983; Ogbor, 2000) or in books or book sections (Sundin & Holmquist, 1989; Mulholland, 1996; Nutek, 1996; Ahl, 2002).

However, if the journals gain a more prominent position in terms of career prerequisites, scholars may not be able to afford to do critical feminist work. Or, there will, as today, continue to be two parallel discussions with little exchange between them, which is also a loss for entrepreneurship research.

In conclusion, the discursive practices that regulate the discourse on women's entrepreneurship serve to produce and uphold a discourse on women entrepreneurs which excludes the social world and which constructs women as secondary. The research recreates women's secondary position in society instead of forwarding the cause of women. Discourse analysis analyzes texts, not intentions, but I have no reason whatsoever to believe that this result was the intention of the authors. Knowing that research on women's entrepreneurship is marginal in the entrepreneurship research field, and that because of this (at least in the USA) it may take a tenured position to be given the opportunity to conduct such research, and knowing that several of the authors have a sincere interest in giving women a more prominent place in research[3], there is good reason to believe that the intentions were actually contrary to the result.

Then why did it turn out this way? The answer is because of the discursive practices. The name of the game produces this particular result. The way to give women a voice in a field where they are marginalized is to speak *through* the normal discourse – which oppresses women. There are many examples of this from the analysis. One was the argument that economic growth motivates research on entrepreneurship. The way to add women to the research agenda is then to say that they also contribute to economic growth. There seemed to be no room in the analyzed entrepreneurship discourse to study women based only on rationales of equality. Another is the reliance on research methods that celebrate findings of differences, however small. When the differences in questions are gender differences, this leads to the reproduction of the idea that men and women are different. The differences imagined are usually those that reconfirm the current social order. Unpacking and questioning these discursive practices, is therefore a necessary step to be able to produce research that constructs women's entrepreneurship differently.

Below is a summary of the discursive practices that produced the above-mentioned result:

- Entrepreneurship as male gendered, but thought of as neutral.
- Four basic assumptions:
  1. Economic growth is good, and entrepreneurship is good since it furthers economic growth.

---

3 See for example a recent research report on women business owners and equity capital by Brush, Carter, Gatewood, Greene, & Hart (2002), which aims at dispelling myths about women entrepreneurs as secondary to men.

2. Men and women are essentially different.

3. A gendered division of a private and a public sphere of life.

4. Individualism.

- Three strategies used to reinforce the second assumption:

  1. Making a mountain out of a molehill, i.e., stressing small differences between men and women while ignoring similarities and large overlaps.

  2. The self-selected woman, i.e., when finding that men and women entrepreneurs seem more similar than different, one proclaims women entrepreneurs to be exceptions from regular women.

  3. Constructing the good mother, i.e., molding an alternative, feminine entrepreneurship model.

- Methodological preferences: Surveys and statistical analysis that looks for differences.

- Theoretical preferences: Theories concentrating on the individual or the individual firm.

- An objectivist epistemology.

- A writing and publishing system, including a blind review process, which shares the basic assumptions and reinforces the theoretical and methodological preferences.

- Institutional support, research financing and an academic career system, which supports the above.

- The training of entrepreneurship researchers, which may reinforce any of the above.

Abandoning the four basic assumptions and changing some of the other discursive practices might enable the production of a different result. Needless to say, the abandonment of the basic assumptions would have implications beyond the positioning of women. Even if this study examined only a small sub-set of the entrepreneurship literature, with a focus on the positioning of women, I think that these practices delimit not only the female entrepreneur, but also the male entrepreneur, and it shapes how the phenomenon of entrepreneurship is conceived.

In the previous sections, I touched upon the issue of the high-achieving rugged individualist as proper, neither as a description, nor as a norm, for entrepreneurs of either sex. Some of the recent entrepreneurship research has abandoned the trait approach, but other assumptions and discursive practices seem to be left unquestioned, such as assumption number one above. The construction of the entrepreneur would therefore comprise an important research object not only for feminist studies, but also for critical studies on men (Hearn, 1997; 1998) as well as for mainstream entrepreneurship research.

How could one research women's entrepreneurship differently?

From a feminist point of view, this study says that there is both good news and bad news. The bad news is that the talk about women's entrepreneurship, while appearing to be such a positive thing for women with associations of personal autonomy, financial self-sufficiency, a chance for self-actualization, and the promise of freedom from subordination, is in fact casting women in a secondary position in society.

The good news is that I can show that this is done and how it is done. The former might take away some of the enchantment around the entrepreneurship discourse and open up this area for more critical perspectives. The latter might provide some tools for reconstruction.

A feminist point of view (defined broadly as recognizing women's subordination to men and wanting to do something about it) includes an interest in the change of practices that reproduce women's subordination. How would one research women's entrepreneurship to avoid constructing women as secondary, or to avoid the attribution of problems to women instead of to social orders? I would suggest the following two steps:

1. Expansion of the research object.
2. Shift in epistemological position.

Improvements could be achieved by either step, and even more so by the two steps in combination. The following matrix illustrates my thoughts:

	Current research object	**Expanded research object**
Objectivist epistemology	Individualist focus and essentialist assumptions	More factors Contingency studies Comparative studies
Constructionist epistemology	Studies of how women entrepreneurs construct their lives and their businesses, how they "do gender"	Studies of how social orders are gendered and of the mechanisms by which this gendering is reconstructed

Figure 8.1: *Expanding the Research on Women Entrepreneurs.*

185

The limitations and consequences of the first square (individuals or in-dividual businesses as objects combined with essentialist assumptions) have been dealt with in detail throughout the thesis. If anything more should be said about this, one might call for more care when interpret-ing research results of statistical differences. Today, findings of differ-ences are favored at the expense of findings of non-differences, and overlaps are ignored. Statistically significant differences are elaborated on at great length, even if the size and nature of the difference seems quite insignificant. As shown in chapter five, findings of non-differ-ences were also interpreted through a mental framework of differ-ences. Is there some sort of bias, which means that finding differences is better? Or are such results more likely to get published? Is there a "drawer problem" of interesting studies showing no differences, which are not even submitted for publication? If so, conclusions about the existence of differences from published work rest, as Nina Colwill (1982) warned, on loose ground.

The second square indicates that one needs not necessarily aban-don an objectivist position to do critical, feminist work. What would be necessary here, however, is to account for factors "outside" the in-dividual entrepreneur or her business, such as legislation, social norms, family policy, economic policy, structure of labor market re-garding the degree and type of women's participation, etc. A contin-gency study approach would study relationships between, for example, family policy and the degree and type of women's entrepreneurship. To avoid a static picture, one also needs to study the effects of changes in these factors. To avoid the risk of not questioning the norms and values of ones own culture, comparative work, with scholars from different countries would be recommended. Such a research agenda makes for international, comparative studies and contingency studies. By comparing different social orders on these dimensions, alternative ways of organizing "the social" with alternative implications for women might come to the fore. Information from such research is valuable for feminist studies, in the same way that statistics from feminist empiricism is valuable. There were two studies that did three-country comparisons among the reviewed articles (Shane et al., 1991; Kolvereid et al., 1993), but these studied the perceptions and motiva-tions of individuals and would thus still be placed in square one.

To do research in squares three and four, one would have to take the more radical step of making a shift in epistemological position, and study how gender is done. As explained in chapter one, a social con-structionist position entails the recognition of language as constitutive of social reality. To understand reality, one needs a language, a pre-understanding of some sort that orders categories in a comprehensible way. This will mold one's understanding in certain directions. The categories are not given although it seems so because they are internalized; they are socially constructed. Categories are necessary, but they do not have to be set in stone. It should be possible to renegotiate them if by doing so would yield a better understanding.

It seems like the foremost mechanism for the recreation of the gender system is the categorization of people in the two categories of men and women. They are loaded with so many assumptions that the result seems inevitable. The radical solution would be to abandon them entirely and just talk about "people". If there was no segregation between men and women, there could be no hierarchy, as Hirdman (1992) pointed out. The reviewed research about women entrepreneurs showed very few differences between men and women anyway, so even if maintaining an essentialist position, there is not really a reason to study sex differences *per se*. It seems like a dead end for research. Imagine instead, for example, a study identifying sixteen discernible groups of entrepreneurs with men and women in each and every one of these. This would not allow the recreation of women as secondary to men.

But from a feminist point of view, this radical, postmodern solution is also problematic. As long as women as a group are subordinated men as a group, this needs to be talked about. Even if nothing necessarily unites different women, working for women's liberation requires that it is possible to speak about women as a group. To be able to substantiate pay discrimination against women, for example, gender based statistics are helpful. But then again, this is in itself not neutral. Statistical aggregates create a false homogeneity, and they can help confirm the aspect of societal hierarchy they were thought to redress (Gastelaars, 2002). For example, statistics showing that women have an average lower education than men could be used to justify an average lower pay. Using gender as body counts as an analytical category and yet avoiding the recreation of the status quo therefore requires constant vigilance. Facts do not speak by themselves.

The post-structural feminist approach is more fruitful where gender is used as a starting point for research, but not an explanation. Gender is used as an analytical category, but instead of taking it for granted, one looks at how it is constructed. Instead of looking at physical men and women and using their sex as an explanatory variable, one can look at how gender is *accomplished* in different contexts. A shift in thought is necessary, from gender as something that *is*, to gender as something that is *done*, from gender as something firmly tied to bodies to gendered anything – concepts, jobs, industries, language, disciplines, and so on. This includes businesses as well. The studies I reviewed seemed to regard the type of business a woman starts as a simple matter of individual choice. Yet businesses are not gender neutral, they are gendered just as most everything else is. Certain types of businesses are more readily available to a woman than others. Certain businesses are compatible with a subject position as "woman" while others are not. The reverse is, of course, also the case. A man who starts a hair salon for women might, in my country, think twice if he prefers a heterosexual, unambiguous "he-man" subject position.

Such a research approach could be used for the purposes of exposing power relations between male and female, as would, for example, a study of how language upholds gender inequalities. It is what I have aimed at in this study, and this is what other scholars did when deconstructing leadership, organization theory, and business administration from a gender perspective (Martin, 1990; Acker, 1992; Calás & Smircich, 1992; Collinson & Hearn, 1996). If one regards gender as a relational concept, as something that is accomplished over and over again, but is different in different contexts, there are many interesting research projects to carry out. These would be placed in squares three and four in figure 10.1. The division between squares three and four is somewhat artificial since a constructionist position entails that it is not meaningful to look at an individual separate from her social world. If separating the constructs, one must acknowledge and study how they constitute each other. The construction of social reality may, however, be studied with either construct in focus. One can use the individual as a lens, or the social.

In square three I envision studies of how individual men and women perform gender in daily interaction. An example is a study by Gherardi (1996) who investigated how professional women in male working environments positioned their own gender identity, and how the others simultaneously positioned the women as they took up complementary positions. There was a discursive limitation to what positions were available. In this space, none of the women were able to position themselves as "full" participants in the work place. They remained outsiders. This study did not simplify explanations for women's subordination to what individual men and women did (or how they were, for that matter), but also accounted for the choices available through the discursive order. So, "the social" was accounted for even if studying individuals. Another example is Fournier's (2002) study of women farmers in Italy. Contrary to the women in Gherardi's study, they actively resisted being cast in categories of otherness, such as woman (to men), peasant (to urban majority), "educated Other" of the farming community, or "entrepreneurial Other" of the "apathetic farmers", etc. They used these categories as it suited them, while at other times denying them. They resisted the researcher's attempts to understand them by piling up these categories of otherness to a uniform picture, but this could only be achieved by their active work of disconnection, by continuously moving "somewhere else".

In square four, focus would be on the gendering of institutional orders and how they are constructed and reconstructed. Business legislation, family policy, support systems for entrepreneurs, cultural norms, how childcare is arranged, gendered divisions of labor, etc., would be objects for study. An example is Nilsson's (1997) study of support systems for women entrepreneurs' in northern Sweden, that was mentioned earlier. The government instituted a program of special, women counselors for would-be women entrepreneurs. The counselors received appropriate training, and the evaluation showed that they did a very good job. However, they were not fully acknowledged by their colleagues in the regular counseling system, which they were part of. A women-only counseling system counted for less than the regular system. Using institutional theory, Nilsson showed the mechanisms by which this result was achieved.

Abandoning the essentialist position and cross-fertilizing with, for example, feminist theory, critical theory, or institutional theory would most likely make entrepreneurship research more rewarding.

Opportunities and Limitations of Feminist Research

Reality is socially constructed by means of repetition. To do research on women entrepreneurs and not recreate the current result, one would have to break the pattern of repetition as suggested above. But no matter how much one challenges and changes the current construction, there will be a new construction, or a new discourse, replacing it, which is likely to privilege some people at the expense of others.

There is a problem when doing feminist research, namely how to study power relationships between men and women without simultaneously reproducing them. To study how women are positioned in relation to men, one needs to be able to talk about women, to categorize people as women. The problem is that studying any category invites an act of comparison. Studying anything "different" implies recognizing it as degrees of the same and implies hierarchy. What is made different, according to Derrida (1978), is also made secondary and suppressed. This makes the dilemma of feminist studies acute. How can one conduct feminist studies without reproducing the status quo? How can one study power relations between women and men, which require the *naming* of men and women, without contributing to the current situation?

This study showed the limitations of the two most common versions of feminist theory used in the articles, namely liberal and social feminist theory. They are caught in this bind of reproducing women as secondary. The first sees women as the same as men, the other sees women as different. Being a woman is then recognized as either a lamentable situation, which one supposedly can remedy by providing women the same opportunities as men get, or it is recognized as a resource to be added to the range of skills that men demonstrate in business. Both versions were used in the articles. Some authors recommended assertiveness training, financial training, etc., for women, to make them more competitive in the business world. Other authors celebrated women's supposed differences in terms of ethics, care and relational skills and saw this as a contribution to business. In both cases, women were placed somewhere on this scale of sameness and difference. They were categorized in relation to a male gendered norm. However, using a female gendered norm, if such a thing could be achieved, would not change the idea of a scale of sameness and difference. The scale would still exist, and it would have colonizing effects. Jumping off the scale altogether, however, seems to be a difficult feat.

The social constructionist/post-structuralist approach taken in this study might be able to avoid some of these traps. Instead of studying men and women on scales of sameness and difference, it studies conditions and practices that produce gender. Yet such a study is still a victim of the categories it studies. For example, I deconstructed the articles' assumptions of a gendered division of labor with the man as a breadwinner and the woman as a caretaker, and pointed to the possibilities of a different order, where men and women share breadwinning, household work, and childcare on equal terms. But in this I still took the standard, heterosexual couple and the normal nuclear family for granted. My deconstruction/construction therefore colonized lesbian women, and women who have no interest in family and children whatsoever, just as the construction I took apart colonized the category woman. And even if I took sexual orientation into account, more categories of people feeling colonized would still be left. I could add age, class, race and ethnic origin, so as to include the currently politically correct categories, but no matter how many categories I add, there will still be people who feel excluded or misrepresented. The very act of categorizing is colonizing in itself.

However, the other side of the coin is a brighter side. Naming a category makes the category visible. The risk of misrepresenting people does not mean that one should stop trying. Even if an individual does not identify herself as, for example, a working-class, woman and immigrant, people around her are likely to do it, which means both that she must relate to these categories and that these categories will have some repercussions on her life. It works much in the same way as gender as seriality does, which was discussed in detail in chapter one. Consequently, even if one cannot avoid some of the negative effects of categorizations, there are also positive ones. And there is still much work to be done both in making marginalized groups visible, and in questioning how dominant discourses contribute to the marginalization of these groups.

Few theoretical fields worry about their colonizing effects. The concerns about colonizing effects in feminist theory are a reflection of the fact that it is utopian in character. A state where women are not subordinated to men is the goal. Utopia can of course never be achieved, since any new construction of social reality will order people in relation to each other somehow. Categories always delimit. But by naming them, and challenging them, one can possibly change them and thereby contribute to a reconstruction of social reality that one finds fairer. Such was Foucault's project:

> To give some assistance in wearing away certain self-evidences and commonplaces ... to bring it about, together with many others, that certain phrases can no longer be spoken so lightly, certain acts no longer, or at least no longer so unhesitatingly, performed; to contribute to changing certain things in people's ways of perceiving and doing things ... If only what I have tried to say might somehow, to some degree, not remain altogether foreign to some such real effects ... And yet I realize how much all this can remain precarious, how easily it can all lapse back into somnolence (Foucault, 1991:83).

That all can easily lapse back into somnolence does not mean that the idea of utopia is fruitless. It is productive, because it stimulates constant questioning, of both the power relationships between men and women (or any other categories of people), and about how feminist theories themselves contribute to the reproduction of such power relations.

Summary

This chapter discussed how the assumptions that are taken for granted – about entrepreneurship as something unequivocally positive, men and women as essentially different, a certain gendered division of a public and a private sphere of life, and an individualist focus – excluded discussions of social and institutional orders. By imposing a male gendered norm for both dependent variables and independent variables, the reviewed research constructed women's entrepreneurship as secondary. The norm was not questioned. The research constructed women's "shortcomings" and made their amendment an individual responsibility. The discussion excluded equality perspectives and issues of power relations between men and women. Even if aiming at the contrary, the academic study of women's entrepreneurship was framed in such a way as to recreate women's position as the Other.

The assumptions that are taken for granted are the most important aspect of the discursive practices upholding this discourse. They work in combination with writing and publishing practices, the review process, academic career prerequisites, and rules on how can speak on this issue and how. This "package" of discursive practices is gaining ground in academia, and at least one of the assumptions, the growth-is-good assumption, is instrumental for the entrepreneurship research community. From a feminist perspective, there is reason for concern.

The chapter ended with suggestions as to how one can research women's entrepreneurship differently, in order to avoid the recreation of their secondary position. I suggested expanding the research object to include social and institutional aspects as well and making an epistemological shift – to study how gender is accomplished rather than study what it is.

Appendix A

The Selection of Research Texts

This is a study of 81 research articles about women entrepreneurs published in academic research journals. This appendix explains how and why I made this selection. Before arriving at my particular selection, I made a number of de-selection choices that I will relate below. To begin with, I write within the broad field of management, organization theory, and entrepreneurship – or business economics, as the field is known in Sweden. Researchers within this field publish in a wide variety of journals. A quick search in research library databases reveals hundreds of journals with titles relevant for these fields, but anyone in academia knows that some journals carry more weight than others. The ones that really count, the so-called "A-journals" have, however, not published much about entrepreneurship. Busenitz et al. (2003, forthcoming) reviewed the leading US based management journals (Academy of Management Journal, Academy of Management Review, Strategic Management Journal, Journal of Management, Organization Science, Management Science, and Administrative Science Quarterly) from 1985 to 1999 and found 97 articles addressing entrepreneurship among a total of 5291 articles, i.e., 1.8%. Only three of these addressed women.

I made a search in some of the leading European journals, using the same search words: entrepreneur (entrepreneurial, entrepreneurship), small business (emerging business), new venture (emerging venture), and founder(s). I began my search at the earliest issue available on ABI/inform or at the JIBS Research Library. The result was even more meager. Organization Studies (searched from 1981) featured four articles on entrepreneurship, Human Relations (from 1982) one, Journal of Management Studies (from 1976) two articles, Organization (from fall 1994) two, and the Scandinavian Journal of Management (from 1993) featured three articles on entrepreneurship. None of these were about women or gender. I concluded that entrepreneurship is marginal in the field of management (and women's entrepreneurship hardly an issue) and that entrepreneurship scholars do not typically publish in the leading management and organization theory journals. So, where do they publish? It turns out that there are a number of specialized research journals on entrepreneurship.

The research library at Jönköping University lists close to forty English language journals with entrepreneur, entrepreneurship, venturing or small business in the title. To identify the most influential ones, I consulted a web page made by Jerome Katz's at Saint Louis University[1], which is well known and respected by entrepreneurship scholars. It presents a comprehensive list of publications that publish entrepreneurship research. The list rates Entrepreneurship, Theory and Practice (ETP), Journal of Business Venturing (JBV), and The Journal of Small Business Management (JSBM) as being generally recognized as the "Big 3" of refereed scholarly journals aimed at entrepreneurship academicians. It recently added Small Business Economics to the list because it is now included in the Social Sciences Citation Index.

Others agree. Meeks et al. (2001) counted ETP, JBV and JSBM as leading journals. Ratnatunga & Romano (1997) published a "citation classics" analysis of articles in contemporary small enterprise research. They identified six core source journals. Besides the four mentioned by the Babson homepage, they included International Small Business Journal (ISBJ) and Asia Pacific International Management Forum. They concluded that of their source journals, only JBV, JSBM and ETP had impacted the citation classics. They also discussed Entrepreneurship and Regional Development (ERD), included in other lists of core journals, but rejected it for being too policy oriented and too new (it commenced publication in 1989) to fit their particular research design. ERD was, however, recently included in the Social Sciences Citation Index, raising its status within the field.

Brush (1992) published an often-cited, comprehensive review of 57 studies on women entrepreneurs in 1992. She identified sources publishing research on women business owners to be the following: JSBM (14), ETP (5), JBV (5), Frontiers of Entrepreneurship Research, which is the proceedings of the Babson College conference (14), USASBE proceedings (3). The remaining studies were from ERD, ICSB pro-

---

1   The address to the homepage is http://www.slu.edu/eweb/booklist.htm

ceedings, Academy of Management Journal, Sociological Review, Wisconsin Small Business Forum and book chapters. The studies were published from 1975 to 1991.

Ten years have passed since Brush's review. The total number of articles on women's entrepreneurship has increased and so has the number of publication outlets. A complete inventory would not be possible since new articles are published continually. My experience so far tells me that such an undertaking would also include some redundancy. To make this review both relevant and reasonable within the time frame of a thesis project, I made the following selection:

- JBV, JSBM and ETP since they are recognized as the leading journals in the citation classics analysis cited above, and consistently included in other listings of core journals.
- ERD since it has published several articles on women's entrepreneurship and had a special issue on this in 1997. Another reason is that it is European based and somewhat counters the US bias of the other three.

I excluded conference proceedings, since they serve as an early publication outlet, and many of these papers do subsequently appear in other journals. For the very same reason, however, and because of its unique standing in the field, I decided to include the latest two issues available of Frontiers of Entrepreneurship Research (1998 and 1999) where I found two very relevant articles.

The articles considered so far often cited, and sometimes built on, work published elsewhere. Through such referrals I selected some relevant articles on women's entrepreneurship from the following journals: International Small Business Journal (ISBJ), Journal of Business Ethics (JBE), Journal of Developmental Entrepreneurship (JDE), Academy of Management Journal (AMJ), and The Sociological Review (SR). Small Business Economics had very few articles on women's entrepreneurship. I included one from the year 2000, of interest for this review. I also included a 1990 Frontiers article not published elsewhere.

This review and Brush's review differ in the choice of sources (I am more selective) and of course time since, writing ten years later, more is available. There is still an overlap of 21 articles. Even though I did not consider a backward cut-off time, the bulk of the articles in my study are fairly recent: 77% are published from 1990 and onwards. An article on women's entrepreneurship in the selected journals first appeared in 1982, and the latest was published at the time of the analysis during fall 2000. The following table gives an overview of the selection.

Table A.1: *Overview of Selected Articles.*

Journal	Number of articles	Percent
JSBM	27	33
JBV	16	20
ERD	14	17
ETP[2]	11	14
JBE	3	4
Frontiers	3	4
ISBJ	2	2
JDE	2	2
AMJ	1	1
SR	1	1
SBE	1	1
Total	**81**	**100**

The selection is limited to scientific journals. Books and book chapters are not included, partly for reasons of time, but mainly because I wanted to concentrate on peer-reviewed work, in order to capture what the scientific community counts as legitimate scholarly work on women's entrepreneurship. Also, authors not using the words "sex, gender, woman/women," or "female" in the title or in the abstract are generally not included, as these were the primary search words.

Below is an overview of the selected articles, arranged according to topic.

Reviewed Studies in Order of Topic

Personal Background and Firm Characteristics

Hisrish & Brush (1984) JSBM   *Personal and business characteristics*
Scott (1986) JSBM   *Personal background, motivation*
Birley, Moss, & Saunders   *Education and training needs*
     (1987) ETP
Holmquist & Sundin (1990) ERD *Personal characteristics*
Carter, Van Auken, & Harms   *Rural firms, firm characteristics*
     (1992) ERD

---

2   ETP was named American Journal of Small Business until spring 1988. The new name was assumed from the fall issue 1988, indicating a more theoretical, as well as international focus.

Dolinsky (1993) ETP — *Effect of education*
Rosa & Hamilton (1994) ETP — *(Co)ownership*
Dant, Brush, & Iniesta (1996) JSBM — *Franchising*
Shabbir & Di Gregorio (1996) JBV — *Personal goals/structural factors, Pakistan*
Zapalska (1997) JSBM — *Profile Polish WBO*
Shim & Eastlick (1998) JSBM — *Profile Hispanic WBO*
Maysami & Goby (1999) JSBM — *WBO Singapore/elsewhere*
Spilling & Berg (2000) ISBJ — *WBO in Norway*

Attitudes towards Entrepreneurship/Intentions to Start a Business

Scherer, Brodzinsky, & Wiebe (1990) JSBM — *Education, motivation, self-efficacy*
Fagenson & Marcus (1991) ETP — *Perceptions of traits of women entrepreneurs*
Matthews & Moser (1995) ERD — *Family background/interest in starting*
Matthews & Moser (1996) JSBM — *Background/interest in starting business*
Kourilsky & Walstad (1998) JBV — *Attitudes to entrepreneurship among youth*

Psychology

Neider (1987) JSBM — *Locus of control, preferences*
Masters & Meier (1988) JSBM — *Risk-taking propensity*
Sexton & Bowman-Upton (1990) JBV — *Personality*
MacNabb, McCoy, Weinreich, & Northover (1993) ERD — *Value systems, personal identity*
Fagenson (1993) JBV — *Value systems entrepreneurs/managers*
Bellu (1993) ERD — *Motivation, attributional style/performance*

Start-up Process

Pellegrino & Reece (1982) JSBM — *Start-up problems*
Goffee & Scase (1983) SR — *Start-up reasons, discrimination experience*

Nelson (1987) JSBM — *Information needs of female starters*
Shane, Kolvereid, & Westhead (1991) JBV — *Start-up reasons across cultures*
Kolvereid, Shane, & Westhead (1993) JSBM — *Start-up difficulties in different cultures*
Marlow (1997) ERD — *Experience starting/owning in Britain*

Alsos & Ljunggren (1998) Frontiers — *Start-up process*

Management Practice and Strategy
Chaganti (1986) JSBM — *Strategy*
Olson & Currie (1992) JSBM — *Value systems/strategy*
Van Auken, Rittenburg, Doran, & Hsieh (1994) JSBM — *Advertising strategies*
Buttner (2001) JBE — *Management style*

Networking
Smeltzer & Fann, 1989) JSBM — *Networking*
Aldrich, Reese, & Dubini (1989) ERD — *Networking US and Italy*
Cromie & Birley (1992) JBV — *Networking, Northern Ireland*
Andre (1992) JSBM — *Networking*
Katz & Williams (1997) ERD — *Weak-tie networking*

Family
Cox, Moore, & Van Auken (1984) JSBM — *Working couples*
Nelson (1989) ETP — *Network/kin support*
Stoner, Hartman, & Arora, (1990) JSBM — *Work-home role conflict*
Dumas (1992) ETP — *Integrating daughter into family business*
Marshack (1994) ETP — *Copreneurs*
Caputo & Dolinsky (1998) JSBM — *Role of financial/human capital of household members*

Access to Capital
Buttner & Rosen (1988) JBV — *Sex-stereotyping by bank loan officers*

Buttner & Rosen, (1989) JBV	*Bias by loan officers*
Riding & Swift (1990) JBV	*Terms of credit, Canada*
Buttner & Rosen (1992) JSBM	*Perception of loan discrimination*
Fay & Williams (1993) JBV	*Bank discrimination, New Zealand*
Fabowale, Orser, & Riding (1995) ETP	*Bank discrimination*
Carter & Rosa (1998) ERD	*Financing/discrimination*
Greene, Brush, Hart, & Saparito (1999) Frontiers	*Venture capital*
Coleman (2000) JSBM	*Access to capital/terms of credit*

Performance

Cuba, Decenzo, & Anish (1983) ETP	*Management practices*
Miskin & Rose (1990) Frontiers	*Factors related to profitability*
Kalleberg & Leicht (1991) AMJ	*Gender/survival & success*
Fischer, Reuber, & Dyke (1993) JBV	*Education, experience, motivation/ performance*
Rosa, Hamilton, Carter, & Burns (1994) ISBJ	*Management/performance*
Chaganti & Parasuraman (1996) ETP	*Management and performance*
Buttner & Moore (1997) JSBM	*Motivation/success*
Lerner, Brush, & Hisrich, (1997) JBV	*Background factors/performance: Israel*
Carter, Williams, & Reynolds (1997) JBV	*Discontinuance in retail*
Carter & Allen (1997) ERD	*Factors affecting size of business*
Cliff (1998) JBV	*Attitudes to growth and size*
Fasci & Valdez (1998) JSBM	*Performance in accounting practices*
Chell & Baines (1998) ERD	*Performance*
Anna, Chandler, Jansen, & Mero (2000) JBV	*Traditional/nontraditional industries/relation to sales*
Boden & Nucci (2000) JBV	*Background factors/survival*
DuRietz & Henrekson (2000) SBE	*Performance*

Other

Stevenson (1986) JSBM	*Review & reflection*
Birley (1989) JSBM	*Review & reflection*

Moore (1990) JBE	*Review & reflection*
Stevenson (1990) JBE	*Review & reflection*
Brush (1992) ETP	*Review & reflection*
Baker, Aldrich, & Liou (1997) ERD	*Neglect of WBO by scholars and mass media*
Nilsson (1997) ERD	*Counseling services – legitimacy dilemmas*
Brush (1997) JDE	*Perceived obstacles and opportunities by women entrepreneurs*
Berg (1997) ERD	*Review & reflection*
Walker & Joyner (1999) JDE	*SBA programs' effect on eliminating discrimination*

Guide to publication acronyms:

AMJ	American Journal of Management
ERD	Entrepreneurship and Regional Development
ETP	Entrepreneurship Theory and Practice
Frontiers	Frontiers of Entrepreneurship Research
ISBJ	International Small Business Journal
JBE	Journal of Business Ethics
JBV	Journal of Business Venturing
JDE	Journal of Developmental Entrepreneurship
JSBM	Journal of Small Business Management
SBE	Small Business Economics
SR	The Sociological Review

Appendix B

Discourse Analysis Techniques

This appendix presents a brief overview of text analytical techniques available for a discourse analysis. This is meant as a background for the detailed description of the techniques I used in the analysis of the research articles on women's entrepreneurship. The description of the chosen techniques is found in Appendix C.

Overview of Text Analytical Techniques

Foucault performed historical analysis, spanning over centuries. In *The Care of the Self*, in *Discipline and Punish* and in *The History of Sexuality*, to mention just of few of his books, he read large volumes of documents, but he did not prescribe a specific technique for analyzing them. His methodological advice was more theoretical than hands-on practical (Foucault, 1969/1972; 1972; 1991; 1993). The characteristic of Foucault's analysis would be the principles, or perspective guiding his reading as discussed in chapter four. In contrast to other historical studies, he looked for contingencies instead of causes. In mainstream history there is an assumption of determinism, that one thing leads to another in a causal manner. Instead, Foucault saw historical development as accidental and contingent, and an exercise in causal logic as futile. Foucault stayed on the surface. He made a compilation of historical statements without looking for any hidden meaning. With a long-time perspective, he focused on one discourse in each study, and studied changes in this discourse over time. Contemporary analyses focusing on shorter time periods are more prone to the discussion of contrasting or competing discourses occurring simultaneously.

Foucault has inspired scholars from fields as diverse as social psychology, political science, linguistics, and management, to mention a few. They differ in the material they analyze, and in the methods they find most appropriate. They all deal with texts, however. They could be written texts or they could be tape-recorded and transcribed conversations, radio or television shows, or political speeches. The field of text analysis is much wider than the field of discourse analysis, but since discourse analysis borrows from other text analytical methods, I have drawn a map below of a methodological territory pertaining to text analysis to help me choose and motivate my method. I used a recently issued text analysis handbook by Bergström & Boréus (2000) as my main source. They provided me with the categorization of text analysis methods into the five groups as shown in table B.1. Bergström & Boréus are political scientists and interested, as I am, in researching power relations produced by texts. Their selection of techniques is made from such a research interest. It is not an exhaustive list, but it is detailed enough for my purposes. I have given the fifth category, discourse analysis, a little more attention, using a handbook by Winther Jörgensen & Phillips (1999). Kendall & Wickham (1999) and Dean (1994) added information about Foucault's work. The ensuing discussion is my own compilation of the information in these books, with the addition of the pre-understanding from Foucault and Berger & Luckmann (1966).

As table B.1 indicates, only the last group of techniques is labeled discourse analysis. As I interpret it, this is mostly because of differences in epistemological departures, not for technical reasons. All of the textbooks about discourse analysis that I have come across advise the analyst to design his or her own study in the way that seems most appropriate for the task at hand, and with a little modification, all of the text analysis approaches below might be applicable for a discourse analysis.

Table B.1: *Text Analysis Techniques.*

Technique	What is it about?	How do you do it?
1. Content analysis	Quantifying elements in the text	Read the texts, develop a coding scheme, code and count
2. Argumentation analysis	Analyzing how people persuade, looking for the power or lack thereof of an argument	Formal, philosophical analysis of the logic of an argument, or rhetorical analysis
3. Idea and ideology analysis	Describing, analyzing or revealing ideologies	No set method; Examples are ideal types or dimensions as analysis grid
4. Linguistic text analysis	Studying language as carrier of conscious or unreflected meaning	Analysis of metaphors, of syntax and grammar and of word choice
5. Discourse analysis *a) Discourse theory*	Looking for discursive struggles – how discourses compete for the definition of meaning	A set of concepts for finding the elements of a discourse rather than an analysis method
b) Critical discourse analysis	Studying social change by looking at how discursive practices change over time	Linguistic analysis, inter-textuality analysis
c) Discourse psychology	Studying how discourses produce social and personal identities, with social effects	Tools borrowed from conversation analysis, rhetorical analysis and ethno methodology

1. Content Analysis

Content analysis is a term that is sometimes used as a description for any kind of analysis of the content of a text. Technically, however, it is a very specific method that is restricted to the quantification of text elements and as such it is not compatible with discourse analysis (Bergström & Boréus, 2000:44). Content analysis identifies certain words, expressions, sentences, metaphors, etc., codes them, sorts them in categories, counts them, and then draws conclusions from this. It counts its own categories, so to say. Using a pre-determined coding scheme, however well designed, means that the text is not allowed "to speak" to the reader. The context in which an utterance is spoken may be missed. The logic behind content analysis is that words and categories that are frequent assume importance. In discourse analysis, the focus is more on what the text creates, than on what it contains in terms of quantities. Frequency does not automatically coincide with importance. It may reflect a language fashion, or an author's habit. How something is said may be more important than how often. Content analysis also looks for manifest elements only, thus neglecting the unspoken, which is so important for discourse analysis. Content analysis has a few comforting sides in comparison to the other techniques, however. It allows large quantities of text to be analyzed, particularly if using a computer program. With a little translation, you could interpret a frequent occurrence of manifest X, as an equally frequent disregard of unspoken Y.

O'Connell (1999) shows how one can use content analysis for critical purposes. He questioned if the growing worry for criminality and the call for more police and prisons in Ireland was based on an actual increase of the crime rate or on distorted media coverage. By counting numbers and types of reported crimes in four Irish newspapers during a two-month period and comparing the results to the police's crime statistics, he found that the distorted media coverage was more likely to be the cause for the increased worry than actual changes.

2. Argumentation Analysis

Political scientists when analyzing political speeches, party programs, and political debates often use argumentation analysis. Bergström & Boréus (2000) describe two such methods, Arne Naess's (1971) *pro et contra* method, and a similar method by Stephen Toulmin (1958). The purpose is to reconstruct and lay bare an argumentation or to show if it is correct and rational – which of course means that ideas of what is correct and rational are present. One can also use it to find holes in an antagonist's argument. Unlike content analysis, implicit arguments or understandings must be inferred through what is called premises. The analysis method is very time consuming and can only be applied to a limited material. It also concentrates on the "logos" aspect of rhetorical analysis. People persuade with "ethos" and "pathos" too, however, and one might consider supplementing (or replacing) argumentation analysis with rhetorical analysis. This is another text analysis method, which perhaps deserves its own rubric in the table above. Examples of rhetorical analyses used to questions the assumptions of economics are Deirdre McCloskey's (1994; 1998) studies of how economists argue. She found them to base their arguments as much on metaphors and literary devices as on fact.

3. Idea and Ideology Analysis

An ideology may be understood as a conception of how things are, how they ought to be, and ideas of how to get there (Czarniawska-Joerges, 1988). It could be used in an organization study as Czarniawska-Joerges did, but the word is usually associated with society and politics. Bergström & Boréus (2000) distinguish no less than five directions in ideology analysis. One purpose is descriptive: to map the existence of different ideologies within an area and/or during a time period. A second direction would be to study the ideology of certain actors, for example a political party. A third is close to argumentation analysis; it looks for the logic in political ideological argumentation. A fourth direction is called functional idea analysis; it looks for the origins or the effects of ideas. A fifth direction is critical ideology analysis, which is associated with Marx, where ideology is associated with power and false consciousness, the latter of course implying the notion of true consciousness. This direction is also associated with the Frankfurt School, Habermas and critical theory where revealing the ideology is the purpose. Discourse analysis is critical, but it is not critical theory in the sense of the Frankfurt school. Critical theory "proposes a dialectic in which the present forms of reason and society are both negated and retained in a higher form" writes Dean (1994:3). Critical theory challenges modernist, progressivist ideas of technological and social change, but it also offers some sort of alternative, higher version of rationality. Reason and rationality and ideas of the possibility of an ultimate harmony exist. This would be foreign to Foucault's thinking. Habermas also sets natural and social sciences apart, leaving the (natural) scientists to go about their business as usual, which, to discourse analysts, is a rather uncritical move. Since ideology analysis can mean so many different things, there is no recipe book. Bergström & Boréus (2000) give examples of studies that have used ideal types as a grid for reading texts, or dimensions such as the optimistic/pessimistic view of the human being.

4. Linguistic Text Analysis

Linguistic text analysis is Bergström & Boréus' (2000) label for a group of techniques that depart from the idea that the use of language and our way of apprehending reality are interwoven. Our language use is only partly reflected and it affects both what and how we see. Analyzing language use on a level that is less explicitly reflected than the level of the argument may thus be enlightening. Included in these methods are analysis of metaphors, analysis of syntax and grammar, and analysis of word choice.

Critical linguists practice analysis of syntax, grammar, and word choice. It requires linguistic training and is suitable for very short texts. Analysis of metaphors (Lakoff & Johnson, 1980) is more readily available for a non-linguist. It concentrates on the content of metaphors as opposed to the intentional use of them as in a rhetoric study. Bergström & Boréus illustrate the technique by quoting a study by Jacobsson & Öygarden, (1996). They studied the metaphors used to describe the economy in Sweden. They found that the economy was described in terms of the weather – sunshine on the markets, change of climate in the economy, the currency being in hard weather – or as something related to the sea, for example the market economy as the anchor, a floating exchange rate, etc. They concluded that the economy is talked about as part of nature, as something one cannot control, with the ideological effect of taking thoughts away from political interventions in the market.

5a. Discourse Theory

Discourse theory draws on Laclau & Mouffe (1985), according to whom discourses construct the social world, and meaning can never be fixed because of the inherent instability of language. Different discourses continually fight for hegemony, which means that they try to lock a certain meaning, to fix language in a certain position. There is discursive struggle going on continually. The aim of the analysis is to "map the processes in which we fight about how the meaning of signs shall be fixed, and how some fixations of meaning become so conventional that we apprehend them as natural" (Winther Jörgensen & Phillips, 1999:36 my translation). Discourse theory does not separate a discursive from a non-discursive reality. An action is a discursive sign as well as a word, and both text and practice could be analyzed in a discourse analysis. Departing from Foucault, Laclau and Mouffe have developed an elaborate conceptual apparatus for defining and labeling different elements in a discourse, which at sight I found very appealing, but in lieu of practical advice on how to use it, I found that Foucault's principles were quite sufficient for my purposes.

5b. Critical Discourse Analysis

Critical discourse analysis (Fairclough, 1995) agrees that discourses shape the social world, but says that discourse is only an aspect of social praxis. Contrary to Laclau and Mouffe, material and economic practices are seen as non-discursive. There is a dialectic relationship between the discursive and the non-discursive. They constitute each other. The idea is to research the relationships between discursive praxis and social and cultural change by studying how discursive praxis reproduces or changes the latter. This is seen by studying intertextuality, that is, by comparing how different texts draw on or diverge from each other. Critical discourse analysis holds on to the ideology concept. Discursive practices are said to contribute to unequal power relationships between social groups. These effects are called ideological. It is critical in the sense that it aims at siding with repressed social groups for a liberating purpose. There is a political engagement for social change. Fairclough, coming from a linguistic background, uses a whole array of tools derived from language theory when analyzing texts. Examples would be interactional control (who is in control of the linguistic interaction), choice of words, and grammar. Critical discourse analysis does, metaphorically, look at the text with a magnifier and dissects it bit by bit. This limits the amount of material you can work with, of course, and critical discourse analytical studies often concentrate on only one or a few short texts.

5c. Discourse Psychology

Discourse psychology (Potter, 1997; Potter & Wetherell, 1987; Wetherell & Potter, 1992) emanates from social psychology where it was formulated as a critique of cognitive approaches. Cognitive psychology perceives the individual as autonomous with a set of personal characteristics. The individual and society are seen as separate, dualistically related units. The individual interprets the world through cognitive processes (mental scripts) that are seen as more or less stable mental structures that govern action. In the light of discourse analysis, cognitive approaches underestimate the social origin of mental states in stressing the universal aspects of them. Discourse psychology sees mental processes not as internal, stable, mental phenomena possessed by the individual but as constituted by social interaction. This is referred to as the non-essentialist view of the self. People's ways of apprehending the world are not universal, but historically and socially specific and thus contingent.

Discourse psychology focuses on discourses in situated social practices. It studies how individual and group identity is created discursively in social interaction, and on how discourse is used as a flexible resource in social interaction. The aim of analysis is not to categorize people, but to reveal the discursive practice wherein the categories are constructed. The analysis also looks for how the discourses are constructed as true, and analyzes their ideological effects. Ideology is defined as discourses that categorize the world in ways that legitimate and reproduce social patterns – but not as false consciousness. The ideological content is judged according to its effect of favoring some groups at the expense of other groups.

The approach draws on ethnomethodology, conversation analysis and rhetorical analysis. Naturally occurring material is favored over interviews that are always in some way affected by the researcher, or "recipient designed" as Silverman puts it (1997, 1998b). Examples would be naturally occurring conversations, scientific texts, media texts, and so on. Naturally occurring talk is tape recorded, transcribed and coded thematically. *Points of crisis*, where something goes awry in the conversation may reveal conflicts between different discourses, as may disfluency or silences. Different pronoun usage may reveal shifts in subject positions. Examples of tools used from rhetorical analysis are metaphor analysis and the concept of "ethos", in which ways a person's character (or identity) is constructed. Discourse analysis studying identity constructions and power implications of discourses for human beings rejects the common view of the individual as an autonomous unit. It therefore tries to avoid the word "individual" because it has the wrong connotations. A more suitable vocabulary has been developed. Instead of "individual", the expression "subject position" is used, to allow for a sense of self that is multiple, fragmented and constituted by discourses. Different discourses allow different subject positions that sometimes compete.

The handbooks I have used suggest picking tools freely from all of the analytical approaches, and designing a study that suits the particular research question asked. The important thing to remember is to integrate elements from the different methods in such a way that the theoretical premises do not collide. The epistemological departures are different in the five groups of methods discussed. Content analysis is often used in an objectivist tradition; counting elements are assumed to reflect meaning and importance. Ideology analysis is usually associated with an epistemology according to which our representations are reflections of outer, material circumstances. The idea of finding holes in arguments in argumentation analysis suggests that there is a norm for what a good (rational, logical) argument is like. Linguistic analysis may be more close to the epistemological departure of discourse analysis, according to which language does not reflect, but rather produces reality.

For reasons of non-compatible theoretical premises, there are several other, common research techniques that do not easily lend themselves to a discourse analysis. The most obvious would be the survey technique. Mail surveys and structured interviews use pre-formulated questions and answers. These are by necessity formulated within a certain discourse, which will delimit the number of discourses a person can draw upon in his or her answer, thus precluding the analysis of how people draw on discourses. Survey techniques usually assume that attitudes are stable, mental phenomena. Discourse analysts do not hold this position. Further, self-contradictory answers are a problem in surveys, but an asset in discourse analysis. It shows the use of several discourses, and it shows how an individual constructs different subject positions.

Discourse analysis does not rest easily with interviews either. An objectivist epistemology in combination with interview techniques, for example, aspires to get clear and unbiased responses from the interviewee, so that the answers may correctly reveal the respondent's underlying attitudes. This is not compatible with discourse analysis. If discourse analysts use interviews, they regard the interview as a social interaction, which both parties construct together and, consequently, the statements made by both parties are equally interesting for analysis. Some question interviews altogether, and prefer to analyze "naturally occurring" data, with the insight that all communication is recipient designed, and information from interviews is not comparable with information in written texts (Silverman, 1997; 1998b).

As with all forms of science, discourse analysis involves interpretation, but it is not interpretation in the sense of hermeneutics. Hermeneutics is a search for the underlying meaning of what is said, sometimes layers of underlying meaning as in the hermeneutical spiral. This is exactly what Foucault advises against. As discussed earlier, he says to stay on the surface. Foucault studied documents, but not for the purpose of interpreting them. Instead, his approach "organizes the document, divides it up, distributes it, orders, arranges it in levels, establishes series, distinguishes between what is relevant and what is not, discovers elements, defines unities, describes relations" (Foucault, quoted in Dean, 1994:15).

Appendix C

Techniques Used in this Research

As suggested by both Bergström & Boréus (2000) and Winther Jörgensen & Phillips (1999), I designed my own approach, picking elements from several of the methods discussed above, and de-selecting those that did not fit, such as those that can only be employed for very short texts. My handbooks suggest starting by familiarizing oneself with the material. I had already written a review article on a smaller selection of the articles (Ahl, 1997). Based on this, and based on the theoretical background presented in this book, I had a good sense of what to look for. I wanted information for an overview of the articles. I also wanted information for a methodological and epistemological discussion. I then wanted to analyze how the research is argued, how women are positioned, and what underlying assumptions may be inferred.

The overview

I began with a content analysis, but it was not an analysis looking for certain words or sentences, but rather more broad categories. I designed a table with the following categories, which I used as a reading guide. For each article, I filled out the relevant information. The result was 100 typed pages which comprised the basis for the overview.

Table C.1: *Reading Guide.*

1. Journal
2. Author(s)
3. Title
4. Country
5. Research problem
6. Reason behind the problem
7. Theory base
8. Presence of feminist theory
9. Method
10. Data sources
11. Measures
12. Analysis
13. Sample type
14. Sample size
15. Comparison
16. Descriptive/explanatory/conceptual
17. Independent variables
18. Dependent variables
19. Results
20. Ontological/epistemological assumptions
21. Construction of the female entrepreneur before study
22. Construction of the female entrepreneur after study
23. Quotes, comments

Most points in table C.1 are self-explanatory. Some merit a clarification. Point six refers to the reasons that the authors have put forward as to why their particular problem is an important one and is worth researching. Theory base refers to if the paper is based on psychology, sociology, economics, etc. Point eight refers to if the authors used feminist theory or not, and in such a case, which theory was used. Point 15 makes a note of whether the study used comparison groups. These were typically male and female groups. Point 20 refers to the ontological and epistemological assumptions (realist, constructionist, etc.) in the paper. These were seldom stated and had to be inferred by other information in the text.

In points 21 and 22, I have noted how the authors envision the female entrepreneur. Talking about a female entrepreneur can only make sense if there is a non-female entrepreneur, which she is not, and which she is constructed as different from. The latter is sometimes only implicit, but yet present in the text. The possible differences put forward reveal how the authors envision the female entrepreneurs. This is most poignant in the formulation of hypotheses. A plain example would be a hypothesis stating that the female entrepreneur is less growth oriented than the male entrepreneur. It is also quite clear in the interpretation of the results and in the discussion of implications. Sometimes there is a change in the construction, as a result of the study. Most often there is not.

Many of the categories above are quite straight-forward and can be presented with descriptive statistics as I have calculated in chapter five. There the reader will find an overview of topics, theory bases, methods, and samples as well as a summary of findings, presented at face value. Directly after follows a discussion and critique of methodology and a discussion of epistemological assumptions.

Analyzing Introductions

For the purpose of the discussion of chapter six, which is an analysis of the researchers' arguments, the positioning of women, and underlying assumptions, the information from the content analysis provided a good basis, but it was not enough. The first part of chapter six, which analyzes the arguments put forward as to why one should research female entrepreneurship, is a content analysis through the eyes of a literary genre analysis. It might also be labeled an argumentation analysis, but not the formal philosophical analysis referred to in the previous appendix (it does not judge if the arguments are logical or not), rather it could be called a genre-specific argumentation analysis.

Scientific journal articles make up their own literary genre with its own distinctive marks. Literary theorist John Swales (1990) has analyzed articles in international science articles[1] and found that they more or less use the same rhetorical moves to create interest and convey their message. The introduction section, in particular, almost always follows the same three-step procedure. First, establish a territory by claiming the centrality or the importance of the research area. Second, establish a niche by indicating a research gap, making a counter claim or raising a question. Alternatively, indicate the continuance of a research tradition. Third, occupy the established niche. This is usually accomplished through the presentation of the work or its purpose and by announcing the principal findings.

The articles in this analysis here were no exceptions. Chapter six examines how steps one and two are achieved in the articles, i.e., how do the authors establish the importance of the "gender and entrepreneurship" research field, and how do they establish their particular

---

1   Swales cites studies on journals in a wide range of disciplines in the natural and social sciences.

niche. The content of the argumentation was of course my main focus, but the reader might be interested in the technicalities of the analysis as well, which is why I present it below.

I began by filling out the following table, adapted from Swales, (1990:141) for each article.

Table C.2: *Introduction Section Structure.*

Move	
1. Establishing a territory	1. claiming centrality and/or
	2. making topic generalization(s) and/or
	3. reviewing items of previous research
2. Establishing a niche	1a. counter-claiming or
	1b. indicating a gap or
	1c. question-raising or
	1d. continuing a tradition
3. Occupying the niche	1a. outlining purposes or
	1b. announcing present research
	2. announcing principal findings
	3. indicating research article structure

Going from top to bottom, there is declining rhetorical effort, weakening knowledge claims and increasing explicitness writes Swales (1990:141). I found that the pattern established by Swales was followed, although the variation in length and elaboration was great. The shortest and most efficient, by far, was the following. The numbers preceding the sentences indicate the order in which they appear in the text.

Table C.3: *Introduction Section Analysis: Example 1.*

Fabowale, L., Orser, B., & Riding, A. (1995). Gender, structural factors, and credit terms between Canadian small businesses and financial institution. *Entrepreneurship, Theory and Practice, 19*(4), 41–65.

1	1 claim centrality	(2) This question, fraught with emotional overtones and inconclusive findings, has received considerable attention in the public press and in academic research.
	2 topic generalization	
	3 review items of previous. research	
2	1a counter-claiming	
	1b indicate gap	
	1c question-raising	(1) Do credit terms differ between female and male small business owners? (3) If, indeed, differences do exist, to what extent are structural differences in borrowers' eligibility account-able?
	1d continue tradition	
3	1a outline purpose	(4) The aim of this study is to report on research that sheds further light on these issues. To this end, the study had three objectives.
	1b announce present research	
	2 announce principal findings	
	3 indicate structure	

All three moves were completed in an elegant opening paragraph of seven lines, whereupon the authors continued with purpose and methods. The moves were not completed in order – the authors began with a question. A more typical example is offered below.

Table C.4: *Introduction Section Analysis: Example 2.*

Riding, A. L., & Swift, C. S. (1990). Women business owners and terms of credit: some empirical findings of the Canadian experience. *Journal of Business Venturing, 5*(5), 327–340.

1	1 claim centrality	(1) The trends toward the increasing numbers of women who are entering the ranks of small business in Canada is well established (+ statistics).
	2 topic generalization	
	3 review items of previous research	
2	1a counter-claiming	
	1b indicate gap	(2) As the number of women business owners has increased, questions of whether or not women business owners behave differently from their male counterparts, and whether or not women receive any different treatment in the capital marketplace, remain unresolved.
	1c question-raising	(3) One aspect of the latter issue that has frequently been raised concerns the question of whether or not women are treated differently from men by credit grantors.
	1d continue tradition	
3	1a outline purpose	(4) The specific purpose of this paper is to use empirical findings to add to our knowledge of this distinctive aspect, with particular reference to whether or not the terms of loans and lines of credit differ significantly between male and female principals of small businesses, and whether or not such differences are attributable to a systematic gender bias or to systematic gender-related differences in the patterns of small business ownership.
	1b announce present research	
	2 announce findings	
	3 indicate structure	(5) Accordingly, this paper is organized as follows.

This was a very straight-forward introduction. Some articles used more space and a more elaborated structure, such as the one below.

Table C.5: *Introduction Section Analysis: Example 3.*

Greene, P. G., Brush, C. G., Hart, M. M., & Saparito, P. (1999). Exploration of the venture capital industry: is gender an issue? *Frontiers of Entrepreneurship Research* (pp. 168–181).

1	1 claim centrality	(1) Entrepreneurship is recognized as the engine of growth in the U.S economy ... Fueling this engine is the spectacular worldwide expansion of the venture capital industry and consequent creation of numerous equity financing operations for growing entrepreneurial firms. (4) The dramatic growth in presence, growth and contributions of women-owned businesses has attracted significant attention ... (+statistics on women owned businesses and research about them).
	2 topic generalization	
	3 review items of previous research	(2) (6) (9)
2	1a counter-claiming	
	1b indicate gap	(3) However, absent from previous research is consideration of gender, either as independent or analysis variable. (5) Yet, research on venture capital ... of women-owned firms is extremely limited. (7) ... found no studies examining women's access to or utilization of equity funding in their ventures.
	1c question-raising	(8) What explains ...?
	1d continue tradition	
3	1a outline purpose	(11) This study addresses the following questions:
	1b announce present research	(10) This study seeks to provide empirical evidence of the dearth of venture capital investments in women-owned businesses.
	2 announce principal findings	
	3 indicate structure	

Here the authors completed the moves in cycles. First, the centrality of entrepreneurship was established, and a gap in entrepreneurship research indicated. Second, the centrality of women's entrepreneurship was established, and another gap, on venture capital, identified before questions were raised and the purpose announced. Previous research was visited and revisited three times to substantiate the claims. The moves were completed in two and a half pages. Although unveiling the rhetorical structure of research articles was not the primary purpose of this exercise, it did provide some interesting insights into how research articles in the field of entrepreneurship research are introduced. First, most of the articles followed the steps indicated by Swales quite faithfully. Of the articles 88% completed all three moves, and nearly all of these did so in the logical order. The average number of steps to complete the moves was 4.6. Most of the articles (73%) used only one cycle. Two cycles were used by 23% and only three articles used three. In the cases where more than one cycle was used, the procedure was usually to establish a territory, review research, and indicate a gap or a contradiction, then review research pertaining to that gap specifically before outlining the purpose.

Thirteen articles deviated from the logical order of the moves. Seven chose to indicate a gap or raise a question before establishing the territory as Fabowale et al. (1995) cited above. Three started with the purpose before completing move 1 and 2, and three articles began with move 1, but introduced the purpose before indicating the gap. All versions seemed to work fine, as long as they were completed within a reasonably short introduction section. As a reader, I got a quick overview of what it was about and an idea of why I should read it. This was not necessarily the case with the eight articles that omitted move 3 from the introduction and introduced it several pages later, for example in the method section. The ones that had a very lengthy introduction with an extensive literature review and discussion before even mentioning the present research were also less efficient in selling their work. One article did not complete move 2, which made me wonder what was interesting about the study or why it should be undertaken at all. I concluded that there is a very good reason for introduction sections being structured the way they are. To put it quite simply – it works.

Hypotheses, research problems and assumptions

After the analysis of the introductions, I analyzed the research problems and the hypotheses to see how they positioned women entrepreneurs. An example would be a hypothesis stating, "women will be less active networkers than men". This positions women as inferior to men in terms of networking. I did not use an elaborate scheme as in the analysis of the introductions, instead I categorized the hypotheses and problems as they occurred and looked for patterns. Again, I found some interesting results that are presented in chapter six.

So far, the analysis resembles a content analysis in that the presence or absence of the investigated aspects was considered for all articles. I have information as to what percent fit into each of my categories. When reading the articles I also found some interesting themes reflecting underlying assumptions that did not lend themselves to this sort of content analysis. An underlying assumption per definition resides under the text, and can hardly be coded in a content analysis. I therefore leave the logic of content analysis, which says that something that is often said is important, and instead rest more fully on the logic of discourse analysis, which says that the presence of a statement, however unusual, indicates that there is a discourse around to be drawn upon to produce this statement and to make this statement possible and legitimate. The presence of a statement in these research articles, however unusual, has also passed this particular discourse community's strict screening devices and is therefore in a double sense legitimate. As signs of legitimate discourses they are interesting to analyze even if they do not appear in all articles.

I went back to my notes from my first reading, looking at the last five points on the list in particular. The themes emerged through this exercise. Having formulated the themes, I went back to the articles relevant for each theme and reread the relevant sections. The themes are discussed in chapters six and seven. They deal with assumptions of gender differences, assumptions about work and family, about what is public and what is private and assumptions about individual versus collective responsibility. Regarding the last few themes, I found some dissenting voices within the body of articles, indicating the presence of conflicting discourses. The choice of themes is of course a reflection of my research interest and feminist theory perspective. The discussion is carried out as a conversation between the selected research texts and myself. I use ample citations from the articles I converse with to show the reader how I came to my conclusions.

References

Abelson, R. P. (1972). Are attitudes necessary? In B. T. King & E. McGinnies (Eds.), *Attitudes, conflict, and social change*. New York and London: Academic Press.

Acker, J. (1992). Gendering organizational theory. In A. Mills & P. Tancred (Eds.), *Gendering Organizational Analysis*. London: Sage.

Ahl, H. J. (1997). Entrepreneuship research with a gender perspective: an overview of past research and suggestions for the future. Paper presented at the 14th Nordic Conference on Business Studies, Bodö, Norway.

Ahl, H. J. (2002). The construction of the female entrepreneur as the other. In B. Czarniawska & H. Höpfl (Eds.), *Casting the Other. The production and maintenance of inequalities in work organizations* (pp. 52–67). London: Routledge.

Ahl, H. J., & Samuelsson, E. F. (2000). *Networking through empowerment and empowerment through networking* (Research report 2000–1). Jönköping: Jönköping International Business School.

Ahrne, G., & Roman, C. (Eds.). (1997). *Hemmet, barnen och makten: Förhandlingar om arbete och pengar i familjen*. Stockholm: Fritzes.

Aldrich, H., Reese, P. R., & Dubini, P. (1989a). Women on the verge of a break-through: networking among entrepreneurs in the United States and Italy. *Entrepreneurship and Regional Development, 1*, 339–356.

Aldrich, H., Reese, P. R., Dubini, P., Rosen, B., & Woodward, B. (1989b). *Women on the verge of a breakthrough? Networking among entrepreneurs in the United States and Italy.* Paper presented at the Frontiers of entrepreneurship research.

Aldrich, H. E. (1999). *Organizations Evolving.* Thousand Oaks; London: Sage.

Allen, S., & Truman, C. (Eds.). (1993). *Women in business: perspectives on women entrepreneurs*. London: Routledge.

Alsos, G. A., & Ljunggren, E. (1998). Does the business start-up process differ by gender? A longitudinal study of nascent entrepreneurs. In P. Reynolds, W. D. Bygrave, N. M. Carter, S. Manigart, C. M. Mason, G. Dale Meyer, & K. G. Shaver (Eds.), *Frontiers of Entrepreneurship Research* (pp. 137–151). Babson Park, MA: Babson College.

Alvesson, M., & Due Billing, Y. (1999). *Kön och organisation*. Lund: Studentlitteratur.

Anderson, W. T. (1990). *Reality isn't what it used to be*. New York: Harper Collins.

Andre, R. (1992). A national profile of women's participation in networks of small business leaders. *Journal of Small Business Management, 30*(1), 66–73.

Anna, A. N., Chandler, G. N., Jansen, E., & Mero, N. P. (2000). Women business owners in traditional and non-traditional industries. *Journal of Business Venturing, 15*(3), 279–303.

Austin, J. L. (1965). *How to do things with words*. New York: Oxford University Press.

Bachrach, P., & Baratz, M. (1963). Decisions and Nondecisions: An Analytical Framework. *American Political Science Review* (57), 641–51.

Baker, T., Aldrich, H. E., & Liou, N. (1997). Invisible entrepreneurs: the neglect of women business owners by mass media and scholarly journals in the USA. *Entrepreneurship and Regional Development, 9*(3), 221–238.

Beasley, C. (1999). *What is feminism? An introduction to feminist theory.* London: Sage.

Bellu, R. R. (1993). Task role motivation and attributional styles as predictors of entrepreneurial performance: female sample findings. *Entrepreneurship and Regional Development, 5*(4), 331–344.

Bem, S. L. (1981). *Bem Sex-Role Inventory.* Palo Alto, CA: Mind Garden.

Berg, N. G. (1997). Gender, place and entrepreneurship. *Entrepreneurship and Regional Development, 9*(3), 259–268.

Berg, N. G., & Foss, L. (Eds.). (forthcoming). *Entreprenörskap og foretaksutvikling i et kjönnsperspektiv.* Oslo: Universitetsforlaget.

Berger, P., & Luckmann, T. (1966). *The social construction of reality: a treatise in the sociology of knowledge.* London: Penguin Books.

Bergström, G., & Boréus, K. (2000). *Textens mening och makt (The meaning and power of text).* Lund: Studentlitteratur.

Beyer, A. (1996). *Den kvinnliga företagarprofilen.* Stockholm: Företagarnas Riksorganisation.

Birch, D. (1979). *The Job Generation Process.* Cambridge, MA: MIT Press.

Birley, S. (1989). Female entrepreneurs: are they really different? *Journal of Small Business Management, 27*(1), 1–37.

Birley, S., Moss, C., & Saunders, P. (1987). Do women entrepreneurs require different training? *American Journal of Small Business, 12*(1).

Bladh, C. (1991). *Månglerskor: att sälja från korg och bod i Stockholm 1819–1846.* Stockholm: Komm. för Stockholmsforskning.

Boden, R. J., & Nucci, A. R. (2000). On the survival prospects of men's and women's new business ventures. *Journal of Business Venturing, 15*(4), 347–362.

Brush, C., Carter, N., Gatewood, E., Greene, P., & Hart, M. (2002). *The Diana project. Women business owners and equity capital: the myths dispelled.* Kansas City: Kauffman Center for Entrepreneurial Leadership.

Brush, C. G. (1992). Research on Women Business Owners: Past Trends, a New Perspective and Future Directions. *Entrepreneurship, Theory and Practice, 16*(4), 5–30.

Brush, C. G. (1997). Women-owned businesses: Obstacles and opportunities. *Journal of Developmental Entrepreneurship, 2*(1), 1–24.

Burr, V. (1995). *An introduction to social constructionism.* London: Routledge.

Busenitz, L., West III, G. P., Shepherd, D., Nelson, T., Chandler, G. N., & Zacharakis, A. (2003 forthcoming). Entrepreneurship research in emergence: past trends and future directions. *Journal of Management.*

Butler, J. (1997). Excitable speech: A politics of the performative. New York: Routledge.

Buttner, E. H. (2001). Examining female entrepreneurs' management style: an application of a relational frame. *Journal of Business Ethics, 29*(3), 253–269.

Buttner, E. H., & Moore, D. P. (1997). Women's organizational exodus to entrepreneurship: self-reported motivations and correlates with success. *Journal of Small Business Management, January*, 34–46.

Buttner, E. H., & Rosen, B. (1988). Bank loan officer's perceptions of the characteristics of men, women and successful entrepreneurs. *Journal of Business Venturing, 3*(3), 249–258.

Buttner, E. H., & Rosen, B. (1989). Funding new business ventures: are decision makers biased against women entrepreneurs. *Journal of Business Venturing, 4*(4), 249–261.

Buttner, E. H., & Rosen, B. (1992). Rejection in the loan application process: male and female entrepreneurs' perceptions and subsequent intentions. *Journal of Small Business Management, 30*(1), 59–65.

Calás, M., & Smircich, L. (1992). Using the "F" Word: Feminist Theories and the Social Consequences of Organizational Research. In A. Mills & P. Tancred (Eds.), *Gendering Organizational Theory*. Newbury Park: Sage.

Calás, M., & Smircich, L. (1996). From "The Woman's" Point of View: Feminist Approaches to Organization Studies. In S. Clegg, C. Hardy, & W. Nord (Eds.), *Handbook of Organization Studies* (pp. 218–257). London: Sage.

Caputo, R. K., & Dolinsky, A. (1998). Women's choice to pursue self-employment: the role of financial and human capital of household members. *Journal of Small Business Management, 36*(3), 8–17.

Carland, J. W., Hoy, F., & Carland, J. A. C. (1988). "Who is an antrepreneur?" is a question worth asking. *American Journal of Small Business* (spring), 33–39.

Carter, N. M., & Allen, K. R. (1997). Size determinants of women-owned businesses: choice or barriers to resources? *Entrepreneurship and Regional Development, 9*(3), 211–220.

Carter, N. M., Williams, M., & Reynolds, P. D. (1997). Discontinuance among new firms in retail: the influence of initial resources, strategy, and gender. *Journal of Business Venturing, 12*(2), 125–145.

Carter, R. B., Van Auken, H. E., & Harms, M. B. (1992). Home-based businesses in the rural United States economy, differences in gender and financing. *Entrepreneurship and Regional Development, 4*(3), 245–257.

Carter, S., & Rosa, P. (1998). The financing of male- and female-owned businesses. *Entrepreneurship and Regional Development, 10*, 225–241.

Chaganti, R. (1986). Management in women-owned enterprises. *Journal of Small Business Management, 24*(4), 19–29.

Chaganti, R., & Parasuraman, S. (1996). A study of the impacts of gender on business performance and management patterns in small business. *Entrepreneurship Theory and Practice, 21*(2), 73–75.

Chell, E., & Baines, S. (1998). Does gender affect business 'performance'? A study of microbusinesses in business services in the UK. *Entrepreneurship and Regional Development, 10,* 117–135.

Chodorow, N. (1988). *Femininum – maskulinum. Modersfunktion och könssociologi.* Stockholm: Natur & Kultur.

Cliff, J. E. (1998). Does one size fit all? Exploring the relationship between attitudes towards growth, gender and business size. *Journal of Business Venturing, 13*(6), 523–541.

Coleman, S. (2000). Access to capital and terms of credit: a comparison of men- and women-owned small businesses. *Journal of Small Business Management, 38*(3), 37–52.

Collinson, D. L. (1992). *Managing the Shopfloor. Subjectivity, Masculinity and Workplace Culture.* Berlin: Walter de Gruyter.

Collinson, D. L., & Hearn, J. (1996). Breaking the silence: on men, masculinities and managements. In D. L. Collinson & J. Hearn (Eds.), *Men as managers, managers as men.* London: Sage.

Colwill, N. (1982). *The new partnership: Women and men in organizations.* Palo Alto, CA: Mayfield Publishing Company.

Connel, R. W. (1995). *Masculinities.* Cambridge: Polity Press.

Cooper, A. C., Markman, G. D., & Niss, G. (2000). The evolution of the field of entrepreneurship. In G. D. Meyer & K. A. Heppard (Eds.), *Entrepreneursip as Strategy* (pp. 115–133). London: Sage Publications.

Cox, J. A., Moore, K. K., & Van Auken, P. M. (1984). Working couples in small business. *Journal of Small Business Management, 22*(4), 25–30.

Cromie, S., & Birley, S. (1992). Networking by female business owners in Northern Ireland. *Journal of Business Venturing, 7*(3), 237–251.

Cuba, R., Decenzo, D., & Anish, A. (1983). Management practices of succesful female business owners. *American Journal of Small Business, 8*(2).

Czarniawska, B. (1997). *Narrating the organization: Dramas of institutional reality.* Chicago: The University of Chicago Press.

Czarniawska, B. (2002). *Social Constructionism and Organization Studies.* Retrieved 2002-03-15, from http://hem.passagen.se/basia/

Czarniawska-Joerges, B. (1988). *Ideological control in nonideological organizations.* New York: Praeger.

Dahl, R. (1957). The concept of power. *Behavioral Science* (2), 201–215.

Danius, S. (1995). Själen är kroppens fängelse. In C. Lindén & U. Milles (Eds.), *Feministisk bruksanvisning* (pp. 297). Stockholm: Norstedts förlag.

Dant, R. P., Brush, C. G., & Iniesta, F. P. (1996). Participation patterns of women in franchising. *Journal of Small Business Management, 34*(2), 14–28.

Davidsson, P. (1989). *Continued entrepreneurship and small firm growth.* Stockholm School of Economics, Stockholm.

Davidsson, P. (1995). *Kultur och Entreprenörskap – en uppföljning* (Research report). Örebro: Siftelsen Forum för Småföretagsforskning.

Davidsson, P., Lindmark, L., & Olofsson, C. (1994). *Dynamiken i svenskt näringsliv.* Lund: Studentlitteratur.

Davies, B. (1989). *Frogs and Snails and Feminist Tales*. North Sydney: Allen & Unwin Australia.

Dean, M. (1994). *Critical and Effective Histories*. London: Routledge.

deBeauvoir, S. (1949/1986). *Det andra könet*. (4 ed.). Stockholm: Norstedts.

Derrida, J. (1978). *Writing and Difference*. London: Routledge.

Dolinsky, A. (1993). The effects of education on business ownership: a longitudinal study of women. *Entrepreneurship Theory and Practice, 18*(1), 43–53.

Douglas, M. (1987). *How institutions think*. London: Routledge & Keagan Paul.

Doyle, J., & Paludi, M. (1998). *Sex and gender: The human experience*. (4 ed.). San Francisco: McGraw-Hill.

Dumas, C. (1992). Integrating the daughter into family business management. *Entrepreneurship Theory and Practice, 16*(4), 41–55.

DuRietz, A., & Henrekson, M. (2000). Testing the female underperformance hypothesis. *Small Business Economics, 14*(1), 1–10.

Eduards, M. (1995). En allvarsam lek med ord. In E. Witt-Brattström (Ed.), *Viljan att veta och viljan att förstå*. Stockholm: Fritzes.

Erkkilä, K. (2000). *Entrepreneurial education: mapping the debates in the United States, the United Kingdom and Finland*. New York: Garland Publishing Inc.

Fabowale, L., Orser, B., & Riding, A. (1995). Gender, structural factors, and credit terms between Canadian small businesses and financial institutions. *Entrepreneurship, Theory and Practice, 19*(4), 41–65.

Fagenson, E. (1993). Personal value systems of men and women: Entrepreneurs versus managers. *Journal of Business Venturing, 8*(5), 409–430.

Fagenson, E. A., & Marcus, E. C. (1991). Perceptions of the sex-role stereotypic characteristics of entrepreneurs: women's evaluations. *Entrepreneurship Theory and Practice, 15*(4), 33–47.

Fairclough, N. (1995). *Critical Discourse Analysis*. London: Longman.

Fasci, M. A., & Valdez, J. (1998). A performance contrast of male- and female-owned small accounting practices. *Journal of Small Business Management, 36*(3), 1–7.

Fay, M., & Williams, L. (1993). Gender bias and the availability of business loans. *Journal of Business Venturing, 8*(4).

Ferguson, K. (1984). *The Feminist Case Against Bureaucracy*. Philadelphia: Temple University Press.

Fischer, E. M., Reuber, A. R., & Dyke, L. S. (1993). A theoretical overview and extension of research on sex, gender and entrepreneurship. *Journal of Business Venturing, 8*(2), 151–168.

Flyvbjerg, B. (1991). *Rationalitet og magt*. Copenhagen: Akademisk Forlag.

Foucault, M. (1969/1972). *The Archeology of Knowledge*. London: Tavistock.

Foucault, M. (1972). The Disourse on Language (L'ordre du discourse), *The archaeology of knowledge & The discourse on language* (pp. 215–237). New York: Pantheon Books.

Foucault, M. (1991). Questions of Method. In G. Burchell, C. Gordon, & P. Miller (Eds.), *The Foucault Effect*. Chicago: The University of Chicago Press.

Foucault, M. (1993). *Diskursens ordning* (Mats Rosengren, Trans.). Stockholm/Stehag: Brutus Östlings Bokförlag.

Foucault, M. (1995). *Discipline & Punish* (Alan Sheridan, Trans.). (Second Vintage Books Edition, May 1995 ed.). New York: Random House.

Fournier, V. (2002). Keeping the veil of otherness: practising disconnection. In B. Czarniawska & H. Höpfl (Eds.), *Casting the other: The production and maintenance of inequalities in work organizations* (pp 68–88). London: Routledge.

Foxall, G. (1984). Evidence for attitudinal-behavioral consistency: implications for consumer research paradigms. *Journal of Economic Psychology*, 5(1), 71–92.

Gartner, W. (1988). "Who is an entrepreneur?" is the wrong question. *American Journal of Small Business, spring*, 11–32.

Gartner, W. B. (1985). A conceptual framework for describing the phenomenon of new venture creation. *Academy of Management Review*, 10(4), 696–706.

Gastelaars, M. (2002). How do statistical aggregates work? About the individual and organizational effects of general classifications. In B. Czarniawska & H. Höpfl (Eds.), *Casting the other. The production and maintenance of inequalities in work organizations* (pp. 7–22). London: Routledge.

Gergen, K. (1991). *The saturated self. Dilemmas of identity in contemporary life*. New York: Basic Books.

Gherardi, S. (1995). *Gender, symbolism and organizational cultures*. London: Sage.

Gherardi, S. (1996). Gendered organizational cultures: narratives of women travellers in a male world. *Gender Work and Organization*, 3(4), 187–201.

Gilligan, C. (1982). *In a Different Voice*. Cambridge: Harvard University Press.

Goffee, R., & Scase, R. (1983). Business ownership and women's subordination: a preliminary study of female proprietors. *The Sociological Review*, 31, 625–648.

Greene, P. G., Brush, C. G., Hart, M. M., & Saparito, P. (1999). Exploration of the venture capital industry: is gender an issue? In P. D. Reynolds, W. D. Bygrave, S. Manigart, C. M. Mason, G. D. Meyer, H. J. Sapienza, & K. G. Shaver (Eds.), *Frontiers of Entrepreneurship Research* (pp. 168–181). Babson Park, MA: Babson College.

Grégoire, D., Déry, R., & Béchard, J.-P. (2001). Evolving conversations: A look at the convergence in entrepreneurship research. Paper presented at the Babson College Kaufmann Foundation Entrepreneurship Research Conference, Jönköping, Sweden 2001.

Greimas, A. J., & Courtés, J. (1982). *Semiotics and Language: An Analytical Dictionary*. Bloomington: Indiana University Press.

Haraway, D. (1991). *Simians, Cyborgs, and Women*. London: Free Association Books.

Harding, S. (1987). Introduction: Is There a Feminist Method? In S. Harding (Ed.), *Feminism and methodology*. Milton Keynes: Open University Press.

Hartmann, H. (1986). Det olyckliga äktenskapet mellan feminism och marxism. För en mer utvecklingsbar förening. In H. e. a. Ganetz (Ed.), *Feminism och Marxism: en förälskelse med förhinder*. Stockholm: Arbetarkultur.

Hearn, J. (1997). The implications of critical studies on men. *Nora, 1997*(1), 48–60.

Hearn, J. (1998). Theorizing men and men's theorizing: Varieties of discursive practices in men's theorizing of men. *Theory and Society, 27*, 781–816.

Hearn, J. (1999). The hegemony of men: on the construction of counter-hegemony in critical studies on men. In P. Folkesson, M. Nordberg, & Smirthwaite (Eds.), *Hegemoni och mansforskning*. Karlstad: Institutionen för samhällsvetenskap, Karlstads Universitet.

Hearn, J., & Parkin, W. (1983). Gender and organizations: A selected review and a critique of a neglected area. *Organizations Studies, 4*(3), 219–242.

Hébert, R. F., & Link, A. N. (1988). *The Entrepreneur: Mainstrean views and radical critiques*. New York: Praeger Publishers.

Herman, E. (1995). *The romance of American psychology: political culture in the age of experts*. Berkeley: University of California Press.

Hirdman, Y. (1992). *Den socialistiska hemmafrun och andra kvinnohistorier*. Stockholm: Carlssons bokförlag.

Hirdman, Y. (2001). *Genus – om det stabilas föränderliga former*. Malmö: Liber.

Hisrish, R. D., & Brush, C. (1984). The woman entrepreneur: management skills and business problems. *Journal of Small Business Management, 22*(1), 30–37.

Hofstede, G. (1984). *Culture's consequences. International differences in work-related values*. London: Sage.

Holgersson, C., & Höök, P. (1997). Chefsrekrytering och ledarutveckling som arenor för konstruktion av ledarskap och kön. In A. Nyberg & E. Sundin (Eds.), *Ledare, makt och kön. SOU 1997:135*. Stockholm: Fritzes.

Holmberg, C. (1993). *Det kallas kärlek*. Göteborg: Anamma förlag.

Holmquist, C., & Sundin, E. (1990). What's special about highly educated women entrepreneurs? *Entrepreneurship and Regional Development, 2*, 181–193.

Hornaday, R. W. (1990). Dropping the E-words from Small Business Research: An Alternative Typology. *Journal of Small Business Management* (October), 22–33.

Huff, A. S. (1999). *Writing for scholarly publication*. Thousand Oaks: Sage.

Iannello, K. (1992). *Decisions without hierarchy. Feminist interventions in organization theory and practice.* New York: Routledge.

Jacobsson, K., & Öygarden, G. A. (1996). Ekonomernas Guernica. Rädslans metaforer och produktion av mening. *Sociologisk Forskning* (2–3).

Jalmert, L. (1999). Lecture at the conference "Kvinna och man inför 2000-talet", Elmia March 5, 1999. Jönköping.

Javefors Grauers, E. (1999). *AB Adam & Eva – en studie av familjeföretag inom ICA. Lic.uppsats.* Linköping: Linköpings universitet.

Kalleberg, A. L., & Leicht, K. T. (1991). Gender and organizational performance: determinants of small business survival and success. *Academy of Management Journal, 34*(1), 136–161.

Kanter, R. (1977). *Men and women of the corporation.* New York: Basic Books.

Kaplan, G., & Rogers, L. (1990). The Definition of Male and Female. Biological reductionism and the sanctions of normality. In S. Gunew (Ed.), *Feminist Knowledge and Construct.* London: Routledge.

Katz, J. A., & Williams, P. M. (1997). Gender, self-employment and weak-tie networking through formal organizations. *Entrepreneurship and Regional Development, 9*(3), 183–197.

Kendall, G., & Wickham, G. (1999). *Using Foucault's Methods.* London: Sage.

King, B. T., & McGuinnies. (1972). Overview: social contexts and issues for contemporary attitude change research. In B. T. King & McGuinnies (Eds.), *Attitudes, conflict, and social change.* New York and London: Academic Press.

Kirzner, I. (1983). Entrepreneurs and the Entrepreneurial Function: A Commentary. In J. Ronen (Ed.), *Entrepreneurship* (pp. 281–290). Lexington MA: LexingtonBooks.

Kolvereid, L., Shane, S., & Westhead, P. (1993). Is it equally difficult for female entrepreneurs to start businesses in all countries? *Journal of Small Business Management, 31*(4), 43–51.

Kourilsky, M. L., & Walstad, W. B. (1998). Entrepreneurship and female youth: knowledge, attitudes, gender differences and educational practices. *Journal of Business Venturing, 13*(1), 77–88.

Kovalainen, A. (1995). *At the Margins of the Economy. Women's Self-Employment in Finland, 1960–1990.* Aldershot: Avebury.

Kuhn, T. (1970). *The Structure of Scientific Revolutions.* (2 ed.). Chicago: University of Chicago Press.

Laclau, E., & Mouffe, C. (1985). *Hegemony and Socialist Strategy. Towards a Radical Democratic politics.* London: Verso.

Lakoff, G., & Johnson, M. (1980). *Metaphors we live by.* Chicago, London: University of Chicago Press.

Landström, H., & Johannisson, B. (2001). Theoretical foundations of Swedish entrepreneurship and small-business research. *Scandinavian Journal of Management, 17*(2), 225–248.

Latour, B., & Woolgar, S. (1979). *Laboratory life: the social construction of scientific facts.* Beverly Hills: Sage Publications, Inc.

Lerner, M., Brush, C., & Hisrich, R. (1997). Israeli women entrepreneurs: an examination of factors affecting performance. *Journal of Business Venturing, 12*(4), 315–339.

Lindén, C., & Milles, U. (1995). *Feministisk bruksanvisning.* Stockholm: Norstedts förlag.

Lindgren, G. (1996). Broderskapets logik. *Kvinnovetenskaplig tidskrift* (1), 4–14.

Low, M., B, & MacMillan, I. C. (1988). Entrepreneurship: Past research and future challenges. *Journal of Management, 14*(2), 139–161.

Lukes, S. (1977). *Power: A Radical View.* London: MacMillan Press.

Lyotard, J.-F. (1979/1984). *The postmodern condition: a report on knowledge.* Manchester: Manchester University Press.

MacNabb, A., McCoy, J., Weinreich, P., & Northover, M. (1993). Using identity structure analysis (ISA) to investigate female entrepreneurship. *Entrepreneurship and Regional Development, 5*(4), 301–313.

March, J., & Olsen, J. (1989). *Rediscovering Institutions.* New York: The Free Press.

Marlow, S. (1997). Self-employed women – new opportunities, old challenges? *Entrepreneurship and Regional Development, 9*(3), 199–210.

Marshack, K. J. (1994). Copreneurs and dual-career couples: are they different? *Entrepreneurship Theory and Practice, 19*(1), 49–69.

Martin, J. (1990). Deconstructing Organizational Taboos: the Suppression of Gender Conflict in Organizations. *Organization Science, 1*(4), 339–360.

Masters, R., & Meier, R. (1988). Sex differences and risk-taking propensity of entrepreneurs. *Journal of Small Business Management, 26*(1), 31–35.

Matthews, C. H., & Moser, S. B. (1995). Family background and gender: implications for interest in small firm ownership. *Entrepreneurship and Regional Development, 7*(4), 365–377.

Matthews, C. H., & Moser, S. B. (1996). A longitudinal investigation of the impact of family background and gender on interest in small business ownership. *Journal of Small Business Management, 34*(2).

Maysami, R. C., & Goby, V. P. (1999). Female business owners in Singapore and elsewhere: a review of studies. *Journal of Small Business Management, 37*(2), 96–105.

McClelland, D. C. (1961). *The Achieving Society.* New York: Van Nostrand Company Inc.

McCloskey. (1985). *The Rhetoric of Economics.* (1 ed.). Madison: The University of Wisconsin Press.

McCloskey, D. (1994). *Knowledge and Persuasion in Economics.* Cambridge: Cambridge University Press.

McCloskey, D. (1998). *The Rhetoric of Economics.* (2 ed.). Madison: The University of Wisconsin Press.

Meeks, M. D., Neck, H., & Meyer, G. D. (2001). Converging conversations in entrepreneurship. Paper presented at the Babson Conference 2001 in Jönköping, Sweden.

Mills, A. (1988). Organization, gender and culture. *Organization Studies, 9*(3), 351–370.

Mirchandani, K. (1999). Feminist insight on gendered work: new directions in research on women and entrepreneurship. *Gender, Work and Organization, 6*(4), 224–235.

Miskin, V., & Rose, J. (1990). Women entrepreneurs: factors related to success. In N. C. Churchill, W. D. Bygrave, J. A. Hornaday, D. F. Muzyka, K. H. Vesper, & W. W. Wetzel Jr. (Eds.), *Frontiers of Entrepreneurship Research* (pp. 27–38). Babson Park, MA: Babson College.

Moore, D. (1990). An examination of present research on the female entrepreneur – suggested research strategies for the 1990's. *Journal of Business Ethics, 9*(4–5), 275–281.

Mulholland, K. (1996). Entrepreneurialism, masculinities and the self-made man. In D. L. Collinson & J. Hearn (Eds.), *Men as managers, managers as men* (pp. 123–149). London: Sage.

Naess, A. (1971). *Empirisk semantik*. Stockholm: Läromedelsförlagen.

Needham, R. (Ed.). (1973). *Right & Left*. Chicago: The University of Chicago Press.

Neider, L. (1987). A preliminary investigation of female entrepreneurs in Florida. *Journal of Small Business Management, 25*(3), 22–29.

Nelson, G. W. (1987). Information needs of female entrepreneurs. *Journal of Small Business Management, 25*(1), 38–44.

Nelson, G. W. (1989). Factors of friendship: relevance of significant others to female business owners. *Entrepreneurship Theory and Practice, 13*(4), 7–18.

Nilsson, P. (1997). Business Counselling services directed towards female entrepreneurs – some legitimacy dilemmas. *Entrepreneurship and Regional Development, 9*(3), 239–258.

Nordberg, M. (1999). Hegemonibegreppet och hegemonier inom mansforskningsfältet. In P. Folkesson, M. Nordberg, & G. Smirthwaite (Eds.), *Hegemoni och mansforskning*. Karlstad: Institutionen för samhällsvetenskap, Karlstads Universitet.

Nutek (Ed.). (1996). *Aspects of women's entrepreneurship*. (Vol. B 1996:10). Stockholm: Nutek.

Nyberg, A. (1997). *Kvinnor, män och inkomster. Jämställdhet och oberoende*. Stockholm: Fritzes.

O'Connell, M. (1999). Is Irish public opinion towards crime distorted by media bias? *European Journal of Communication, 14*(2).

Ogbor, J. O. (2000). Mythicizing and reification in entrepreneurial discourse: ideology-critique of entrepreneurial studies. *Journal of Management Studies, 37*(5), 605.

Olson, S. F., & Currie, H. M. (1992). Female entrepreneurs in a male-dominated industry: personal value systems and business strategies. *Journal of Small Business Management, 30*(1), 49–57.

Parker, I. (1992). *Discourse dynamics: critical analysis for social and individual psychology*. London: Routledge.

Payne, J. W., Bettman, J. R., & Johnson, E. J. (1992). Behavioral decision research: a constructive processing perspective. *Annual Review of Psychology, 43*, 87–131.

Pellegrino, E. T., & Reece, B. L. (1982). Perceived formative and operational problems encountered by female entrepreneurs in retail and service firms. *Journal of Small Business Management, 20*(2), 15–24.

Persson, I., & Wadensjö, E. (Eds.). (1997). *Kvinnors och mäns löner – varför så olika?* Stockholm: Fritzes.

Persson, R. S. (1999). Exploring the meaning of gender: Evaluating and revising the Bem Sex-Role Inventory (BSRI) for a Swedish research context (BSRI-SE) (INSIKT 1999:1). Jönköping: Högskolan för Lärarutbildning och Kommunikation.

Potter, J. (1997). Discourse Analysis as a way of Analysing Naturally Ocurring Talk. In D. Silverman (Ed.), *Qualitative Research. Theory, Method and Practice*. London: Sage.

Potter, J., & Wetherell, M. (1987). *Discourse and Social Psychology*. London: Sage.

Proposition. (1993/94:140). *Bygder och regioner i utveckling*. Stockholm: Riksdagstryck.

Puxty, A. G. (1993). *The Social & Organizational Context of Management Accounting*. London: Academic Press.

Ratnatunga, J., & Romano, C. (1997). A "Citation Classics" Analysis of Articles in Contemporary Small Enterprise Research. *Journal of Business Venturing, 12*, 197–212.

Reed, R. (1996). Entrepreneurialism and Paternalism in Australian Management: A Gender Critique of the 'Self-Made' Man. In D. L. Collinson & J. Hearn (Eds.), *Men as Managers, Managers as Men* (pp. 99–122). London: Sage.

Riding, A. L., & Swift, C. S. (1990). Women business owners and terms of credit: some empirical findings of the Canadian experience. *Journal of Business Venturing, 5*(5), 327–340.

Robert, R., & Uvnäs Moberg, K. (1994). *Hon & han, födda olika*. Stockholm: Bromberg.

Rosa, P., & Hamilton, D. (1994). Gender and ownership in UK small firms. *Entrepreneurship theory and practice, 18*(3), 11–27.

Rosa, P., Hamilton, D., Carter, S., & Burns, H. (1994). The impact of gender on small business management: preliminary findings of a British study. *International Small Business Journal, 12*(3), 25–32.

Saussure, F. d. (1970). *Kurs i allmän lingvistik*. Staffanstorp: Cavefors.

SBA. (1998). *Women in Business*. Retrieved 2002-02-15 from http://www.sba.gov/advo/stats/wib01.pdf

Scherer, R. F., Brodzinsky, J. D., & Wiebe, F. A. (1990). Entrepreneur career selection and gender: a socialization approach. *Journal of Small Business Management, 28*(2), 37–43.

Schumpeter, J. A. (1934/1983). *The Theory of Economic Development*. (Reprint 1971 ed.). New Brunswick: Transaction Publishers.

Scott, C. E. (1986). Why more women are becoming entrepreneurs. *Journal of Small Business Management, 24*(4), 37–44.

Sexton, D. L., & Bowman-Upton, N. (1990). Female and male entrepreneurs: psychological characteristics and their role in gender-related discrimination. *Journal of Business Venturing, 5*(1), 29–36.

Shabbir, A., & Di Gregorio, S. (1996). An examination of the relationship between women's personal goals and structural factors influencing their decision to start a business: the case of Pakistan. *Journal of Business Venturing, 11*(6), 507–529.

Shackleton, V. (1995). *Business Leadership*. New York: Routledge.

Shane, S., Kolvereid, L., & Westhead, P. (1991). An exploratory examination of the reasons leading to new firm foundation across country and gender. *Journal of Business Venturing, 6*(6), 431–446.

Shane, S., & Venkataraman, S. (2000). The promise of entrepreneurship as a field of research. *Academy of Management Review, 25*(1), 217–226.

Shane, S., & Venkataraman, S. (2001). Entrepreneurship as a field of research: a response to Zahre and Dess, Singh, and Erikson. *Academy of Management Review, 26*(1), 13–16.

Shim, S., & Eastlick, M. A. (1998). Characteristics of Hispanic female business owners: an exploratory study. *Journal of Small Business Management, 36*(3), 18–34.

Silverman, D. (1997). Kundera's Immortality: The Interview Society and the Invention of the Self. *Qualitative Inquiry, 3*(3), 304–325.

Silverman, D. (1998a). *Harvey Sacks – social science and conversation analysis*. Cambridge: Polity Press.

Silverman, D. (1998b). The Quality of Qualitative Health Research: The Open-Ended Interview and its Alternatives. *Social Sciences in Health, 4*(2), 104–118.

Singh, R. P. (2001). A comment on developing the field of entrepreneurship through the study of opportunity recognition and exploitation. *Academy of Management Review, 26*(1), 10–12.

Smeltzer, L. R., & Fann, G. L. (1989). Gender differences in external networks of small business owner/managers. *Journal of Small Business Management, 27*(2), 25–32.

Smith, N. R. (1967). *The Entrepreneur and His Firm: The Relationship between Type of Man and Type of Firm*. East Lansing, MI: Michigan State University.

Sommestad, L. (1992). *Från mejerska till mejerist: en studie av mejeriyrkets maskuliniseringsprocess*. Lund: Arkiv.

Spilling, O. R., & Berg, N. G. (2000). Gender and small business management: the case of Norway in the 1990:s. *International Small Business Journal, 18*(2), 38–59.

Statistics Sweden. (2000). *På tal om kvinnor och män – Lathund om jämställdhet 2000. Retrieved 2002-03-15, from http://www.scb.se/publkat/levnadsforh/lathund.asp*

Stevenson, H. (1984). A Perspective on Entrepreneurship. In H. Stevenson, M. Roberts, & H. Grousebeck (Eds.), *New Business Venture and the Entrepreneur* (pp. 3–14). Boston, MA: Harvard Business School.

Stevenson, L. (1990). Some methodological problems associated with researching women entrepreneurs. *Journal of Business Ethics, 9*(4–5), 439–446.

Stevenson, L. A. (1986). Against all odds: the entrepreneurship of women. *Journal of Small Business Management, 24*(4), 30–36.

Steyaert, C. (1995). *Perpetuating Entrepreneurship through Dialogue. A Social Constructionist View. Doctoral dissertation.* Leuven: Department of Work and Educational Science, Kathoelieke Universiteit Leuven.

Stider, A. K. (1999). Hemma hos firmafamiljen. *Kvinnovetenskaplig tidskrift, 20*(1), 21–31.

Stoner, C. R., Hartman, R. I., & Arora, R. (1990). Work-home role conflict in female owners of small businesses: an exploratory study. *Journal of Small Business Management, 29*(1), 30–38.

Sundin, E. (1988). Osynliggörandet av kvinnor – exemplet företagare. *Kvinnovetenskaplig tidskrift, 9*(1), 3–15.

Sundin, E., & Holmquist, C. (1989). *Kvinnor som företagare*. Malmö: Liber.

Swales, J. M. (1990). *Genre Analysis: English in academic and research settings.* Cambridge: Cambridge University Press.

Söndergaard, D. M. (1999). *Destabilising Discourse Analysis* (Working Paper 7, Kön i den akademiske organisation). Copenhagen: Institut for Statskundskab, Köbenhavns Universitet.

Sörensen, B. (1982). Ansvarsrasjonalitet: om mål-middeltenkning blant kvinner. In H. Holter (Ed.), *Kvinner i felleskab*. Oslo: Universitetsforlaget.

Tannen, D. (1990). *Du begriper ju ingenting* (Anette och Gunnar Rydström, Trans.). 1993: Wahlström & Widstrand.

Theobald, H. (2002). Individual vs collective action: gender inequality and women's action strategies in German and Swedish business firms. In B. Czarniawska & H. Höpfl (Eds.), *Casting the Other* (pp. 104–118). London: Routledge.

Toulmin, S. (1958). *The Uses of Argument.* Cambridge: Cambridge University Press.

Wahl, A. (1996a). Företagsledning som konstruktion av manlighet. *Kvinnovetenskaplig tidskrift* (1), 15–27.

Wahl, A. (1996b). Molnet – att föreläsa om feministisk forskning. *Kvinnovetenskaplig tidskrift* (3–4), 31–44.

Walker, D., & Joyner, B. (1999). Female entrepreneurship and the market process: gender-based public policy considerations. *Journal of Developmental Entrepreneurship, 4*(2), 95–116.

Van Auken, H. E., Rittenburg, T. L., Doran, B. M., & Hsieh, S.-F. (1994). An empirical analysis of advertising by women entrepreneurs. *Journal of Small Business Management, 32*(3), 11–27.

Watson, J. (2002). Comparing the performance of male- and female-controlled businesses: relating outputs to inputs. *Entrepreneurship Theory and Practice, 26*(3), 91–100.

Veblen, T. (1926). *Den arbetsfria klassen (The Leisure Class)*. Stockholm: Wahlström & Widstrand.

Wetherell, M., & Potter, J. (1992). *Mapping the Language of Racism: Discourse and the Legitimation of Exploitation*. Hemel Hempstead: Harvester Wheatsheaf.

Wicker, A. W. (1969). Attitudes v. actions: the relationship of verbal and overt responses to attitude objects. *Journal of Social Issues, 25*, 41–78.

Wiklund, J., Davidsson, P., Delmar, F., & Aronsson, M. (1997). Expected consequences of growth and their effect on growth willingness in different samples of small firms. In P. Reynolds, N. Bygrave, N. Carter, P. Davidsson, W. Gartner, C. Mason, & P. McDougall (Eds.), *Frontiers of Entrepreneurship Research* (pp. 1–16). Babson Park, MA: Babson College.

Winther Jörgensen, M., & Phillips, L. (1999). *Diskursanalyse som teori og metode*. Roskilde: Roskilde Universitetsforlag.

Young, I. (1995). Gender as Seriality. In N. L & S. S (Eds.), *Social Postmodernism*. Cambridge: Cambridge University Press.

Zapalska, A. (1997). A profile of woman entrepreneurs and enterprises in Poland. *Journal of Small Business Management, 35*(4), 76–82.

Index